PUBLIC GOODS AND PUBLIC POLICY

COMPARATIVE POLITICAL ECONOMY AND PUBLIC POLICY SERIES
Volume 3: Public Goods and Public Policy

Series Editors:

CRAIG LISKE, *University of Denver*
WILLIAM LOEHR, *University of Denver*
JOHN F. McCAMANT, *University of Denver*

PUBLIC GOODS
AND
PUBLIC POLICY

edited by

WILLIAM LOEHR

TODD SANDLER

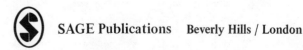 **SAGE Publications**   Beverly Hills / London

For information address:

SAGE PUBLICATIONS, INC.
275 South Beverly Drive
Beverly Hills, California 90212

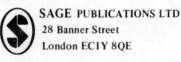

SAGE PUBLICATIONS LTD
28 Banner Street
London EC1Y 8QE

Printed in the United States of America

Library of Congress Cataloging in Publication Data

Main entry under title:

Public goods and public policy.

   (Comparative political economy and public
policy series ; v. 3)
      1. Public goods—Addresses, essays, lectures.
2. Externalities (Economics)—Addresses,
essays, lectures. 3. Policy sciences—Addresses,
essays, lectures. I. Loehr, William.
II. Sandler, Todd.
HJ192.P8   330'.01   77-17865
ISBN 0-8039-0965-9
ISBN 0-8039-0939-X pbk.

FIRST PRINTING

CONTENTS

PREFACE

The ever accelerating introduction of technology into the activities of man continues to draw the nations of the world into a closer degree of interaction with respect to decisions concerning allocation, stability, distribution, and growth. The joint space venture between the United States and the European Space Agency (an eleven nation group), which provides for transnational utilization of a space lab, is one example of this interaction. Other examples include the development of an external communication system (i.e., INTELSAT) that links, via satellite, 95 nations; the signing of pollution agreements (e.g., the Baltic Pact) that seek to clean waterways; the convening of the Law of the Seas conference that attempts to assign property rights to the mineral wealth of the oceans; the creation of multinational transactions between the private and public sector that permit the marketing of natural resources. In the near future, more exotic cooperative ventures may involve the construction of space docks, the development of weather modification systems, the establishment of scientific communities on extraterrestrial bodies, the utilization of extrasensory communication networks, and the creation of a world-wide water project which uses polar ice.

If intelligent decisions are to be reached with respect to international interactions, then researchers in the social sciences, especially economics and political science, must develop principles that apply to the emerging transnational community. Without sound principles for cooperation, future scenarios may involve increased inefficiency in resource allocation and increased reliance on conflict to solve contingencies. As the pantries of Spaceship Earth are exhausted, the exigency for transnational cooperative action will become increasingly evident.

Since present and future collaborations concern problems that are associated with public goods (e.g., communication networks, ecomonitoring systems, and ecocontrol mechanisms), externalities (e.g., pollution), property rights, and the operation of market and nonmarket structures, these five areas of study must be given top priority whenever transnational interactions are analyzed. The purpose of this book is to present an analysis of these five areas of inquiry in order to promote a better understanding of public policy within both the present and future international spheres.

The book is partitioned into three parts. In the first part, the economic and political theories of public goods and externalities are presented. Additionally, many empirical studies of these problems are surveyed. Part I is written to be a self-contained survey of the theory of public goods and externalities which we hope will be a useful introduction for the uninitiated reader. Furthermore, the three initial chapters define and present the tools and principles of analysis that are employed in Parts II and III. The informed reader can skip Part I and read the essays in the later parts in any order, since each essay is independent of the others. Part II contains a series of essays that analyze nonmarket structures including the Olympic Games, supranational bodies, and military alliances. Finally; Part III examines other transactions in the international arena involving trade, the assignment of property rights, and taxation.

By presenting both the theoretical development (Part I) and the application of this theory to specific problems (Parts II and III), this book seeks to establish the importance and relevancy of economic and political theory in achieving a clearer understanding of transnational interactions.

William Loehr
Todd Sandler

PART I:

ASPECTS OF PUBLIC GOODS

Chapter 1

ON THE PUBLIC CHARACTER OF GOODS

W I L L I A M   L O E H R
University of Denver

T O D D   S A N D L E R
University of Wyoming

I. INTRODUCTION

Public goods theory is barely out of its infancy, and therefore, it is not surprising that important issues remain unresolved. A substantial body of principles has been developed in recent years that has proven to be of interest to economists and others concerned with the analysis of public policy. The purpose of this paper is to briefly survey the literature in public goods theory with an eye to developing a selected number of these principles critical to an analysis of public policy, viewed from the public goods perspective. Since the other papers in this volume use this perspective to analyze a variety of public issues, our objective here is to draw out the elements of public goods theory which appear as useful background for these analyses. On the other hand, the points discussed here are general ones and should permit the reader to begin to apply these principles to situations not of direct concern to the authors of this volume.

Throughout this paper the conventional normative objective of Pareto optimality is employed in addressing the efficient provision of public goods. Pareto optimality is a position where an improvement in the well-being of one individual cannot be made without a reduction in the well-being of at least one other individual. We pursue this objective after clearly distinguishing between purely public and private goods. Furthermore the paper examines some of the allocational problems related to public goods (Section II). We analyze explicitly the case of "impure" public goods (Section III), externalities (Section IV) and the joint production of goods with both public and private properties (Section V). Toward the end of our discussion (Section VI), we present some of the major considerations entering into the political

AUTHORS' NOTE: We appreciate comments provided by Robert Shelton.

economy of public goods provision and extend the analysis into the time dimension (Section VII) where public goods may span time as well as individuals. Oftentimes, reference is made to the papers in this volume, thereby relating them to specific areas within the theory of public goods. References to articles in this volume will be made in parentheses without the use of a date.

II. THE ECONOMICS OF PUBLIC AND PRIVATE GOODS

The economic nature of the public good is vividly dramatized by considering the polar case of a pure public good juxtaposed against a private good. The private good is perfectly divisible in that it can be parcelled out to different individuals. Given a fixed amount of such a good, increased consumption by one community member reduces the quantity available to other members by an equivalent amount. As a result of the private good's property of perfect divisibility, potential consumers can be excluded from consuming the good (e.g., to exclude from consumption those who do not pay for the items consumed). Mathematically, the concept of divisibility can be expressed as:

(1) $y = y^1 + y^2 + \ldots + y^n$

where y is the total amount of the private good available which is made up of the amount of y owned (consumed) by individual 1 (y^1) plus that owned (consumed) by individual 2 (y^2) and so forth through individual n.

The outstanding property of a pure public good[1] is that, upon its production, it is equally consumed by all members of the community. As a result, one member's consumption of the pure public good does not reduce the quantity or quality available to other members. The pure public good is perfectly indivisible in that it cannot be divided up and parcelled out to individual members of the community. Furthermore, once it is produced, it is either impossible or prohibitively costly to exclude any member or group of members in the community from consuming it. For instance, a community member can consume a pure public good despite the fact that the member has not contributed to its cost of production. Mathematically, we see a pure public good as:

(2) $X = X^1 = X^2 = \ldots = X^n$

Superscripts again represent consuming parties and X is the total amount of the pure public good available. In this case, however, the amounts of X consumed by each of the individuals, 1 through n, are the same as the total, X. The equality signs in equation (2) indicate both the complete indivisibility of the pure public good and the fact that individuals cannot be excluded from consuming it once the good is produced. On the other hand, the addition sign in equation (1) specified the additive but separable properties of the pure private good with respect to the consuming individuals.

The concepts of private and public goods, expressed in equations (1) and (2) respectively, can also be cast in a format which leads to the derivation of the demand curve for each type of good. Rather than produce a separate diagram, we show in Figure 3 panels (b), (d) and (e), that, due to the divisibility of private goods, the total demand for a private good is simply the sum of the amounts that each individual would want to consume at each price. The total demand curve in panel (b) is the horizontal sum of the demand curves of each individual (assuming two individuals). With a pure public good, however, the total amount is consumed by all, and therefore, the overall demand curve for a public good is a vertical summation of the demand curves of each individual. To determine the overall "price" which the community is willing to pay for a given amount of a public good we must add the amount that individual A is willing to pay for that amount, plus the amount that individual B is willing to pay for the same amount, etc. This is shown as Figure 3(a) for a two person community.

A. A GENERAL EQUILIBRIUM MODEL OF A WORLD WITH TWO PRIVATE GOODS

Unique Pareto optimality when two private goods are concerned is illustrated geometrically in Figure 1.[2] Units of one private good (y_1) are measured along the horizontal axis, while units of the other private good (y_2) are measured along the vertical axis. The curve PP' is a production possibility curve depicting society's menu of choices regarding the production mix of goods (y_1) and (y_2). Any point on the curve PP' represents a situation where society's resources are fully employed assuming the best existing technology is used. Consequently, points that lie outside of PP' are unobtainable. Points located inside of PP', such as E', indicate unemployment or inefficient use of resources and are, therefore, suboptimal.

The contours M_1M_1' and M_2M_2' are two social indifference curves representing two levels of society's aggregated preferences for goods (y_2) and (y_1).[3] In reality, there are an infinite number of social indifference curves, one for each level of community satisfaction, that pass through the private good commodity space, although only two are depicted in Figure 1. A particular social indifference curve is a locus of points, or various combinations of (y_2) and (y_1), that yield a constant level of satisfaction or utility to society. Furthermore, the general nature of a given set or map of these social indifference curves reflects a particular distribution of income, wealth, and power.

Social welfare is at a maximum where the "highest" contour is reached subject to the production possibility frontier. In Figure 1, M_2M_2' is the welfare maximizing contour, stipulating that society consume OC of y_2 and OC' of y_1. At any point on the production possibility other than E, the private good (y_1) is either being underproduced (at point U for example) or overproduced (at Z).

More specifically, the slope of a line drawn tangent to PP' is called the marginal rate of transformation of y_1 into y_2 (abbreviated MRT_{12}). At E, the slopes of the community indifference curve and production possibility frontier are equal. This notion can be expressed as:

(3) $MRS_{12} = MRT_{12}$

The left-hand side indicates the rate at which the community is willing to substitute y_1 for y_2 taking into account each individual's marginal preference

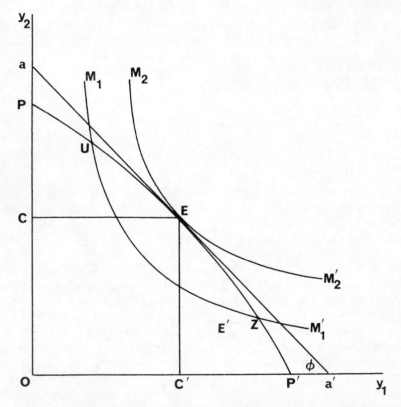

Figure 1: Pareto Optimality with Private Goods

for y_2 and y_1 within the community. On the right, the MRT_{12} indicates the rate at which the community is able to substitute y_1 for y_2 (or vice versa) by shifting resources from the production of one to the other, given the technical properties of the production function. It is of interest to note that the community MRS_{12} shown in equation (3) is a representation of all individuals in the community. For Pareto optimality it is necessary to note that:

$$(3') \quad MRS_{12}^1 = MRS_{12}^2 = \ldots = MRS_{12}^n = MRS_{12} = MRT_{12}$$

Equation $(3')$ specifies that the rate at which each and every individual in society is willing to trade y_1 for y_2 is equal to everyone else's trade-off and that all trade-offs are equal to MRT_{12}. If these trade-off ratios were unequal and individual 1 had a higher marginal rate of substitution of y_1 for y_2 (i.e., he valued y_2 more highly relative to y_1) than everyone else, he would offer more y_1 in exchange for y_2 in the market than everyone else. Two things would happen simultaneously: 1) some individuals would trade y_2 for individual 1's y_1, raising their MRS_{12} and lowering 1's MRS_{12}; and 2) more y_2 and less y_1 will be produced, supplying individual 1's demand for y_2 instead of y_1, and because of increasing costs, raising MRT_{12}. Pareto optimality could only occur therefore where equation $(3')$ was satisfied.

B. A WORLD WITH PURE PUBLIC GOODS

The Pareto-optimal condition when public goods are present is similar to that shown for private goods in equation $(3')$. In a system containing two goods, a purely public good X and a purely private good y, Pareto optimality may be expressed as:[4]

$$(4) \quad \sum_{i=1}^{n} MRS_{Xy}^i = MRT_{Xy}$$

where MRS_{Xy}^i is the *ith* individual's marginal rate of substitution of the public good X for the private good y. This optimality condition is for a community of n individuals. Due to the indivisibility of the public good, a true measure of the marginal benefit of the public good, in terms of the private good, requires a summing of the marginal rates of substitution over all n individuals. Equation (4) is Pareto optimal because only at that point is the rate that society is willing to substitute X (the public good) for y (the private good) equal to the rate that society can substitute X for y. If this situation does not prevail, then it is possible for society to reach a higher level of well-being by changing the production and consumption mix of X and y. In other words, if equation (4) does not hold, then the public good is either being overproduced or underproduced.[5]

C. THE PUBLIC GOOD PROBLEM

The political nature of the pure public good is closely related to its economic nature. This relationship is, again, most clear when the public good is presented in its pure form. Since the pure public good is completely indivisible, it cannot be parcelled out, priced, and subsequently sold to members of the community in the manner that the pure private good is priced and sold through the market system. In view of this basic feature of public goods, their allocation poses a distinct problem (see Shaffer).

On the other hand, if the individuals who comprise a community express their true preferences for public goods, they can each be assigned a tax-share (or price) according to these preferences. In this instance, the public good dilemma disappears and the solution is structurally similar, although different in character, to that solution that would prevail in a free market system. The fundamental problem, however, is that community members are aware of the fact that their tax-share is dependent upon their preference revelation. Furthermore, they are cognizant of the fact that they will not forego any of the public good benefits once the public good is produced as it is either impossible or prohibitively costly to exclude nonpaying community members from consuming it. Therefore, individuals can conserve their scarce personal resources and best serve their self-interest by understating their evaluation of the pure public good. Indeed, it is quite possible for members to reveal no preference for the good in anticipation of receiving a "free ride." They can enjoy the benefits of public goods provided through the expenditures of others while contributing nothing themselves. In terms of equation (4), some individuals claim that their $MRS_{Xy} = 0$, i.e., that they are unwilling to give up the private for the public good, when in fact their $MRS_{Xy} > 0$.

Because of this free rider behavior, a decentralized market system ultimately fails to attain Pareto optimality in a world with public goods. Moreover, the emergence of the free rider is most critical in the instance when the public good is in its pure form. Where free riding is prevalent, collective goods must be financed through some compulsory taxing scheme (see Morgan-Shelton).

In reality, however, most economic goods and services are neither purely public nor purely private. In fact, the vast majority of goods fall somewhere between the two extremes put forth above and therefore, exhibit properties of both "publicness" and "privateness" (see DeSerpa, Hanson). Since most public goods are not pure and in view of the fact that the appropriateness of solutions to public good problems depends upon the degree of a particular good's pureness, the following sections will examine the nature of the less than pure public goods as well as specifying the general Pareto-optimal conditions for these goods.

III. SPECTRUMS AND TAXONOMIES

Examples of pure public goods are difficult to discover, and thus, impure public goods continue to command increasing attention.[6] Impure public goods include such items as information systems, game reserves, canals, satellite communication networks, etc., that are partially indivisible and/or partially nonappropriable. Essentially, the "public character" of goods is related to three spectrums—i.e., the degree of indivisibility, the extent of nonappropriability of the good's benefits, and the size of the interacting group that consumes the benefits of the good.

In Figure 2, the three axes[7] denote these three spectrums. Full appropriability exists anywhere on the OABC plane; whereas, total nonappropriability is shown on the EFGD plane. Full indivisibility corresponds to distance OC on the x-axis, and divisibility occurs at the origin. Furthermore, the size of the interacting group varies along the y-axis from one person (at 0) to the entire world (at A). Therefore, the vertical planes, numbered 1 through 5,

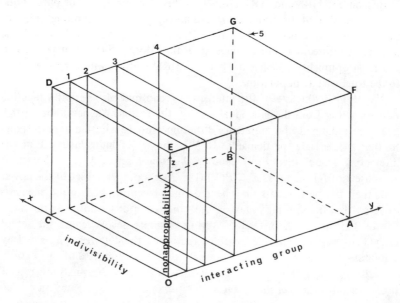

Figure 2: Classification Scheme

depict a group size of a region, a state, a nation, an international group, and the world, respectively.

Any good can be located on the diagram. For instance, private goods lie along line OA, depending upon the interacting group's size, because these goods are fully divisible and appropriable. A worldwide pure public good (e.g., monitoring the ozone layer, plutonium waste removal) is placed at point G. Local impure public goods (e.g., tennis courts, swimming pools), which are partially indivisible and fully appropriable, are placed on the OABC plane between plane OEDC and plane 1. In this volume, the Morgan-Shelton paper considers public goods of an interregional nature that are located between planes 1 and 3. The Shaffer, Amacher-Tollison, and the DeSerpa pieces examine public goods (i.e., defense, ocean pollution and the Olympic spirit) that are situated between planes 3 and 5 near the upper portion of the box.

A. SIZE OF INTERACTING GROUP

Each of the three spectrums in Figure 2 can be associated with the form of the Pareto-optimal provision conditions. For private goods, the size of the group (i.e., n is group size) determines the number of MRSs that must be simultaneously equated to the MRT. Hence, if n = 10, then $MRS^1 = MRS^2 = \ldots = MRS^{10} = MRT$ represents the provision condition (subscripts on the MRS and MRT terms have been suppressed). For pure public goods, the size of the interacting group determines the limiting index of summation with respect to the MRSs. That is, if the good provides indivisible benefits to three adjoining states (see the Morgan-Shelton paper), then provision optimality is reached when $\sum_{i=1}^{n} MRS^i = MRT$, where n corresponds to the total tristate population.

Variation in the size of the interacting group may also permit a redefinition of actors from the individual to, say, the nation. Whenever the participants are redefined, the preference structure must be adjusted to correspond to that of the new participants. If N is the set of individuals within the interacting group, then $P(N)$ denotes the power set of N (i.e., the set of all subsets of N). Suppose $K \subset P(N)$ (i.e., K is a proper subset of the power set), then the participants may be redefined to correspond to the elements of K so that the limiting index on the summation of the MRSs is the number of elements of K instead of N. For example, let N denote the set of individuals within four allied nations that share the deterrence provided by a military arsenal, and let the K consist of the four subsets of $P(N)$ corresponding to the sets of individuals within each of the four nations, respectively. In this example, the social welfare function that aggregates the preferences of the nation's individuals becomes the relevant preference structure. Moreover, provision optimality occurs when $\sum_{i=1}^{4} MRS^i = MRT$ is satisfied, where the MRS^i corresponds to the trade-off associated with the social welfare function of the *ith* nation (see Sandler and Cauley, 1975; Olson and Zeckhauser, 1966). Redefinition of the participants, as above, can transform a "large numbers" problem into a "small numbers" problem. Hence, the defense example alters the relevant participants from all individuals in four nations to four participants representing four governmental entities.

B. INDIVISIBILITY SPECTRUMS

Public goods may be less than perfectly indivisible because of two influences—accessibility, and/or crowding. Each of these factors generates the same impact on the optimal provision conditions; i.e., the MRS terms must be weighted when summed. In the case of crowding, increased utilization of a public good creates congestion costs which detract from the satisfaction derived from the good. On the other hand, increased provision gives rise to benefits in the form of congestion relief, whenever utilization remains unchanged.

An example of congestion costs may be that of a public swimming pool which, once produced, is available to all citizens. As increasing numbers of people use the facility, congestion costs are imposed upon people already using the pool. The latter find that with the addition of each new pool user, their own satisfaction from using the pool declines. It is even possible that the increase in satisfaction to the new pool user is less than the decrease in satisfaction to the people already using it. Thus, increased use may have an overall negative impact on community welfare. If new pools are constructed in the community, however, the users are spread over a large number of pools and satisfaction rises to all pool users (congestion costs are reduced).

These opposing effects can be captured by the introduction of k, measuring the average utilization rate of a unit of the impure public good (see Oakland, 1972; Sandler, 1975). The essential ingredients of the model are depicted in equations (5) - (7):

(5) $\quad C^i = C^i(k,X)$ where $k = \sum\limits_{i=1}^{n} X^i/X$

(6) $\quad X^i \leqslant X$

(7) $\quad U^i = U^i(y^i, C^i)$ with $\partial U^i/\partial y^i > 0$ and $\partial U^i/\partial C^i < 0$

Equation (5) represents the congestion (i.e., C^i) experienced by the *ith* individual, in which increases in average utilization augment congestion and increases in the public good (i.e., X) relieve congestion. In equation (6), the impurity of the public good is underscored, since the i*th* individual's consumption (i.e., X^i) may be less than the amount of the public good supplied. The utility function of the i*th* individual is shown to depend positively on private good consumption (i.e., y^i) and negatively on congestion (see equation (7)).

As k varies from 1 to n, the nature of the good changes from being divisible to being fully indivisible. If the good is divisible, then $\sum_{i=1}^{n} X^i = X$ and k is 1; however, when the good is indivisible, $X^i = X$ for all i and k equals n. Partial divisibility occurs when $1 < k < n$.

Provision optimality is achieved when $\sum_{i=1}^{n} c^i MRS^i = MRT$. c^i corresponds to a weighting factor that measures for each individual, the reduction in congestion that results from a unit increase in the public good. Each of the MRS^i terms denotes the individual's marginal benefit, in terms of the numeraire, from congestion relief.

Congestion costs have been dealt with extensively in what has come to be known as the "Theory of Clubs" (Buchanan, 1965; Ng, 1973). "Clubs" can be organized such that only members enjoy public goods provided by the membership. A larger membership, all else equal, implies congestion costs for current members. In this volume, the DeSerpa paper illustrates an interesting application of the theory of clubs. Optimal toll and membership requirements can be derived for impure public goods that are appropriable through the erection of an exclusion mechanism (e.g., a turnstile, a guard). These conditions[8] appear in equations (8) and (9) (see the derivations in Oakland, 1972; Sandler, 1975):

$$(8) \quad \sum_{i=1}^{n} MCC^i = MB^i \quad \text{(Toll)}$$

$$(9) \quad \int_0^{X^i} (\sum_{i=1}^{n} MCC^i) ds^i \leqslant \int_0^{X^i} MB^i ds^i \quad \text{(Membership)},$$

where s^i is a dummy of integration.

The optimal toll must equate, at the margin, the benefits from an additional unit of utilization with the additional congestion costs imposed on the membership (i.e., $\sum_{i=1}^{n} MCC^i$, where MCC^i is the marginal congestion costs experienced by the i*th* individual). The toll is set equal to the left-hand side of equation (8). Furthermore, efficient membership requires that the membership benefits for any individual must equal or exceed the total congestion costs that his membership creates for the interacting group.

Partial indivisibility may also result from limited accessibility owing to the location of the public good vis-a-vis the individuals. If accessibility is unequal between participants, then many individuals will consume less than the total public good supplied. This consideration requires the introduction of weights (i.e., A^i) on each individual's consumption of the public good—i.e., $X^i = A^iX$. As A^i approaches 1, the good becomes more indivisible. When equation (10) is satisfied, optimality in provision is achieved (Mohring and Boyd, 1971: 353-354).

$$(10) \quad \sum_{i=1}^{n} A^iMRS^i = MRT$$

C. NONAPPROPRIABILITY

If a good is appropriable at zero cost, then the provision conditions are unaffected; however, the expenditure of exclusion costs, which transforms a nonappropriable good into an appropriable good, will affect provision requirements. The extent of exclusion costs can be related to the nonappropriability spectrum in Figure 2. The larger the degree of nonappropriability, then the greater will be the necessary exclusion costs. Presumably, fully nonappropriable goods are associated with infinite exclusion costs, while appropriable goods require zero exclusion costs.

When an impure public good is subject to crowding and requires exclusion costs in order to force toll payments, then equation (11) represents the condition for optimal provision (Oakland, 1972: 351-355).

$$(11) \quad \sum_{i=1}^{n} c^iMRS^i = MRT + MEC$$

In equation (11), the sum of marginal production costs and marginal exclusion costs must be equated to the benefits from congestion relief. The introduction of marginal exclusion costs reduces the optimal quantity of the good as compared with the case of zero marginal exclusion costs.

The relationship between nonappropriability and exclusion costs is crucial in resolving whether markets or nonmarket structures, e.g., supranational structures (see Knoer and Amacher-Tollison) should provide the good. For instance, if both market and nonmarket provision render equivalent benefits, then a comparison between exclusion costs required by market allocation and the operation costs of the nonmarket structure determines which is a more viable allocative mode (see Arrow, 1970; Bator, 1958; Auster and Silver,

1973; Ruggie, 1972; Russett and Sullivan, 1971; Sandler and Cauley, 1977). Obviously, the nonmarket structure is preferable if and only if operation costs are less than exclusion costs.

IV. EXTERNALITIES AND PUBLIC GOODS

An externality exists whenever the consumption or production activities of one individual affects, either positively or negatively, the economic activities of another individual and where no mechanism exists to compensate (to charge) those bearing external costs (benefits).[9] Externalities may exist between two or more producers; between two or more consumers; or between producers and consumers. Moreover, producers and consumers may correspond to firms, individuals, or nations. Within this volume, the Smith paper and the Amacher-Tollison paper examine aspects of international externalities such as international pollution (e.g., pollution of the seas, destruction of the ozone layer by the SST).

If costs and benefits of externalities are unrecognized when allocative decisions are reached, inefficiency results in the form of suboptimal provision of some desirable activities, and superoptimal provision of some undesirable activities. For example, suppose nation A dumps PCB (a carcinogenic substance) into a river that flows into nation B. Failure to recognize the damage to the environments of both nations leads to a larger level of PCB pollution than would occur if the costs to B are included within the production costs of the polluting nation A. Essentially, a production externality causes a divergence between private cost of production and social cost of production, where social cost includes both private costs and costs imposed outside the producer.

When costs are recomputed to include all relevant social costs, the externality is said to be internalized, resulting in efficient allocation. Four fundamental methods permit internalization of an externality: 1) A tax-subsidy scheme can be implemented in order to equate social and private costs or benefits (see Morgan-Shelton, Smith); 2) The parties can bargain (see Amacher-Tollison); 3) A court can impose a liability assignment that internalizes the externality (see Amacher-Tollison); 4) A nonmarket structure can regulate the level of the externality (see Knoer, Hanson).

The second solution is most relevant to situations involving only a small number of participants so that benefits from cooperation are easy to recognize and inexpensive to achieve. The other three solutions necessitate the existence of a specialized institution, i.e., a fiscal mechanism, a court or a nonmarket structure. For many international problems, the relevant institutions are nonexistent.

Public goods are closely related to externalities since a special class of consumption externalities can be analyzed as a public good (Mishan, 1971; Evans, 1970). If x^{ij} represents the ith individual's consumption of the jth good and x^{ij} is a public good to the interacting group, then the welfare conditions for this consumption externality are equivalent to that of a public good—i.e., $\sum_{i=1}^{n} MRS^i = MRT$, where MRS^i refers to the marginal benefits derived from x^{ij} by each individual. Thus, a consumption externality that all individuals' experience is equivalent to a public good. An example might be the immunizations against communicable disease which are received by some people and not by others. Those individuals not receiving the immunization receive some benefit, since the probability of coming into contact with the disease is reduced by those who have been immunized.

In a similar fashion, activities which impose external costs on second parties can be construed as "public bads." In the equation $\sum_{i=1}^{n} MRS^i = MRT$, if the marginal rates of substitution which are summed do not include those trade-offs of parties adversely affected by the externality, then the activity causing the externality is being done in superoptimal amounts. Inclusion of the external costs will cause $\sum_{i=1} MRS$ to decline since the MRS of individuals suffering external costs is negative. (Negative MRS implies that these individuals are willing to "pay," in private goods terms, to have the external cost reduced). The externality causing activity must therefore be curtailed so as to again equate $\sum_{i=1}^{n} MRS^i = MRT$, where $i = 1, \ldots, n$ includes everybody.

V. JOINT PRODUCTS AND PUBLIC GOODS

As in the study of private goods, joint products are an important consideration for public goods. Joint production requires that the same intermediate input(s) produces two or more outputs (e.g., oil produces gasoline, kerosine and synthetic fibers; a steer produces a hide and meat). For public goods, an intermediate input may produce one or more pure public goods as well as private or impure public goods.[10] For example, defense expenditures by an alliance (see Shaffer) produces deterrence (a pure public good), earned foreign exchange for nations that host military bases (a private good), and protection against attack (an impure public good).

Although joint products complicate the form of the provision conditions, these conditions for joint products are essentially a conglomerate of previously stated forms. If each unit of an intermediate input, say z, produces one unit of x, a pure public good, and one unit of y, a pure private good, then equations (12) and (13) represent the provision conditions for z (see Holtermann, 1972; Mishan, 1969).

$$(12) \quad \sum_{i=1}^{n} MRS_x^i + MRS_y = MRT_z$$

$$(13) \quad MRS_y = MRS_y^1 = \ldots = MRS_y^n$$

In these equations, each of these MRS and MRT terms show the trade-off between the good in question and a private numeraire good (r). The r subscript has been deleted in order to simplify notation. Equation (12) states that the marginal benefit of the public output (i.e., $\sum_{i=1}^{n} MRS_x^i$) must be added to the marginal benefit of the private output (i.e., MRS_y), and that this sum must be equated to the marginal cost of the intermediate input (i.e., MRT_z) in order to satisfy Pareto optimality. The "private" aspects of the optimality conditions are captured in equation (13), which states that each individual's MRS must be simultaneously equated.

The five panels of Figure 3 depict the graphical solution when two individuals, say A and B, consume the private and public outputs that are

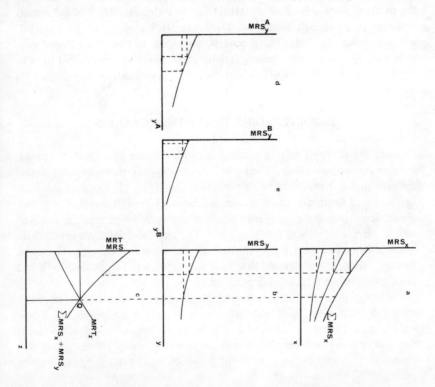

Figure 3: Vertical and Horizontal Summations of Demand Curves

produced by good z. In Figure 3, the vertical axes measure the MRSs and the MRT, and the horizontal axes measure the units of the respective goods. Furthermore, the diagram assumes that z produces x and y in fixed proportions in which each unit of z renders one unit of both x and y. Both horizontal and vertical summations are required for optimality to be satisfied. That is, the MRSs for the public good are vertically summed over the individuals in panel a; whereas, the MRSs of the private good are horizontally summed in panel (d), (e), and (b). Finally, the marginal benefits for the public and private goods must be vertically summed, as shown in panels (a), (b), and (c), if all marginal benefits derived from z are to be depicted. Optimality is achieved at point Q in panel (c) by equating both the marginal benefits and costs associated with z. Thus, Figure 3 graphically depicts both requirements of optimality as stated in equations (12) and (13).

If good z produces more than one pure public and private good, then additional vertical summations, a summation for each public good, and additional horizontal summations, a summation for each private good, are imperative. Additionally, impure public outputs from the intermediate input are handled like the pure public outputs except that weighted, instead of unweighted, MRSs are vertically summed.

VI. PUBLIC GOODS AND PUBLIC INSTITUTIONS

Very often, in view of public goods and/or externalities, public policy analysts are quick to recommend public intervention in the markets where externalities exist. This "naive approach," (Burkhead and Miner, 1971: 112) rarely includes an attempt to compare the benefits to be expected from the public intervention with the costs of doing so. Subsidies and taxes are usually recommended so as to force private parties to bear all costs of their actions or be rewarded for all benefits created thereby. Often, little account is taken of the costs involved in determining the relevant amount of the tax (subsidy) nor of the further distortions which may be introduced into the economy because of the tax (subsidy) payments.

An even more fundamental problem arises out of what has come to be called the "theory of second best," (Lipsey and Lancaster, 1956-1957). The main thrust of that theory is that taxes (subsidies) designed to bring one sector of the economy toward Pareto optimality, while resources in other sectors remain nonoptimally allocated, do not insure an overall improvement in societal welfare.[11] Taxes (subsidies) can introduce distortions of their own, albeit at the same time removing distortions of another type (see Morgan-Shelton). For example, an income tax as a replacement for an equal yield excise tax may relieve the economy of the distortions in relative prices resulting from the latter, but can introduce entirely new distortions. The income tax introduces a distortion in the "prices" of work and leisure for all persons whose income is subject to tax. A judgment in favor of one or the other tax cannot be made on the basis of Pareto optimality since each leaves some of the necessary conditions for optimality unsatisfied (Burkhead and Miner, 1971: 114).

Should we therefore stand by in despair waiting for the unlikely event that we are able to correct all distortions simultaneously? We think not. Dealing more with the likelihood of a welfare improvement than its certainty, Mishan (1962) thinks it reasonable to expect a welfare improvement if the sectors within which adjustments are to be made are small relative to the remaining ones. Secondly, the likelihood of a welfare gain increases as the discrepancies in the marginal relationships between the sectors where adjustments are to be made and the rest of the economy becomes relatively large. There are indeed some sectors of the economy where interactions with other sectors are small. Intervention in these relatively isolated sectors, in the quest for optimality, is unlikely to cause significant distortions elsewhere, and therefore could be considered (operationally at least) not significantly different from a "first-best" solution.

A. THE COSTS OF RAISING REVENUE

To the public policy analyst, a relevant question should be whether an imperfect (costly) market, or public intervention is the most efficient institutional structure for the treatment of externality and public goods problems. Market solutions have the advantage of providing a wealth of information about the relative values of goods and services, but the more markets are distorted by public intervention, the more distorted this information becomes. In any "real world" situation, the analyst must consider policies which are to be applied where other public policies not of direct concern, as well as markets which handle both purely private goods and externalities, already exist. It is to his advantage to have access to the greatest amount of undistorted information possible. Public policy intervention always involves some costs directly attributable to the search for such information and agreement on the appropriate policy. Probably more important from the microeconomic point of view, however, public policy intervention implies a distortion in the prices which would be established by market transactions, and therefore, impose indirect costs upon sectors of the economy not of concern to the policy analyst. Since it is these prices which provide information to all remaining sectors of the economy, we must take care that policy implementation does not cause costly distortions affecting sectors of the economy where no public intervention is intended.

B. THE "FORCED RIDER"

Tanzi (1972) has clearly shown us that welfare costs may be involved in providing public goods which differ in how individuals may be excluded from consuming them. In standard public goods analysis, we often assume that consumption of the public good can be extended to all individuals at zero marginal cost, and that it is either impossible to prevent individuals from consuming the good, or that they can be excluded from consumption only at some cost. This imperfect ability of the public good producer to exclude some people as consumers gives rise to the "free rider" problem alluded to earlier.

Taking a different point of view, however, we see a whole set of public goods which people are forced to consume, whether they like them or not, and this gives rise to the problem of the "forced rider." In the case where the consumer can choose to consume the good or not, no problem arises, since no consumer will choose voluntarily to consume an item which reduces his well-being. A public park or a television program—both public goods—need not be consumed by those individuals who value their services negatively. Such a consumer need only stay at home or turn off the television, and he excludes himself from consuming the goods. If he so chooses, he can go to the park or watch the program at zero marginal cost, and at that time, the normal public goods analysis applies. Pareto optimality requires that consumers be charged tax prices which reflect each one's marginal evaluation of the public good. Clearly, since each consumer consumes the same amount of the pure public good, it is likely that each individual's marginal utility from that given amount will be different from other individuals' marginal utility, since different people will value the marginal unit of the equal amount of the public good differently. Therefore, for Pareto optimality, each must be charged a different tax price, so as to equate each individual's ratio of marginal utility to tax price.

On the other hand, we have a set of goods—defense is the best example—where not only is it impossible to exclude some individuals from consuming, but individuals cannot exclude themselves either. It is entirely possible that the welfare of some individuals might fall when a marginal unit of the public good is provided. In the case of defense, people who oppose military activities for philosophical, religious, or political reasons would undoubtedly be affected in this way. They become "forced riders" by having consumption forced upon them. Whenever some individuals are negatively affected in this way, the search for Pareto optimality gives rise to the need for negative tax prices (subsidies) for these individuals. To ensure that the marginal utility to tax price ratios for all persons in the economy are equated, individuals with negative marginal evaluations must be "charged" negative tax prices. Those who suffer a welfare loss by public good provision must be compensated for the loss.

This problem becomes particularly acute in that tax policy—as an expediency—does not distinguish between "forced riders" and other public good consumers. A pacifist, for example, must pay the same tax price charged for defense as any other individual, his negative marginal evaluation notwithstanding. The true cost to the economy of providing defense in this case must include the welfare losses falling upon all relevant "forced riders."

C. COSTS OF AGREEMENT

The costs of public goods provision discussed above clearly may fall upon specific individuals in the society. They, of course, will react, either to prevent those particular public goods from being provided, or to modify the way in which they are provided. If some goods or services are to be provided by the public sector, decision rules must be worked out so that the members of the society can agree among themselves as to the quantity of public goods and the methods of provision. The costs involved in the process of agreement and decision will stem mainly from two sources. First, any decisions which create "forced riders" or other economic distortions impose costs on a segment of the population. If these people are engaged in the decision-making process at all, bargaining must take place to arrive at some form of compensation for their welfare reduction. Without compensation, no agreement can be reached. Second, where the agreement of more than one person is needed to reach a decision, some costs will be involved in communication among them; (i.e., bargaining, and the time and effort expended to come to a final settlement).

Unanimity among all persons affected by public policy is the only decision rule which can remove costs of the "forced rider" type, and the only rule which is Pareto optimal. (A decision is a Pareto-optimal move only if it makes at least one individual better off, without making another individual worse off). Under a rule of unanimity, any individual who would have a noncompensated cost imposed upon him by a public decision has an effective veto power over that policy. To gain his consent, others in the society have to offer compensation or modification of the policy to alleviate these costs for the dissenting individual. In any "real world" situation, however, unanimity is likely to be an unrealizable goal as a decision-making tool due to the relatively high bargaining costs which are likely to accompany it.

Buchanan and Tullock (1962) have devoted considerable attention to the interaction of these costs in constitutional choice. Here we will employ their basic framework, with modifications, in the consideration of more specific decisions, ignoring, for the moment, the choice of constitutions. Our chosen

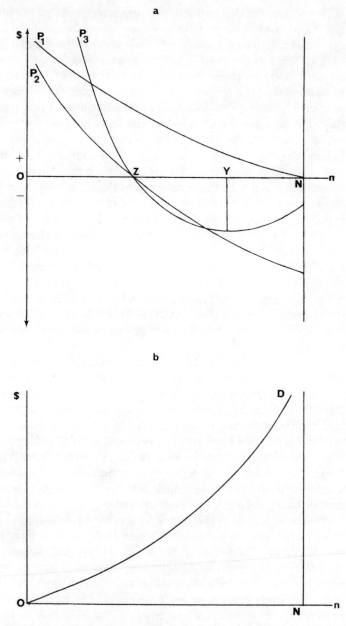

Figure 4: Expected Net Indirect Costs and Benefits

model remains crude, but will lead us, nevertheless, in the direction of discovering a most optimal form of government for handling decisions on externalities, including public goods. In Figure 4 we have drawn hypothetical relationships between the net indirect costs imposed upon persons affected by public decisions (the vertical axis), and the number of persons (n) needed to reach agreement on public action (horizontal axis). ON represents the total number of persons in the decision-making community. Costs are net in that they take into account all indirect costs imposed upon the individual. For example, curve P_1 represents costs imposed upon a person who bears some burden under all decision rules with the exception of unanimity. The individual might be a "forced rider" for the type of public action under consideration and will, therefore, agree to the action only when adequately compensated, so his net costs become zero only at N, where the entire population is in agreement. His cost function P_1 is downward sloping, since the greater the proportion of the population needed for agreement, the more likely persons similar to himself (but not identical to him) will be wooed by the early proponents of the public action. Bargains struck to bring a larger and larger proportion of the population into agreement are likely to provide compensation and policy modification which make the action less and less costly to the individual concerned. Only at N, however, will his own personal costs reach zero, since only then will he receive full compensation to satisfy his own personal tastes.

Since we are concerned here with a specific public good decision, there will be n net indirect cost curves, one for each individual. There is no reason to believe that the curves will always show that a cost is being imposed. Cost curve P_2, for example, might pertain to a person who will suffer a cost if less than OZ/ON of the population is needed to sustain a decision, but who has net indirect benefits (negative cost) bestowed upon him if a greater proportion is required. He might, for example, be able to become a "free rider" if greater-than-OZ/ON are in on the decision. Some of the decisive proportion might consist of persons like himself, who can strike bargains so as to impose costs on others and enjoy a free ride themselves.

Another individual might possess a curve like P_3, indicating that he would be suffering a loss if less than OZ/ON were needed for a decision, but beyond that, would be a net free rider. A point may be reached, however, where the need to form larger and larger coalitions would force bargains between free riders and those who suffer losses. Free riders would have to relinquish some of their free-ride benefits to pay compensation to those who had suffered costs before. As drawn, P_3 would begin to turn upward after a proportion of OY/ON was passed, indicating that the individual represented by P_3 would be relinquishing some of his free-ride benefits in an attempt to draw more people into the decisive coalition. Note that, as in the case of P_2, the cost curve need not end at zero costs when unanimity is reached. Some free riders may still exist, even where everyone is in agreement on the policy of concern.

It is safe to make the generality that these individual cost curves would be generally downward sloping as larger and larger proportions of the population are needed for a decision. Some may turn up, but most likely only as large proportions are needed. It is easy to conceive of some curves that are positively sloped throughout, as would be the case with a potential dictator. If only one person is needed for a decision, the curve of that particular person would begin far below the horizontal axis, since he could bestow upon himself the maximum free ride. As more and more persons were brought into the decision, and dictatorial powers were eroded, the X-dictator's curve would rise steadily, probably into the positive quadrant as unanimity were approached. It is safe to assume, however, that the number of potential dictators is small, and that the majority of curves would look like those shown. Summation of these individual costs would lead to a community cost function which looks roughly like the one labeled C in Figure 5.[12]

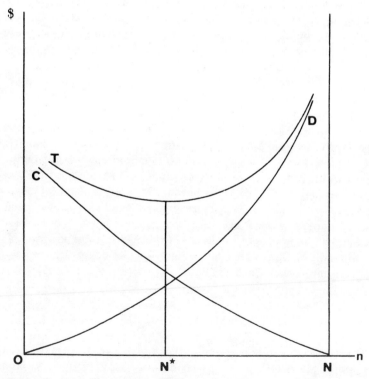

Figure 5: Net Indirect Costs

The second type of decision-making cost is represented by the curve D in Figure 4(b). It would most likely have the positive slope and roughly the shape shown since the need to form larger and larger decisive blocs would imply a greater expenditure in time, effort, and bargaining on the part of all decisionmakers. The need for unanimity might send costs infinitely high, as the majority tries to make concessions to the last individual to gain his agreement on the policy in question.

Both types of costs can be placed on the same diagram and summed, as they are in Figure 5. The resultant total indirect cost curve, T, would generally possess a minimum at some point, such as X, which occurs when a coalition of ON*/ON is needed. Each specific policy would imply a different set of costs for each individual concerned, and probably different bargaining costs as well. Both C and D, therefore, could be expected to occupy different positions for any given decision, and T's minimum would likely occur at differing proportions of the population.

If we now reason that decisions on public policy should be made where community costs are minimized, we are abandoning, in effect, Pareto optimality. Anything short of unanimity does just that. If, in reality, it is not possible to obtain unanimity—and therefore, Pareto optimality—we should not throw up our hands in despair. A second-best solution is better than no solution, and establishing a decision rule which minimizes decision-making costs is a desirable second best.

Our diagrams have dealt only with a single, specific decision. As yet we cannot say how government should be organized so as to minimize decision-making costs when "government" makes many different decisions, each of which could be expected to impose minimum costs at different-sized coalitions. If ON in Figure 5 represents a nation, and 0 represents the individual, each point between 0 and N represents some different-sized group. ON* might constitute one state or province within the nation, while ON*/2 might be a municipality. On the other hand, ON* might represent all urban dwellers, or all persons of a given racial background. Exactly how persons are lined up along ON has not been specified, and probably cannot be specified without some knowledge of the decision to be made. At this point, we cannot say who will be in the decisive coalition, and we doubt that we can (see Buchanan and Tullock 1962: 112).

VII. INTERGENERATIONAL PUBLIC GOODS

The introduction of intergenerational public goods that are public between and within generations provide a considerably more complicated problem than the normal one posed above. For example, a unit of plutonium waste that is removed from the atmosphere benefits not only the present world population, but it also benefits future generations, owing to plutonium's long half-life of 2400 years (Sandler and Smith, 1976). Future technological developments can be expected to create public goods and bads of an intergenerational character.

Intergenerational public goods are even more difficult to provide, since indivisibility and nonappropriability concern both present and future generations. Without a time machine, provision optimality cannot be implemented through voluntary exchange, because the relevant bargaining parties cannot meet. Moreover, if the present generation fails to include benefits derived by future generations (beyond those benefits that are included by altruistic motives) when production is decided, underprovision of intergenerational public goods will result. Underprovision of these goods lends support for the creation of nonmarket structures that attempt to link generations in order to more optimally supply intergenerational public goods. These structures must decide the proper rate of discounting, intergenerational financing of public goods, and the extent of intergenerational altruism.

International externalities, as discussed by Amacher-Tollison and Smith, can be intergenerational in character. In these instances, present internalization schemes break down unless liabilities and bargains can be imposed across generations. In fact, all of the problems discussed in this volume have an intergenerational analog that is difficult to tackle, especially with traditional tools. Future developments in public goods and public policy must examine the intergenerational aspects of publicness.

VIII. SUMMARY

In summary, this paper (see Section II) explored the Pareto-optimal requirements for the polar cases of the pure public good and the private good. Moreover, the essence of the public good problem (i.e., the need for government provision) is depicted. Section III presented a taxonomy of public goods that related the public character of goods to three spectrums—i.e., the degree of indivisibility, the extent of nonappropriability of the good's benefits, and the size of the interacting group that consumes the benefits of the good. Furthermore, Section III depicted the Pareto-optimal conditions for impure public goods. The following section analyzed the relationship between externalities and public goods; whereas, Section V presented the relationship between joint products and public goods. In Section VI, the feasibility of public provision of public goods is studied within an approach that included political considerations. Finally, Section VII discussed intergenerational public goods. The remaining essays in the volume will employ the definitions and tools presented in this paper.

NOTES

1. See Samuelson (1954, 1955). In reality, most public goods do not manifest themselves in their pure form. We will examine impure public goods in detail below. For the moment, however, we continue to make the simplifying assumption of absolute purity.

2. For a complete derivation of unique Pareto optima see Ferguson (1966) and Bator (1957).

3. For the moment, we assume that these social indifference curves satisfy Arrow's (1951) five axioms. For a specification and discussion of these see Henderson and Quandt (1971: 282-86).

4. The assumptions of this model are as follows:

   (1) There exist two general types of goods: pure public goods and private goods.
   (2) All individuals possess a consistent set of preferences for both the private goods and the public goods that are well-behaved (i.e., smooth and convex to the origin throughout). Furthermore, these preferences are assumed to be fully revealed.
   (3) The production possibility frontier, which depicts society's menu of choices regarding levels and composition of public and private good production, is assumed to be smooth and concave to the origin (i.e., that it possesses a continuous and diminishing marginal rate of transformation).
   (4) There are no "Veblenese Effects," (i.e., interdependencies among utility functions).
   (5) There exists a given distribution of factor ownership.
   (6) The supply of all factors is perfectly inelastic.

5. For a diagrammatic treatment of the pure private good world see Bator (1957) and for the public good world, Samuelson (1955).

6. The literature on impure public goods is quite extensive. Some representative pieces include Buchanan (1965; 1968), DeSerpa (1976), Evans (1970), Litvack and Oates (1970), McGuire (1972; 1974), Mishan (1969), Ng (1973; 1974), Oakland (1969; 1972), Pauly (1970), Sandler (1975), Winch (1973).

7. James Buchanan (1968: 171-177) introduced the size of the interacting group as an important consideration for public good classification. The three-dimensional box is an extension of the two-dimensional box developed by Buchanan; however, we define the interacting group somewhat differently from Buchanan. In Buchanan, the interacting group corresponds to those individuals consuming a unit of the good; whereas, our definition refers to the group consuming the benefits from the supply of the good (see Sandler and Cauley, 1977).

8. These conditions generalize the membership conditions of Buchanan's (1965) theory of clubs, since homogeneity of individuals is no longer assumed. Also, see McGuire (1972; 1974), Ng (1973; 1974), Ng and Tollison (1974), and Tollison (1972.

9. The literature on externalities has grown significantly in the last 15 years. Important works include those by Buchanan and Stubblebine (1962), Davis and Whinston (1962), Dolbear (1967), Evans (1970), Gifford and Stone (1973), Holtermann (1972), Kamien et al. (1973), Marchand and Russell (1973), Mishan (1969; 1971), and Mohring and Boyd (1971).

10. On public goods and joint products, refer to Evans (1970), Mishan (1969), Oakland (1969), Holterman (1972), Samuelson (1969).

11. Many of the points introduced here are found in Burkhead and Miner (1971).

12. There is no reason to expect that the total indirect cost curve, C, of Figure 5 need hit the horizontal axis at N. Where it touches the axis, whether it touches it, and whether or not it turns upward, depends upon the mix of costs and free rides imposed by the specific decision being considered.

BIBLIOGRAPHY

ARROW, K. J. (1970) "The Organization of Economic Activity: Issues Pertinent to the Choice of Market Versus Nonmarket Allocation." Pp. 59-73 in R. Haveman and J. Margolis (eds.) Public Expenditures and Policy Analysis. Chicago: Markham Publishing Co.

––– (1951) Social Choice and Individual Values. New York: John Wiley.

AUSTER, R. and M. SILVER (1973) "Collective Goods and Collective Decision Mechanisms." Public Choice 14(Spring): 1-17.

BATOR, F. (1958) "The Anatomy of Market Failure." Quarterly Journal of Economics 72(August): 351-379.

––– (1957) "The Simple Analytics of Welfare Maximization." American Economic Review 47(March): 22-59.

BEER, F. (1972) "The Political Economy of Alliances: Benefits, Costs, and Institutions in NATO." Sage Professional Papers in International Studies. Beverly Hills: Sage Publications.

BUCHANAN, J. (1968) The Demand and Supply of Public Goods. Chicago: Rand McNally.

––– (1965) "An Economic Theory of Clubs." Economica 32(February): 1-14.

BUCHANAN, J. and W. STUBBLEBINE (1962) "Externality." Economica 29(November): 371-384.

BUCHANAN, J. and G. TULLOCK (1962) The Calculus of Consent. Ann Arbor: The University of Michigan Press.

BURKHEAD, J. and J. MINER (1971) Public Expenditure. Chicago: Aldine.

DAVIS, O. and A. WHINSTON (1962) "Externalities, Welfare, and the Theory of Games." Journal of Political Economy 70(June): 241-262.

DeSERPA, A. (1976) "Multi-dimensional Public Goods." Working Paper, Arizona State University.

DOLBEAR, F. (1967) "On the Theory of Optimum Externality." American Economic Review 57(March): 90-103.

EVANS, A. (1970) "Private Good, Externality, Public Good." Scottish Journal of Political Economy 17(February): 79-89.

FERGUSON, C. E. (1966) Microeconomic Theory. Homewood, Illinois: Richard D. Irwin.

GIFFORD, A. and C. STONE (1973) "Externalities, Liability, and the Coase Theorem: A Mathematical Analysis." Western Economic Journal 11(September): 260-268.

HENDERSON, J. M. and R. E. QUANDT (1971) Microeconomic Theory: A Mathematical Approach. New York: McGraw-Hill Book Co.

HOLTERMANN, S. (1972) "Externalities and Public Goods." Economica 39(February): 78-87.

KAMIEN, M., N. SCHWARTZ and D. ROBERTS (1973) "Exclusion, Externalities, and Public Goods." Journal of Public Economics 2(July): 217-230.

LIPSEY, R. G. and K. LANCASTER (1956-57) "The General Theory of Second Best," Review of Economic Studies 63: 11-32.

LITVACK, J. and W. OATES (1970) "Group Size and the Output of Public Goods: Theory and Application to State-local Finance in the United States." Public Finance 25(No. 1): 42-58.

MARCHAND, J. and K. RUSSELL (1973) "Externalities, Liability, Separability, and Resource Allocation." American Economic Review 63(September): 611-620.

MCGUIRE, M. (1974) "Group Segregation and Optimal Jurisdictions." Journal of Political Economy 82(January/February): 112-132.

――― (1972) "Private Good Clubs and Public Good Clubs: Economic Model of Group Formation." Swedish Journal of Economics 74(February): 84-99.

MISHAN, E. (1969) "The Relationship Between Joint Products, Collective Goods, and External Effects." Journal of Political Economy 77(May/June): 329-348.

――― (1971) "The Postwar Literature on Externalities: An Interpretative Essay." Journal of Economic Literature 9(March): 1-28.

――― (1962) "Second Thoughts on Second Best." Oxford Economic Papers 14(October): 206-217.

MOHRING, H. and H. BOYD (1971) "Analyzing 'Externalities': Direct Interaction vs. 'Asset Utilization' Framework." Economica 38(November): 347-361.

NG, Y. (1974) "The Economic Theory of Clubs: Optimal Tax/Subsidy." Economica 41(August): 308-321.

――― (1973) "The Economic Theory of Clubs: Pareto Optimality Conditions." Economica 40(August): 291-298.

NG, Y. and R. TOLLISON (1974) "A Note on Consumption Sharing and Non-exclusion Rules." Economica 41(November): 446-450.

OAKLAND, W. (1972) "Congestion, Public Goods, and Welfare." Journal of Public Economics 1(November): 339-357.

――― (1969) "Joint Goods." Economica 36(August): 253-268.

OLSON, M. and R. ZECKHAUSER (1966) "An Economic Theory of Alliances." Review of Economics and Statistics 48(August): 266-279.

PAULY, M. (1970) "Optimality, Public Goods, and Local Governments: A General Theoretical Analysis." Journal of Political Economy 78(May/June): 572-585.

RUGGIE, J. (1972) "Collective Goods and Future International Collaboration." American Political Science Review 66(September): 874-893.

RUSSETT, B. and J. SULLIVAN (1971) "Collective Goods and International Organization." International Organization 25(Autumn): 845-865.

SAMUELSON, P. (1969) "Contrast Between Welfare Conditions for Joint Supply and for Public Goods." Review of Economics and Statistics 51(February): 26-30.

――― (1955) "A Diagrammatic Exposition of a Theory of Public Expenditure." Review of Economics and Statistics 37(November): 350-356.

――― (1954) "The Pure Theory of Public Expenditures." Review of Economics and Statistics 36(November): 387-389.

SANDLER, T. (1975) "Pareto Optimality, Pure Public Goods, Impure Public Goods, and Multiregional Spillovers." Scottish Journal of Political Economy 22(February): 25-38.

SANDLER, T. and J. CAULEY (1977) "The Design of Supranational Structures: An Economic Perspective." International Studies Quarterly 21(June): 251-76.

――― (1975) "On the Economic Theory of Alliances." Journal of Conflict Resolution 19(June): 330-348.

SANDLER, T. and V. K. SMITH (1976) "Intertemporal and Intergenerational Pareto Efficiency." Journal of Environmental Economics and Management 2(February): 151-159.

SANDMO, A. (1973) "Public Goods and the Technology of Consumption." Review of Economic Studies 40(October): 517-528.

TANZI, V. (1972) "A Note on Exclusion, Pure Public Goods and Pareto Optimality." Public Finance 27(1): 75-78.

TOLLISON, R. (1972) "Consumption Sharing and Non-exclusion Rules." Economica 39(August): 276-291.

WINCH, D. (1973) "The Pure Theory of Non-pure Goods." Canadian Journal of Economics 6(May): 149-163.

Chapter 2

EMPIRICAL ESTIMATION AND THE
THEORY OF PUBLIC GOODS: A SURVEY

JON CAULEY
University of Hawaii–Hilo

In view of the fact that the power of theoretical arguments increase dramatically when coupled with an integrated empirical test of the real world, Chapter 2 will address the empirical literature associated with the models presented in Chapter 1 above.[1] Despite this focus, it needs to be mentioned that adequate empirical tests ultimately rest upon logical and rigorously specified theoretical models and as a result, it is impossible if not misleading, to discuss empirical work without at least tangential reference to theory.

The purpose of this Chapter is twofold as indicated in Figure 1 by the squares labeled (A) and (B), whereas the sequence of the presentation is indicated with arrows. First, a representative survey of the existing literature will be presented. The survey is classified into three major categories: demand estimation approaches, supply estimation approaches, and other approaches that do not fit well into the two previously mentioned schemes. Each of the subcategories in section (A) will be developed in the following manner. Initially, the fundamental problem posed by the public good will be dealt with as well as the method of resolving it. An attempt is made to position the problem and its empirical resolution within an international institutional context. Next, the statistical procedure will be specified and amplified upon. Subsequently, criticisms of the literature and directions for future research will be suggested in section (B).

A. SURVEY

From an economic perspective, the logic of the first two subsections of (A) rests upon the impending fact that value in an economic system is either explicitly or implicitly determined by the interaction of the demands and supplies of individual economic units. As optimal resource allocation in the private and/or public sectors requires an assessment of this value, it is fundamental that the empirical nature of these schedules be ascertained.[2] In a smoothly functioning international market system, a determination of value and its effective resolution is a somewhat trivial matter. To the contrary, in

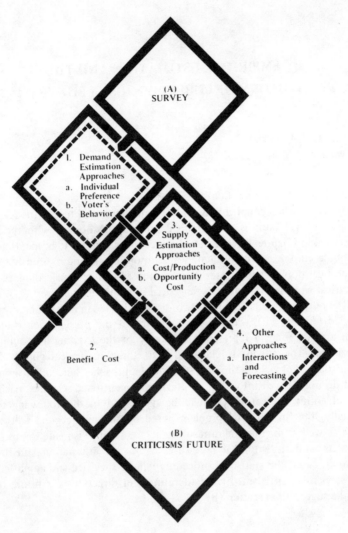

Figure 1: Flow Diagram of Part II

an international arena plagued with public goods (bads), efficient transnational resource allocation policy is predicated upon knowledge of the sort concealed within the demand and supply schedules for these goods. On the other hand, there exist other types of empirically orientated socio-economic research that should be portrayed in a survey of this nature, providing a rationale for the third subsection of (A).

1. Demand Estimation: The Individual Preference Approach

As a first case and in order to illustrate the problem of demand estimation in which an individual preference approach is employed, a recreation example is developed within the framework of the international arena. In general, the extent to which the individual economic preference approach is useful in estimating the demand for an international public good depends upon the degree of publicness associated with the good. More specifically, the ability to apply the technique presented here is inversely related to the pureness of the public good involved. In other words, the closer the good is to the pure public end of the private-public good spectrum, the less appropriate is the econometric procedure expressed here.

Nevertheless, the basic problem is that of any public good, the fatal inability to directly apply the "measuring rod" of money. Since recreational land utilization typically carries a zero price tag, the ability to evaluate this good in pecuniary terms becomes problematic. Subsequently, a dilemma is posed with respect to efficient resource allocation. In particular, assessing the optimal utilization of land in recreation as opposed to, say, commercial use, where a rate of return on investment can be readily ascertained, is at best, woefully inadequate.

For concreteness, suppose that a supranational structure (SS) has been formed by two countries, Alphaland and Betaland, in an effort by both countries to "share" a common lake. These two countries have been motivated to communality regarding the lake because resources, especially human resources, are mobile between countries and because of the circumstance that three of the most ideal spots for recreational parks lie on Alphaland and Betaland's jurisdictional boundary (see Figure 2). The purpose of the (SS) is to jointly finance and administer the recreational areas with an eye toward securing the highest economic return to the aforementioned public lands in terms of their best alternative use—commercial use. The (SS) is confronted with questions like: should park number 3 be closed and a new park built in some other location, or, should a portion of private land in Alphaland be secured through the (SS)'s "eminent" domain and transformed into a park?

Additionally, for purposes of tractability, assume that concentric zones around each recreational area have been delineated and that members of Alphaland and Betaland can be identified with these zones (e.g., zip code zones or their equivalent). Furthermore, each zone contains the same number of people and the distance within each zone to a particular recreation area is the same (see Figure 3, where R designates a representative recreational area).

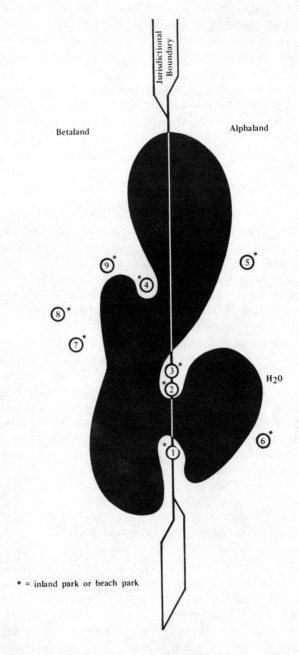

Figure 2: Map of Inland Parks and Beach Parks

The method for obtaining the information that the (SS) needs to fulfill its decision-making responsibilities with has been referred to as the back-door approach to obtaining information of the kind generated by market prices in the private sector.[3]

The essence of the method is that, although zero entrance or gate fees prevail, park users do spend time and money traveling to them. The fact that they are willing and able to incur these associated private costs, provides explicit evidence of willingness and ability to pay for the services produced by the park whether it be swimming, boating or consuming the park's aesthetic endowments. As a result, the necessity to place a value on each separate activity is obliviated while at the same time the unique properties of the sundry parks are recognized.

In view of the above stated problem and associated suppositions, two pieces of information are needed in order to estimate demand relationships for the parks, ultimately allowing the (SS) to place dollar values on them so that the value of land in recreational use can be compared with the value of the land in commercial use as well as facilitating comparisons between and among different parks in Alphaland and Betaland: (1) the number of visits made by each person and (2), the zone in which each person resides.

Figure 3: Concentric Distance Zones Around Recreational Area R

Table 1 and Table 2 present the information presumed above. First, observe that already one point on the demand curve is determined in a straightforward manner (i.e., the point: $0.00, 75 visits). In addition, notice that it costs fifty cents more to travel to Zone II than from Zone I, and so on. Next, assume that an entrance fee of fifty cents is levied. Persons residing in each zone now incur costs that are equal to the zero entrance fee of the next zone that is further away. For example, Zone I residents would now pay $1.00 per visit and according to the "law of demand," the expectation is that visits will become less frequent (i.e., in particular, 20 times a year in lieu of 30 times a year). The same relative situation confronts the residents of all zones. For instance, at a fifty-cent entrance fee the total number of visits would be $20 + 15 + 10 = 45$ visits per year. This procedure gives another point on the demand curve (i.e., a price-quantity demand combination of: $0.05, 45 visits). In a similar manner and by assuming successively higher gate

Zone	Visits per year	Ave. Distance, d (miles)	d x 5¢/mile ($)
I	30	10	$ .50
II	20	20	1.00
III	15	30	1.50
IV	10	40	2.00
V	0	50	2.50

Table 1: Visitation Rates at Zero Gate Fee (at Zero Entrance Prices)

Gate Fee	Total Visits Per Year
$ .00	75
.50	45
1.00	25
1.50	10
2.00	0

Table 2: Demand Schedule

fees, further points on the demand curve can be obtained and a demand curve can be derived (see Table 2 and Figure 4). Once the demand curve has been estimated, the gross value to a representative resident can be estimated.

Price-dependent demand functions are estimated utilizing standard least-squares regression techniques. Following the procedure established by Burt and Brewer (1971: 818-827), rates of visitation to each recreational area would be estimated with equations of the following general form.

$$(1) \quad V_{ij} = b_{oj} + \sum_{l=1}^{n} b_{lj} P_{il} + e_{ij}$$

$$(2) \quad V_{ij} = \hat{b}_{oj} + \sum_{l=1}^{n} \hat{b}_{ij} P_{il}$$

In equation (1), V_{ij} is the number of visits per 10,000 members of the populations of Alphaland and Betaland to park (j) from zone (i). Moreover,

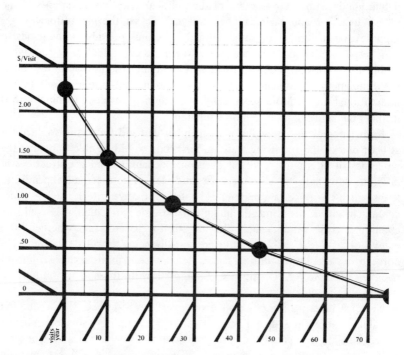

Figure 4: Recreational Demand Curve

P_{il} are travel costs (proxy prices), from zone (i) to recreational area (l); where $l=1, \ldots, j, \ldots, n$ recreational areas. The error term is e_{ij}. In a subsequent stage the actual demand functions are derived employing the methodology of Knetsch (1963). Equations of the general form depicted in equation (2) are solved and the values of V_{ij} are converted[4] into absolute visits in order to get the quantity demanded (i.e., number of visits from zone (i) given a zero price, or entry fee).[5] Subsequently, arbitrary prices are introduced and a new, converted V_{ij} figure is obtained. This process is repeated for each zone, and the estimated visits from each zone at each price are summed yielding various combinations of prices and quantities demanded (i.e., a demand curve for a particular recreational area). Next the area under the demand curve is calculated[6] and a dollar value associated with a given recreational area is obtained.[7]

2. Demand Estimation: Voter's Behavior Approach

In instances where the individual economic preference approach is deemed inappropriate or when the investigator would like to analyze the demand for public goods within the context of the political mechanism, variants of the voter's behavior approach can be utilized.[8] To set the institutional stage, suppose that a number of supranational structures provide public goods to their respective jurisdictional members which are comprised of nation-states. Within the context of concern for the efficient allocation of world resources, the fundamental problem is again, the presence of public goods in the international arena. More specifically, a method is developed whereby (SS) member demand functions can be estimated.[9]

Knowledge of the individual (SS) member demand functions is valued for at least one of the following reasons. First, one would be able to predict the outcomes of alternative political decision mechanisms and tax structures in different supranational structures. Second, tax structures and expenditure levels which satisfy certain preferenced-based normative criteria, such as those contained within the Lindahl equilibrium specified in Chapter 1, could be computed. This would enable the investigator to ascertain whether "too many" or "too few" public goods were actually being provided relative to the norm being employed. For instance, defense contributions of participant members of the NATO Alliance juxtaposed with those contributions of Warsaw Pact members.[10]

Next, an investigation of "scale economies" to (SS) size in the production of public goods such as defense and/or deterrence in military alliances could be undertaken. Finally, predictions of projected changes in values of economic and demographic variables on quantities of public goods to be supplied in different supranational structures could be made.

By employing the following assumptions regarding the nature of the political process in each (SS), garnered information can be utilized for making inferences concerning the responses of individual member demands for public goods with respect to price, gross national product and other variables.

1. Units of measurement for a given jurisdictionally supplied commodity can be chosen in such a way that each jurisdiction (j) is able to supply the commodity at constant unit cost q_j.
2. For each member (i) there is a tax share T_i such that (i) must pay the fraction T_i of the total cost of jurisdictional expenditures in the community. Member (i's) tax share may depend upon wealth, gross national product or some other individual member characteristics, but does not vary with the size of expenditures nor with the way in which the member expresses desires for jurisdictional public goods.
3. Any member (i) of jurisdiction (j) is aware of its "tax price," $T_i q_j$ and is able to determine the quantity of the collective commodity which the member would choose for the jurisdiction given that the specified member must pay the fraction T_i of its total cost. In order to do so, the member merely needs to maximize "its preferences" subject to a linear "budget" constraint where its tax price for the jurisdictional good is $T_i q_j$.
4. In each jurisdiction, the quantity supplied of the public good is equal to the median of the quantities demanded by its members.
5. In each jurisdiction the median of the quantities demanded is the quantity demanded by the member with the median gross national product for that jurisdiction.

In order to more clearly show how the assumptions, which underly the theoretical model, relate to the estimating procedure, and precisely how the statistical procedure can generate the kind of information necessary to resolve the issues mentioned above, reconsider the assumptions, especially assumption 4. In Figure 5, one of the infinite many social preference functions for the member country with the median GNP is depicted, namely I_i, the one that maximizes its social welfare subject to its "budget constraint," bb'. If assumption 4 prevails, there is a majority voting system such that the quantity selected represents half of the members who want more and half that want less than the quantity offered by the (SS) in a Walrasian tâtonnement process for providing public good. This puts the country with the median GNP in a decisive voting position within the (SS). In Figure 5, this quantity will be O$\bar{q}$.

More accurately, if assumptions 4 and 5 are not false, the quantity of the public good chosen by a particular (SS) will be the same as that desired by

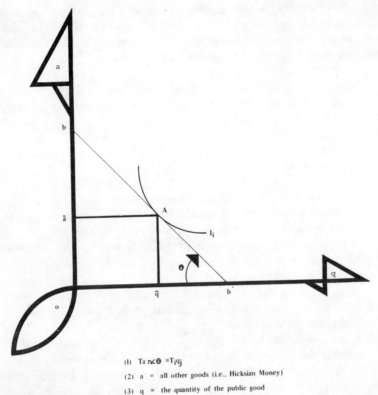

(1) $\tan \angle \theta = T_i q_j$

(2) a = all other goods (i.e., Hicksian Money)

(3) q = the quantity of the public good

Figure 5: Specific Price and Quantity Combination of Country with Median Gross National Product

the country with the median gross national product. Moreover, given the assumption about the constancy of T_i and q_j, the expenditures of any (SS) can be treated as an observation on the demand curve (i.e., a specific price and quantity combination is determined), of the country with the median gross national product where the price that country pays for the public good is proportional to its tax share.

The public issues postulated in the first portion of this subsection, as well as others,[11] can be subjected to an empirical test with a multiple regression model used to fit the log-linear function delineated in equation (3).

(3) $\log E = c + \alpha \log n + \delta \log \hat{t}$

$$+ \epsilon \log \hat{Y} + \sum_{i=1}^{k} B_i X_i$$

The symbols are defined as follows:

E = The expenditures of a jurisdiction on a specified category of public goods in a given jurisdiction. In particular, separate regressions can be run for different definitions of E such as the following.
  (a) E = Police expenditures.
  (b) E = Parks and recreation expenditures.
  (c) E = Total jurisdictional expenditures.
n = The number of members in a jurisdiction.
$\hat{t}$ = The tax share of a member with the median GNP for a jurisdiction.
$\hat{Y}$ = Median GNP in a jurisdiction.
δ = Price elasticity.
ϵ = GNP elasticity.
$\gamma(1+\delta)$ = Elasticity of demand with respect to population.
ξ = Elasticity of tax share with respect to GNP.[12]

3. Demand Estimations: The Benefit/Cost Approach

In situations where it is impossible to ingeniously tap "market type" information in the manners demonstrated above, or when an administration is concerned with a more comprehensive evaluation of expenditure policy, the benefit/cost approach is available. When the benefit/cost tool is perceived in its most general way, from a general equilibrium welfare point of view, both the demand and the supply sides of the "value scissors" are transversed. In order to embellish this notion, consider the following statement by Seneca and Taussig (1974:16): "Benefit-cost analysis . . . means a systematic evaluation of all the advantages and disadvantages of any actual or hypothetical change in society's production and consumption arrangements."

Although, in the past, benefit/cost analysis has been utilized primarily as an evaluative tool for looking at specific projects or as an instrument to select alternative government projects within the constraint of a "fixed purse," a general theory of nonmarket investment lends itself to this theoretical apparatus and, as such, provides a foundation for empirical study. Moreover, insofar as transaction costs and benefits are modeled, then this technique can be employed to determine whether or not activities should come under the domain of the "state" (i.e., in this case, a supranational structure), or whether they should be left to the free workings of the international system.[13]

The problem is to comprehensively estimate social benefits and costs with respect to alternative international resource allocations that stem from the existence of public goods. One part of the problem is that the exact dimensions of the benefits and/or costs are not known by the interested parties. For example, how would one place a dollar value on the benefits that an alliance

member receives relative to its contributions? Second, there are many benefits and costs that accrue over a period of time, severely complicating the
estimating problem.[14]

Another set of riddles is present if the domain of inquiry is extended to
encompass uncertainty (e.g., international information systems, satellite communication networks and property right's situations). Additionally, an empirical estimation of benefits and costs of income and distribution policies are
extremely elusive, especially in view of the incomparability of data among
countries.

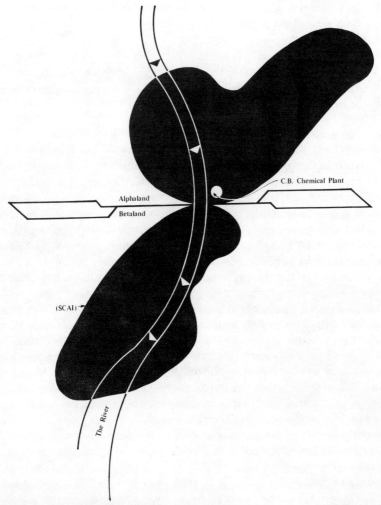

Figure 6: Benefit/Cost Map

In order to put forth a specific problem framed in an institutional context and to foster an understanding of the complexities involved with a systemic approach to evaluating international social welfare empirically, consider the heuristic circumstance that follows.[15] Let three be an ecosystem with two countries and consider a stream that cuts through their two political jurisdictions (see Figure 6).

In Alphaland the C.B. Chemical factory proceeds to utilize the river water as a means to dispose of its waste, and in doing so, degrades the water quality to a point where Sugar Cane Associates, Inc. (SCAI), located downstream will be forced out of business.[16] An ad hoc committee composed of members from both countries has been formed and mandated to secure an efficient social allocation of resources.

The spillover problem that the ad hoc committee is charged to look into can be broken down into three parts. First, the committee must determine if the difference between net social gains and net social losses is greater, less than, or equal to zero. Formally, the problem is specified in equation (4).

(4)　Net Social Gain (NSG) − Net Social Loss (NSL) $\lesseqgtr$ 0, where
　　　NSG = $V_c - V_f^c$ and
　　　NSL = $V_s - V_f^c$

Additionally, V_c is the value of chemical production, V_f^c is the value of the factors in their best alternative use other than chemical production, V_f^s is the value of the factors in their best alternative use other than sugar cane production, and V_s is the value of the sugar cane crop. Finally, T_c and T_b are transaction costs and benefits respectively as defined.

Assuming for the moment that net transaction benefits are equal to zero (i.e., $T_b - T_c = 0$), and NSG is greater than NSL, then the committee should dissolve as social welfare cannot be improved. In other words, the net gains to society by allowing the pollution to continue are greater than the net losses. On the other hand, if NSL is greater than NSG, then it is possible that the creation of a supranational structure could enhance social welfare from the point of view of the committee and its associated mandate. A potential improvement in social welfare could result if the costs associated with the creation and operation of the (SS) were less than the absolute value of the difference expressed in equation (4).

If indeed this is the case, the committee should proceed to select a (SS) such that net transaction benefits are at a maximum. Given this selection, it will be up to the (SS) to administer optimal pollution abatement policy, providing the fundamental rationale for the last part of the committee's task. In particular, this would be a determination of an optimal level of pollution abatement.

Of course, a number of empirical estimations must be made in order to ascertain benefit/cost information necessary for the committee to fulfill its mandate. For instance, optimal pollution abatement is determined where marginal social benefits (MSB), or the additional benefits rendered to society from additional units of pollution abatement, are equal to the marginal social costs (MSC), or additional social costs associated with the production of additional units of pollution abatement. These two functions, as well as the others implied in the discussions above, can be estimated with ordinary least squares regression equations of the general form depicted in equation (5).[17]

$$(5) \quad Y_i = a_o + \sum_{i=1}^{k} b_i X_i + e_t$$

where:

Y_i = MSB or MSC
X_i = Variables representing units of pollution abatement $9i = 1, \ldots, k$).
a_o = Intercept value.
b_i = Regression coefficients
e_t = An error term.

4. Supply Estimation: Estimation of Production Costs

The supply side "of the value coin" is juxtaposed to that of demand and a knowledge of it is necessary for securing an optimal allocation of resources. Moreover, as one might expect, many of the same problems that plague a viable estimation of benefits hamper empirical investigations with respect to public sector supply functions. In addition to data problems, at least two major difficulties are: the lack of an unambiguous quantity and/or quality dimension that can be employed to measure output and, the absence of a rigorously specified theory of governmental supply that can be subjected to an empirical test.

Both of these problems are relevant to the estimation of production and cost functions. With regard to the former, for example, a given quality dimension could be extracted from within a number of different evaluative contexts such as the consumer, the government or some research analyst. Furthermore, how does one go about unambiguously delineating the quality of an advanced degree if the output under consideration is education? Or, how is the output of national defense to be measured? Additionally, it is difficult to construct meaningful empirical tests of the supply of many public goods as no agreed upon theory exists. For instance, do regulated firms or agencies strive to minimize costs and if not, what are the relevant motivational postulates?

Be that as it may, for illustrative purposes, suppose that two countries, Alphaland and Betaland, share a common border and the sea. Both countries are interested in building a desalinization plant due to intermittent fresh water shortages. An ad hoc committee is formed to investigate the possibility of a joint desalinization venture. The question that the committee has been commissioned to answer is, could significant per unit cost savings be achieved if a joint venture was undertaken in lieu of separate nation-state provision of fresh water procured from two distinct desalinization plants.

Estimation of classical supply conditions, due to an application of duality theory, can proceed along two lines: estimation of cost functions, or estimation of production functions. This is a result of the fact that, given certain assumptions, cost and production functions are dual to each other.[18] However, it is most suitable to directly estimate production functions when levels of output are endogenous. On the other hand, if the level of output is exogenous, then it is preferable to estimate cost functions.

Given available cross-section data, the question before the ad hoc committee can be answered with information obtained from an estimation of the following translog cost function.[19]

$$(6) \quad \ln C = \alpha_0 + \alpha_y \ln Y + 1/2 \, \gamma_{yy} (\ln Y)^2$$

$$+ \sum_i \alpha_i \ln P_i + 1/2 \sum_i \sum_j \gamma_{ij} \ln P_i \ln P_j$$

$$+ \sum_i \gamma_{yi} \ln Y \ln P_i$$

where: C = Total Cost, Y = Output and P_i is the price of the ith factor input. More specifically, scale economies are defined as the proportionate increase in cost resulting from a small proportionate increase in the level of output and this information is derived from the estimating equation specified in equation (6).[20] In other words, the measure of scale economies is equal to the elasticity of total cost with respect to output. The elasticity term, $\partial \ln C / \partial \ln Y$, is subtracted from unity so that positive values are associated with economies of scale and negative values with diseconomies. Depending upon the sign and magnitude of this elasticity, the ad hoc committee can determine whether or not a joint venture will produce significant per unit cost savings.

5. Supply Estimation: Estimation of Opportunity Costs

In the preceding subsection, the supply phenomenon was couched within its traditional perspective. A more general approach, one that includes the social costs of production, will be presented next. Interpreted in a most comprehensive manner, the opportunity cost of supply approach transgresses the typical demand-supply dichotomy. As Heyne (1976:57) has put it, "demand determines costs, costs determine prices. Prices for alternative goods determine the demand for particular goods. Everything depends upon everything else in the opportunity cost way of thinking."

The basic logic of the opportunity cost approach is that resources should be valued in their best alternative use. The fundamental problems associated with this approach are essentially the same as those of the previous subsection and some specifics will be elucidated upon in the following example. Suppose country A, Alphaland, is a member of a military alliance and in this capacity, the central government contributes a "sizable" portion of its public funds toward this defense goal. Certain governmental representatives would like to know the "opportunity cost" of defense provision in connection with this alliance membership so that more efficient internal resource allocation deci-

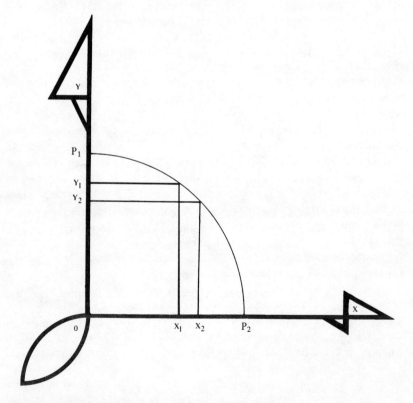

Figure 7: The Opportunity Costs of Providing Defense

sions can be made. In other words, these representatives would like to know what price the people of Alphaland are paying for their alliance membership.

The situation is depicted with the production possibility curve $P_1 P_2$ in Figure 7. Initially, dichotomize two classes of expenditures such that X = expenditures on the military alliance that Alphaland belongs to and Y = a specific nonalliance category of Alphaland GNP expenditures. Assuming full employment and the best utilization of the arts, if Alphaland chooses to increase the production of X from X_1 to X_2 then it must sacrifice $Y_1 Y_2$ of an alternative expenditure category in order to do so (e.g., expenditures on domestic education). From a dollar and cents point of view, the administration would like to present the social cost of additional military alliance expenditures so that it can make more intelligent budgetary decisions.

The requisite information is contained within the estimating equation (7).

(7) $(Y_i/GNP) = b_o + b_i (M/GNP) + e_t$ where

M = Military alliance expenditures by country Alphaland and,

$Y_i = Y_1 \ldots \ldots Y_n$, where the $Y_i 1_2$ are relevant expenditure categories.

Depending upon the sign of the regression coefficients (i.e., the b_i's), it can be estimated whether or not a military alliance tradeoff exists for the various expenditure categories (i.e., the X_i's). More specifically, if the sign of a regression coefficient is negative, the interpretation is that as military alliance expenditures increase,[21] a category of nonalliance expenditures decrease. In addition, the estimated magnitude of a given tradeoff is expressed in the value of the regression coefficient. For instance, if $b_1 = -.30$ and Y_1 is personal consumption expenditures, then the inference is that a one dollar increase in alliance expenditures will, other things being equal, lead to a thirty-cent sacrifice in personal consumption expenditures.[22]

6. Other Relevant Empirical Investigations: Estimations of Economic and Political Interactions and Forecasting

In addition to the empirical research regarding public goods and bads that readily fit into a demand and supply framework, there are other types of research in this area that should be, at least, alluded to in a survey of this sort. The general nature of these investigations is outlined in Figure 8, a diagram of a total politico-economic system.[23] Two major problems are contained within the confines of this model. The first problem concerns interactive processes that occur between and/or among sectors or regions of the international economic system or the international political system. Moreover, interactions can take place between the economic and political systems, interactions that play an important role in the shaping of the international arena.[24] Secondly, in many instances, it is of critical importance to view these interactions from a dynamic perspective so that forecasts of the future can be estimated, providing an empirical basis for the formation of world policies.

Since the dynamic interactive processes that operate between the economic and political systems in the international arena are extremely complex, it is troublesome to model these phenomena in a comprehensive manner. Usually, only a portion of the total system is modeled empirically. As an example of this research, consider the following situation. Suppose that a supranational structure has been created to assess the economic structure of the world in the year 2000.[25] Although thinking up until very recently has been concerned with only one country or jurisdiction in the present time period, it is the stated purpose of the (SS) to engage in an analysis of all countries in the future. To facilitate the above task, five variables are modeled within the context of a simulation model: population, industrial output, food production, depletion of nonrenewable resources, and pollution of the environment.

The (SS) simulates two polar scenarios. Initially, assume that the Green Revolution recently introduced in India and other developing countries takes place in a region of the world. The application of modern technology to the agricultural sector expands food supplies rapidly. As a result of the reduced

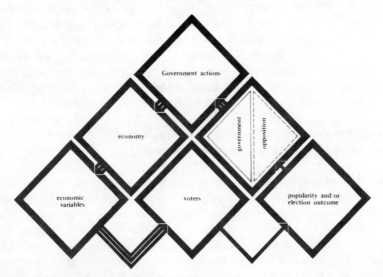

Figure 8: Total Politico-Economic Model

mortality rate that the increased food supply engenders, birth rates begin to climb.

As time passes, however, the use of fertilizer, pesticides and herbicides pollutes streams which in turn, will ultimately pollute the ocean. The expanding food supply provides a basis for the expansion of the industrial sector. This facet of the interdependency creates a depletion of mineral resources as well as environmental pollution of sundry types (e.g., water, air, etc.). The high birth rates coupled with declining resources and environmental pollution create a feedback loop that begins to impinge on the general quality of life (e.g., eventually the crude death rate, after dropping due to the expansion of the food supply, begins to rise dramatically). Other interdependent factors come into play which result in a collapse of the world system.

On the other hand, disaster is averted by a zero economic growth policy and a zero population growth policy. There is a structural shift of the economy, for example, to recycling and to the production of goods and services that do not utilize resources at such a rapid rate. Or, advances in technology thwart off impending disaster in some way or another (e.g., the use of solar energy in lieu of the fossil fuels).

B. CRITICISMS AND DIRECTIONS FOR FUTURE RESEARCH

In this section a number of general and specific criticisms pertaining to the empirical investigation of public goods in the international arena will be suggested along with recommendations for future research in the area. To begin with, consider the two general criticisms that follow. First, although a sizable body of public good empirical research exists at the nation-state level and below, very little effort has been expended to estimate relationships that prevail at the international level (see Figure 9).

Despite this fact, in many instances the same econometric of politometric[26] techniques can be employed in the investigation of international problems analogous to those that occur at lower layers of the world hierarchical system. That is to say, in principle, it turns out that problems encountered within national boundaries (e.g., regional spillover problems) are quite similar in nature to those that occur between and/or among national boundaries. Hence, both the theoretical and empirical models that have been previously developed could be productively applied to an empirical investigation of the international system.[27]

A second general criticism of the empirical research in the area transversed in this survey is that the theoretical and empirical models have not been fully integrated. For example, many of the empirical tests are carried out with little, if any, reference to a rigorously specified theoretical model. In these instances, the appropriate econometric specification and the choice of data

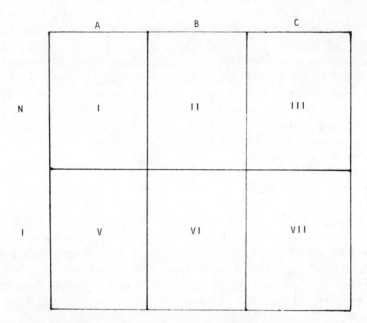

Figure 9: Empirical Investigation, General Classification Scheme Matrix

are severely hampered. Moreover, if theoretically and empirically integrated models do not exist, there are no meaningful guidelines that can be used as a foundation for the collection of future data. To be sure, a great deal of past data has been collected on a somewhat arbitrary basis in terms of its relevance to a tightly meshed theoretical and empirical modeling procedure. On the other hand, if viable modeling procedures exist, they can be used as a guide for the collection of meaningful data. In particular, as exemplified in the other parts of this book, much of the theory is framed within the context of marginal relationships while most of the data are that of totals or averages. This forces the researcher to utilize inappropriate data or perform gross manipulations of the data which impair the accuracy of statistical interpretations.

In addition to the general criticisms outlined above, specific criticisms of the empirical procedures contained in the survey section can be made. Two illustrations will suffice to demonstrate the nature of these criticisms. First, recall the international recreational example developed in Section (A1). The fundamental methodology here is that of the so-called cost-incurred type. However, other methods for evaluating recreational areas exist and it is not clear that the presented method is superior. For example, there exists the user charge and merit-weighted user day approaches.

Second, the estimation of recreational benefits with the cost-incurred approach assumes that cost-incurred is an accurate proxy for the price of admission to a given recreational area. It may or it may not be. Some persons driving to recreational areas may receive net positive increments of utility on their way if the views are beautiful or if they are visiting someone on the way.

Furthermore, the opportunity cost of time travel must be calculated along with the opportunity cost of the time spent in the park if an accurate and comprehensive estimation of park benefits is to be made. This is at best a difficult concept to empirically measure, and at worst, impossible.

As a second elucidation regarding specific criticisms, consider the simulation (or forecasting) model put forth in Section (A6).[28] This simulation model consists of a set of mathematical equations based upon a set of assumptions governing the feedback between and/or among a selected number of aggregated variables. Hence, the validity of the projections that emanate from the model depend upon the assumptions, the particular variables delineated, and the manner in which the interaction process has been depicted.

Initially, focus upon an assumption of the model, and its alleged plausibility. Suppose that this assumption specifies the relationship between industrial production and pollution. Since prices are not explicitly incorporated into the model and because price changes may very well affect the adequacy of the assumption governing the relationship between industrial production and pollution, one can hardly be confident in projections that stem from it.

Moreover, since technological change is not formally and specifically modeled, not only is the above relationship suspect as well as others not mentioned, but the list of variables is imbued with a shadow of doubt. For instance, a new scientific discovery applied to society may engender a significant variable that would not be accounted for in the simulation process.

Be that as it may, despite these criticisms of existing research, a great deal of public sector empirical research within the world system remains to be tackled. In order to more clearly point to potential directions for future research, consult the research matrix presented in Figure 9. Most of the empirical studies to date have been done from a nation-state perspective. Row N of the matrix is, relatively speaking, well represented with respect to examples of empirical research. On the other hand, Row I of the matrix is sparsely represented.

There are, no doubt, a number of reasons for the dearth of empirical research associated with these cells among which are: lack of data, lack of comparability of data among countries, and/or lack of the ability to collect data. This observation suggests the following comments regarding the typology depicted in Figure 9.

1. A class of studies that should have been done, but for some reason

have not been done (e.g., due to lack of data or inadequate methodology).

2. A class of studies that should have been done and could have been
   done, but have not been done (i.e., there does not appear to be any
   reason that these studies have not been done other than neglect).
3. Studies that could and should be done in the future when appropriate data are collected or appropriate methodology is developed, etc.
4. Studies that should not have been done because the data was not
   appropriate or because methodological tools were not adequately
   developed.

Within the view of Figure 9, and the four comments presented above, the
directions for future research seem to be rather clear cut. Generally speaking,
Row I of the research matrix needs to be filled. In terms of this necessity,
priorities are difficult to specify. Certainly, however, neglected research (i.e.,
comment number 2), is a prime candidate. The other area of immediate
interest could be delineated by number 1 comment. Focus of attention in this
area would not only address itself to the two general criticisms outlined
previously, but would expand the domain of number 1 of the classification
scheme. Other directions of the future are present and will be left up to the
reader's imagination.

NOTES

1. Throughout Chapter 2, due to considerations of space, only selected examples
will be developed for purposes of illustration. References, and/or references cited
therein, however, will provide those readers that are unfamiliar with the modeling
procedure or for those readers who have not come in contact with a particular type of
econometric specification previously, with the necessary leading information.

2. Although primary emphasis is placed upon the efficiency of resource allocation
in Chapter 2, this is not to say that distribution (or equity) and stabilization considerations are not of immense importance, especially in the international arena, or that these
areas are not worthy of empirical investigation.

3. The discussion here follows that of Moncur (1972:53-64). Also, see Moncur
(1975:301-311). The basic estimating procedure was put forth by Hotelling (1949).
Later, extensions were made by Boyet and Tolley (1966:984-1001), Clawson (1959),
Clawson and Knetsch (1966), Burt and Brewer (1971:818-827), and Knetsch
(1963:1148-1157).

4. Since parks other than the specific park under consideration may be substitutes,
the prices of alternative parks are included in the regression equations.

5. By expressing visits from each zone as visits per thousand population in the zone,
the assumption of equal-population distance zones can be readily dropped (i.e., multiply
the population of zone (i) by V_{ij}).

6. The area under the demand curve can be estimated as the sum of areas of
trapezoidal figures under the curve and between successive "price-quantity" point. If

(P_k, Q_k) represents the ktn price-quantity point, then the area under the demand curve is:

$$\sum_{k=1}^{n} [(P_k + P_{k+1})/2] \times (Q_k - Q_{k+1}).$$

7. In practice, a questionnaire survey that covers only a fraction of the year (e.g., two weeks) would be utilized for obvious reasons. This being the case, a yearly dollar value is extrapolated under the assumption that the two weeks sampled are representative ones.

8. A great deal of the empirical analysis regarding this approach has its roots in the theory of public choice. For an excellent survey of both the theory and empirical work in this area, see Mueller (1976:359-433).

9. The material in this section is taken from Bergstrom and Goodman (1973:280-296). For other similar approaches see Borcherding and Deacon (1972:891-901), Deacon and Shapiro (1975:943-955), Barr and Davis (1966:149-165), and Barlow (1970:1028-1039). Additionally, it should be noted that these approaches can be applied to taxation. See Davis and Haines (1966:274).

10. Empirical investigations of the sort outlined in this subsection would be an important extension of the existing alliance research. For example, if defense expenditures possess properties of publicness, it has been hypothesized that larger (SS) members will consume more of this good resulting in a disproportionate sharing of the defense financing between and/or among alliance members. See Olson and Zeckhauser (1966:266-279), Pryor (1969:96-99), Starr (1974:521-532), Russett (1970:91-126), and Mushkat (1975:20-33).

11. Given the assumptions, there are a number of interesting notions that can be empirically tested in terms of the theoretical model, two of which that have particular relevance in terms of Chapter 1 and will be briefly discussed here. First, a congestion term is embodied in the demand function allowing for the empirical estimation of congestion. Z is the quantity of the public good and $Z^* = n^{-\gamma} Z$, with $1, \ldots, n$ countries involved. Given that the social preference function of country (i) is of the functional form $u^i(X_i, Z^*)$, and X is private good, when $\gamma = 0$, then the public good is Samuelsonian pure. If $\gamma = 1$, then congestion is present in the sense that each country receives the fraction $1/n$ of the total amount of the public good. In this connection, see also Cicchetti and Smith (1976:183-200).

Second, given the assumptions of the model, it is possible to answer the question of whether or not the public good is being overproduced or underproduced from the point of view of standard economic criteria. A particular resource allocation that satisfies assumptions (1-4) is called a Bowen equilibrium by Bergstrom and Goodman and, in general, the Bowen is not Pareto optimal. On the other hand the Lindahl equilibrium is More specifically, when price elasticities are negative, the Lindahl equilibrium quantity of the public good will exceed the Bowen quantity, provided that the tax share of the country with the median GNP is lower in the Lindahl equilibrium. In countries where empirical estimates suggest that this assumption is valid, the conclusion is that less than the Lindahl (or Pareto optimal) equilibrium quantity of the public good will be provided. provided.

12. The elasticities, with the exception of demand elasticity with respect to population discussed in the text below, are derived in the following manner where:

$Y = GNP$
$D = Demand$

The demand function is of the following general functional form:

$$D\ (Y, T^i\ (Y), n^i, x^i).\ \text{Take}\ dD/dY = \partial D/\partial Y + (\partial D/\partial T)\ (\partial T/\partial Y).$$

In terms of elasticities, $(Y/D)\ (dD/dY) = \epsilon + \delta\xi$, and

$$\xi = (Y/T^i)\ (\partial T^i/\partial Y).$$

13. For example, the Pareto-optimality conditions of international arrangements that are derived from the new theory of consumption model provide the theoretical basis for this kind of interpretation, since "bads" as well as "goods" are included on the benefit side of the equation (i.e., the right-hand side of the equations in Chapter 1). Additionally, if all costs are included in the left-hand side of the equations, then transaction costs are included, as indeed they should be. In more sophisticated estimation procedures that rely on the new theory of consumer demand (or household production theory as it is sometimes called), "hedonic" prices can be estimated. As Rosen (1974:34-55) points out, "Observed product prices and the specific amounts of characteristics associated with each good define a set of implicit or 'hedonic' prices." Also see Muellbauer (1974:977-994), and references cited therein.

14. See the subsection in Chapter 1 regarding intergenerational public goods.

15. For other examples of international spillovers that lend themselves to the benefit/cost approach see Weisbrod (1968, 1969a and 1969b), Margolis (1957), and Bhagwati (1976a and 1976b).

16. It is implicitly assumed that the two firms are operating independently and will not cooperate unless forced to do so by a higher authority and that a private market for property rights does not exist. Also, it is assumed that the value of the sugar cane crop is just large enough to keep SCAI producing sugar cane, that output of pollution abatement is subject to increasing costs, and that the public values initial units of pollution abatement more highly than subsequent units of pollution abatement.

17. Either one of these functions, or both, may be nonlinear and hence would be empirically modeled in log-linear form. Also see Gerhardt (1972) and Pratt (1974).

18. For example, Christensen and Greene (1976:658) point out that, "The specification of a production function implies a particular cost function, and vice versa. Thus, the structure of production can be studied empirically using either a production function or a cost function." Also see Christensen, Jorgenson and Lau (1971:255-256), Christensen, Jorgenson and Lau (1973:28-45), Lau and Yotopoulos (1972:11-17) and Lau and Yotopoulos (1971:96-109).

19. It should be noted that the translog estimating equation yields demand information in addition to supply information. In particular, Christensen and Greene (1976:659) indicate that, "Recent developments in duality theory have enhanced the appeal of the cost function approach. Every cost function implies a set of derived demand equations. Functional forms for cost functions have been developed which have two attractive features: they imply derived demand equations which are linear in the parameters, and at the same time they represent very general production structures, even though they cannot be derived from explicit production functions. It places no prior restrictions on substitution possibilities among the factors of production. Equally important, it allows scale economics to vary with the level of output. This feature is essential to enable the unit cost curve to attain the classical U shape."

20. For the derivation, see Christensen and Greene (1976:659-661).

21. For an excellent discussion of problems associated with the estimating procedure, see Russett (1971:29-50).

22. As an actual example, for the U.S.A. Russett (1969:412-426) estimated that a one dollar increase in defense spending led to a forty-two cent sacrifice in personal consumption expenditures and a twenty-nine cent sacrifice in fixed investment expenditures.

23. See Frey and Schneider (1975:339-360) for a more complete discussion.

24. For some intra and international examples here, see Cauley and Shelton (1975:261-276), Crowley (1971:27-43), Marr (1974:416-421), Frey and Schneider (1975:339-360), Oates (1972:195-202) and Pryor (1969).

25. See Meadows, Meadows, Randers and Behrens (1972).

26. Frey and Schneider (1975:339-360) have referred to this term. In particular, they state that, "The empirical estimation of politico-econometric models may in analogy to econometrics be termed politico-econometrics or for short, politometrics."

27. These problems, however, differ in both the magnitude and the international nature of the cooperative effort which is required from a theoretical point of view and hence must be taken into account when formulating politometric models.

28. For a more detailed discussion here, see Morganstern, Knorr and Heiss (1973:145-168).

BIBLIOGRAPHY

BARLOW, R. (1970) "Efficiency Aspects of Local School Finance." Journal of Political Economy 78(September/October):1028-1039.

BARR, J. and O. DAVIS (1966) "An Elementary Political and Economic Theory of the Expenditures of Local Governments." Southern Economic Journal 33(October):149-165.

BERGSTROM, T. C. and R. P. GOODMAN (1973) "Private Demands for Public Goods." American Economic Review 63(June):280-296.

BHAGWATI, J. N., ed. (1976a) The Brain and Taxation: Theory and Empirical Analysis. Amsterdam: North-Holland Publishing Company.

––– (1976b) Taxing the Brain Drain: A Proposal. Amsterdam: North-Holland Publishing Company.

BORCHERDING, T. and R. DEACON (1972) "The Demand for the Services of Non-Federal Governments." American Economic Review 62(December):891-901.

BOYET, W. E. and G. S. TOLLEY (1966) "Recreational Projection Based on Demand Analysis." American Journal of Agricultural Economics 48(November):984-1001.

BURT, O. R. and D. BREWER (1971) "Estimation of Net Social Benefits from Outdoor Recreation." Econometrica 39(September):818-827.

CAULEY, J. and R. B. SHELTON (1975) "National Defense and Legislative Decision-Making" in Craig Liske, William Loehr and John McCamant (eds.) Comparative Public Policy: Issues, Theories and Methods. New York: John Wiley and Sons, Inc:261-276.

CHRISTENSEN, L. R. and W. H. GREENE (1976) "Economics of Scale in U.S. Electric Power Generation." Journal of Political Economy 84(August):655-676.

CHRISTENSEN, L. R., D. W. JORGENSON, and L. J. LAU (1971) "Conjugate Duality and the Transcendental Logarithmic Production Function." abstract Econometrica 39(July):255-256.

––– (1973) "Transcendental Logarithmic Production Frontiers." Review of Economics and Statistics 55(February):28-45.

CICCHETTI, C. J. and V. K. SMITH (1976) "The Measurement of Individual Congestion

Costs: An Economic Application to Wilderness Recreation." Pp. 183-200 in Steven
A. Y. Lin (ed.) Theory and Measurement of Economic Externalities. New York:
Academic Press.

CLAWSON, M. (1959) "Methods of Measuring the Demand for the Value of Outdoor
Recreation." Washington, D.C.: Resources for the Future, Inc. (February).

CLAWSON, M. and J. L. KNETSCH (1966) Economics of Outdoor Recreation. Baltimore: Johns Hopkins Press for Resources for the Future.

CROWLEY, R. N. (1971) "Long Swings in the Role of Government: An Analysis of
Wars and Government Expenditures in Western Europe Since the Eleventh Century."
Public Finance/Finances Publiques 26:27-43.

DAVIS, O. A. and G. H. HAINES, Jr. (1966) "A Political Approach to a Theory of
Public Expenditures: The Case of Municipalities." National Tax Journal 19(September):259-275.

DEACON, R. and P. SHAPIRO (1975) "Private Preference for Collective Goods Revealed Through Voting on Referenda." The American Economic Review 65(December):943-955.

FREY, B. S. and F. SCHNEIDER (1975) "On the Modeling of Politico-Economic
Interdependence." European Journal of Political Research 3:339-360.

GERHARDT, P. H. (1972) "Air Pollution Control: Benefits, Costs, and Inducements."
Pp. 153-171 in Selma J. Mushkin (ed.). Public Prices for Public Products. Washington: The Urban Institute.

HEYNE, P. (1976) "The Economic Way of Thinking." Chicago: Science Research
Associates, Inc.

HIRSCH, W. Z. (1973) Urban Economic Analysis. New York: McGraw-Hill Book
Company.

HOTELLING, H. (1949) "An Economic Study of the Monetary Evaluation of Recreation in the National Parks." (June 18, 1974) U.S. Department of the Interior
National Service: Letter quoted by R. E. Prewit.

KNETSCH, J. L. (1963) "Economics of Including Recreation as a Purpose in Eastern
Water Projects." Journal of Farm Economics 96(November):1148-1157.

LAU, L. J. and P. A. YOTOPOULOS (1972) "Profit, Supply and Factor Demand
Functions." American Journal of Agricultural Economics 54(February):11-17.

——— (1971) "A Test for Relative Efficiency and Application to Indian Agriculture."
The American Economic Review 61(March):96-109.

MARGOLIS, J. (1957) "Secondary Benefits, External Economics and the Justification
of the Public Investment." Review of Economics and Statistics (August):284-291.

MARR, W. L. (1974) "The Expanding Role of Government and Wars: A Further
Elaboration." Public Finance/Finances Publiques 29:416-421.

MEADOWS, D. H., D. L. MEADOWS, J. RANDERS, and W. BEHRENS (1972) The
Limits to Growth. New York: Universe Books.

MONCUR, J. E. T. (1975) "Estimating the Value of Alternative Outdoor Recreations-
Facilities Within a Small Area." Journal of Leisure Research 71:301-310.

——— (1972) The Value of Recreation Areas on Oahu. State of Hawaii: Department of
Budget and Finance.

MORGENSTERN, O., K. KNORR, and K. P. HEISS (1973) Long Term Projections of
Power. Cambridge, Mass.: Ballinger Publishing Company.

MUELLBAUER, J. (1974) "Household Production Theory, Quality, and the 'Hedonic
Technique.' " The American Economic Review 64(December):977-994.

MUELLER, D. C. (1976) "Public Choice: A Survey." Journal of Economic Literature
14(June):395-433.

MUSHKAT, M. (1975) "The Theory of Public or (Collective Goods) and Defense Spending in the Arab League." Co-Existence 12:20-33.

OATES, W. E. (1972) Fiscal Federalism. New York: Harcourt, Brace, Jovanovich, Inc.

OLSON, M. and R. ZECKHAUSER (1966) "An Economic Theory of Alliances." Review of Economics and Statistics 48(August):266-279.

PRATT, J. W., ed. (1974) Statistical and Mathematical Aspects of Pollution Problems. New York: Marcel Dekker, Inc.

PRYOR, F. (1969) Public Expenditures in Capitalist and Communist Nations. Homewood, Ill.: Richard D. Irwin.

ROSEN, S. (1974) "Hedonic Prices and Implicit Markets." Journal of Political Economy 82(January/February):34-55.

RUSSETT, B. M. (1970) What Price Vigilance? The Burden of National Defense. New Haven, Connecticut: Yale University Press.

――― (1971) "Some Decisions in the Regression of Time-Series Data." Pp. 29-50 in J. F. Herdon and J. C. Bernd (eds.) Mathematical Applications in Political Science V. Charlottesville: The University of Virginia Press.

SENECA, J. J. and TAUSSIG, M. K. (1974) Environmental Economics. New Jersey: Prentice-Hall, Inc.

STARR, H. (1974) "A Collective Goods Analysis of the Warsaw Pact After Czechoslovakia." International Organization 3(1974):521-532.

WEISBROD, B. (1968) "Income Redistribution Effects and Benefit-Cost Analysis," Pp. 177-222 in S. B. Chase (ed.). Problems in Public Expenditure Analysis. Washington: Brookings.

――― (1969a) "Collective Action and the Distribution of Income: A Conceptual Approach." In Joint Economic Committee of the Analysis Evaluation of Public Expenditures. 91st Congress.

――― (1969b) "Geographic Spillover Effects and the Allocation of Resources to Education." Pp. 192-206 in Julius Margolis (ed). The Public Economy of Urban Communities. Baltimore, Maryland.: The Johns Hopkins Press.

Chapter 3

TOWARD AN UNDERSTANDING OF POLITICS
THROUGH PUBLIC GOODS THEORY: A REVIEW ESSAY

ROGER A. HANSON
Reed College

The economic theory of public goods has been used to make contributions to specific areas of political analysis. Applications of public goods theory stem, in great measure, from Olson's (1965) principle of collective action. The principle asserts, somewhat negatively, that as the potential beneficiaries of a public good increase, the amount of the good provided is less optimal. Despite the richness of Olson's model,[1] and the extensive economic literature on public goods, the theory of public goods has been applied to a limited set of political topics such as interest groups, alliances, and the organization of local governments.[2] In addition, Olson's principle has stimulated the development of a competing theory only in the area of political leadership.

The abstract nature of public goods makes it difficult for political analysts to incorporate it into their research repertoire without investing time and effort in understanding the economic principles behind the concept. Yet, political analysts who have the skills to manipulate mathematical formulations appear to have focused their attention on other political decision-theories, such as coalition theory, electoral competition, and the paradox of voting, which are at least as demanding in rigor and precision as public goods theory. Recent reviews of the literature in formal political theory indicate that public goods theory has resulted in fewer theoretical studies and empirical tests than other collective decision-making models (Shepsle, 1974; Kramer and Hertzberg, 1975; Taylor, 1975). If this is an accurate reflection of the relative status of public goods theory, it is appropriate to assess the political theories that have used this economic framework.

A stocktaking effort should confront the puzzling problem of how a theory that is very appealing, at least initially, has not captured the imagination of researchers across a broader range of political questions. From this perspective, several interrelated questions need to be addressed in order to begin to uncover both the knowledge that has been gained and the factors that inhibit future theoretical advances and verification of testable proposi-

---

AUTHOR'S NOTE: I wish to thank Karen A. Feste for helpful comments.

tions. Some of these questions are as follows: What are some of the positive expectations about the theoretical significance of public goods? On the basis of past work, what knowledge has been gained? Do the successes outweigh the failures? Looking ahead, whither the political analysis of public goods? What areas of inquiry may be dead ends? What important methodological problems remain unresolved? What areas of investigation seem most promising?

The objective of this essay is to appraise the potential and past uses of the concept of public goods in political analysis. The first section describes the ways in which public goods theory may serve to illuminate traditional political questions and to uncover new ones. In the second section, an assessment is made of the contributions to political knowledge by major studies in the field. Here a review is undertaken of both theoretical structures and efforts at hypothesis-testing. Finally, the third section raises ideas about research topics that seem to be charted in the direction of nonobvious explanations.

I. INITIAL POSITIVE EXPECTATIONS

The purpose of this section is to unpack the advantages of public goods for systematic political analysis that both unabashed advocates of public goods theory as well as other political analysts would consider appealing.[3] Presumably, positive expectations play a role in leading individuals to consider a public goods perspective. For the purpose of understanding those expectations we must ask the question, what can the theory of public goods do for the study of politics?

1. The defining characteristics of public goods highlight information about political factors that political scientists have hitherto overlooked. Public goods are considered to possess one or both of two properties (Samuelson, 1954, 1955, 1958; Head, 1962; Head and Shoup, 1969). First, public goods are indivisible, i.e., the consumption or use of the good by one individual does not diminish the ability of others to use the same good.[4] Second, they are subject to non-excludability, i.e., once a good is provided, it is not economically feasible to prevent individuals from enjoying the benefits of the good.

According to Samuelson's (1954) first effort to formulate a pure theory of public expenditure, goods are one of two two-polar opposite types. First, "pure collective consumption goods" provide joint satisfaction in the sense that one individual's consumption of the good does not diminish another individual's consumption of the same good. In contrast, with "pure private consumption goods," one individual's consumption does reduce the amount of the good that may be used by others accordingly.

Despite the restrictive nature of Samuelson's dichotomy, the concept of public goods draws attention to certain features of political variables that simply were not considered previously. The potential significance of the concept is revealed by the activities to which the term refers. The list of variables begins with Samuelson's suggestion of defense as a public good.

Every political analyst would agree that defense is a factor of fundamental importance. It provides the critical element of security. And it serves as a form of capital in the essentially political process of bargaining. Moreover, it is reasonable to believe that the long-standing, intuitive ideas about defense are consistent with the more precise properties of joint consumption and non-excludability.

The potential value of the public goods has been amplified by modifying Samuelson's initial, restrictive assumptions about the dimension underlying public goods. More recent formulations of the concept by economists have led to the development of the "impure" public good (Buchanan, 1968). Impure public goods are neither absolutely indivisible nor absolutely divisible. Rather, they are partially divisible, which means that they can be made available in varying amounts to some individuals.

The introduction of the impure public good may serve to enhance even further the understanding of political variables. For example, Sandler and Cauley (1975: 333-35) have proposed a typology of defense by comparing the nature of the services provided by military units (purely defensive services, which serve only as a means of protection in case of attack; deterrent services; and combination defense and deterrent services) against the nature of a good (pure public good, impure public good, and private good). Their typology illustrates how additional information is gained by viewing more traditional distinctions of defense, such as, defensive systems versus deterrence forces, in light of public goods categories.[5]

While the research of Sandler and Cauley may exemplify the potential benefits to be gained in analyzing defense as a public good, the concept of public goods must refer to more than defense. While defense is a uniquely political factor, it is not the primary research topic of most political analysts. Hence, in order to know what can be gained through the theory of public goods, it is imperative to ask the question, what is the range of objects and activities that have been deemed to be public goods? Theoretical studies have focused on the following public goods: defense (Sandler and Cauley, 1975), local educational, police, and fire protection services (Bish and Ostrom, 1973), air pollution control (Bish, 1971), general expenditures (Breton, 1974) and public law (Feeley, 1970). Empirical studies have considered the following items as public goods: defense (Olson and Zeckhauser, 1966; Burgess and Robinson, 1969; Russett, 1970; Russett and Sullivan, 1971; Starr, 1974), state and local government expenditures (Bergstrom and Goodman, 1973; Borcherding and Deacon, 1972).

The point of this review is to demonstrate that the concept of public goods has not been seen, at least initially, as an ethereal notion floating above the world of politics. Moreover, despite the early criticism raised by some economists (e.g. Margolis, 1955) that Samuelson stipulated an empirically vacuous concept, a range of politically important variables have been interpreted as public goods. Hence, the concept appears to be regarded as a tool for shedding light on some traditional political concerns and uncovering some new problems.

2. A second striking feature of public goods theory is that it promises to be a superior explanation of some political problems than previous theories. This expectation is grounded in the fact that initial applications of public goods theory are considered to have challenged, perhaps overturned, prior conceptualizations. Here the two most notable applications that have seriously questioned established theories are Olson's analysis of groups and V. Ostrom's account of the organization of local governments.

Concerning the question of whether or not individuals will join groups such as labor unions and farm organizations, Olson (1965) questions the traditional argument that rational individuals will seek to further their individual interests by joining a group that seeks to promote the common interests of all individuals. Instead, Olson advances the counterassertion that as long as a potential group member can receive the benefits of a good without contributing to its supply, he has an incentive to withhold his contribution (not join). From this fundamental premise based on the idea of the free rider, Olson claims that unless the group is small, it must use special positive or negative incentives to obtain contributions. He seeks to support this conclusion by an interpretation of the relationships between the incentives offered by actual groups and their membership size. While Olson does not test a set of deduced hypotheses, his theory is noteworthy because it suggests a body of theoretically relevant facts about incentives that previous theories overlooked because they assumed that individuals would work for their common benefits.

Concerning the organization of local governments, V. Ostrom and others (V. Ostrom, Tiebout, and Warren, 1961; Warren, 1964; Bish, 1971; Bish and Warren, 1972; E. Ostrom, 1972; Bish and V. Ostrom, 1973; E. Ostrom and V. Ostrom, 1976) question a reform-oriented tradition that seeks to change the structure of multiple units of government to greater consolidation of policy-making authority. It is believed that the existing fragmentation and overlapping authority inhibit policy effectiveness and efficiency.

Vincent Ostrom has brought this belief into some question by a twofold argument. He claims that the configuration of local units of government actually reflects citizens' preferences for public goods, among other things. As a result, citizens likely would prefer community control to a metropolitan government. Second, Ostrom believes that it is efficient for local units of government to contract for the supply of public good with competitive private producers. For this reason, he argues against the creation of a single urban government acting as a monopolistic supplier of public goods. Despite the fact that Ostrom's arguments are more complex than these brief comments suggest, this summary version indicates that public goods play a critical role in his opposition to the reasoning behind the reformers' policy prescriptions.

Thus, if the theoretical arguments set forth by Olson and V. Ostrom are considered to reflect reality accurately, they indicate that public goods theory promises to produce results that are negative and sweeping. And certainly all political scientists should be interested in an analytical framework that contributes to the falsification of extant political theories.

3. An appealing quality of public goods theory is that it may be applied to a variety of political decision-making problems. As a result, it can lead to the development of new theories rather than being limited to refuting political theories as discussed above. Here the work of Frohlich, Oppenheimer and Young exemplifies how public goods theory plays a role in the construction of a formal theory of the distinctively political mechanism of leadership.

The concept of leadership by itself does not entail the coordination necessary to produce public goods. If, as Olson says, non-leaders have little incentive to contribute toward the supply of public goods, then the amount of resources that a leader can control is trivial. Because the leader gains meager satisfaction despite the time and effort spent in organization activities, he has limite; incentives to work for the supply of public goods. Consequently, if leadership is to play a role in effecting the supply of public goods, it must be shown how leaders can raise revenues from non-leaders and then extract some profit for themselves.

Frohlich, Oppenheimer and Young contribute toward the establishment of a theory of leadership by identifying types of revenues that leaders may raise. They relate these revenues to the decision-making calculus for leaders. The calculus specifies the nature and relationship between different cost and benefit terms affecting an individual's decision to exercise leadership. Hence, the calculus reveals the conditions under which an individual will choose to lead and when not to lead. Thus, Frohlich, Oppenheimer and Young's first effort points to the way in which the theory of public goods may promote, in some way, rigorous explanations of topics that have generally been dealt with in loose frameworks. Presumably, future research will be able to attack other problems in the same creative manner as Frohlich, Oppenheimer and Young have begun to do for the problems of leadership.

4. Public goods theory is important because it may clarify the use of coercion in a democratic society. Economists, such as Samuelson, believe that the free-rider problem is a justification for coercive actions, e.g., taxes, rather than reliance on voluntary payments to supply public goods. While Samuelson's idea may be true, it fails to specify the ways in which political institutions should incorporate coercive elements.

However, other analysts have attempted to extend Samuelson's suggestion in two directions. First, Feeley (1970) has broadened the concept of public goods to include a wide range of laws that promote order and the general welfare, not just laws that back up tax policies. This extension is one that should be of interest to political scientists because it focuses attention on the political problem of compliance. As a result, it is worthwhile for political scientists to determine if laws, conceived of as public goods, can be linked with other concepts to explain compliance.

Second, Frohlich and Oppenheimer (1974) have attempted to identify the optimal mixture of coercion, e.g., taxes, threats, and positive inducements in the raising of revenue to supply public goods. Instead of explaining how the revenue can be raised exclusively on one type of sanction, Frohlich and Oppenheimer combine both negative and positive sanctions in their model. Moreover, they examine how leaders may come to choose an optimal package for a set of taxpayers. Thus, it is reasonable to expect that research along the lines begun by Feeley and Frohlich and Oppenheimer will contribute to a richer understanding of complex political processes.

5. Public goods theory merits attention because it permits us to test a theory about the public goods character of actual public policies. It is important to know if policies in the real world provide indivisible as opposed to divisible benefits. This information would supplement current policy studies which have succeeded primarily in predicting expenditure levels and changes in expenditure patterns over time.

In summary, the theory of public goods is appealing to the extent that the following conditions hold: (1) there is a wide range of political variables that can be treated as public goods; (2) there is a large number of political problems that involve questions of the demand and supply of public goods; (3) the richness and complexity of political determinants, processes, and outcomes can be explained by abstract models that generate principles of behavior.

II. WHAT HAS BEEN GAINED BY THE
APPLICATION OF PUBLIC GOODS THEORY?

The previous section contains some of the reasons why political analysts may find the concept of public goods initially appealing. Interest in the concept is likely to wane, however, unless its applications to political questions prove to be relatively successful. This means that it is essential to know exactly what has been gained by these applications. Because the applications are devoted to different substantive issues, they are best arranged according to the general headings of theory construction and theory-testing. Under each heading, the attempt is made to note the contributions made by the major studies to date.

1. THEORY CONSTRUCTION

Public choice theorists tend to agree that the derivation of nonobvious, unambiguous propositions from a model (or an axiomatic set of premises) is a basic criterion of theoretical structures. Because the political analyses of public goods are conducted by public choice specialists, it seems reasonable that these analyses be judged according to the same criteria applied to other public choice theories. With this criterion in mind, let us consider the nature of theoretical results in three areas: (A) Special Interest Groups, (B) Leadership, and (C) Local Government Organization.

(A) Special Interest Groups

A fundamental problem confronting individuals is the decision whether or not to join a group that seeks to achieve the common interests of the group members. Considerable importance has been attached to the role of groups in both domestic and international politics. In domestic systems, special interest groups such as farm organizations, labor unions, and business clubs, are considered to serve the critical function of articulating, and perhaps aggregating, demands. And in the international system, countries may promote their joint interests, e.g., defense, through alliance formation.

Despite the critical role of groups, the application of the concept of public goods has shown that individuals (or countries) will not necessarily act to further their mutual concerns. If the common interests of the group members are interpreted as public goods, then the factors that work against the supply of public goods apply to the formation of voluntary groups. Hence, the traditional political problem of whether or not an individual will either join or not join a group is now seen as being equivalent to the question: will an individual voluntarily contribute to the supply of a public good?

In an initial application of public goods theory to this question, Olson (1965) argues that only under certain conditions will individuals act to supply public goods. Unless coercion is applied, selective incentives offered, or the number of individuals is small, public goods will not be provided. Because group size is the most readily manipulatable condition, it plays a greater role in Olson's efforts to deduce propositions from a mathematical model.[6] His conclusions concerning the effects of group size (the number of possible contributors in some undifferentiated mass public) relate to both the absolute and the relative amount of the public good that is provided. They are as follows:

(1) As the size of the group increases, the actual amount of the public good supplied decreases (absolute).
(2) As the size of the group increases, the amount of the good supplied becomes more suboptimal (relative).

While Olson is generally credited with having raised the question of how and why group size affects the supply of public goods, his answer is not universally accepted. In fact, there is considerable disharmony in the answers that other theorists provide to the problem of the relationship between size and the supply of public goods. Some brief references to leading works in the field will serve to illustrate the widespread disagreement.

First, Chamberlin (1974) claims that increases in group size may effect an absolute level of public goods that is just the opposite of Olson's prediction. If a public good is inclusive (and not an inferior good), the amount of the good that is provided increases, not decreases, as the size of the group gets larger.[7] Olson's second conclusion is challenged by Riker and Ordeshook (1973: 72-74) who purport to show that the conclusion does not follow from the explicit components in the model. Contrary to Olson's conclusion, Riker and Ordeshook argue that in the case of pure public goods (perfect indivisibility) the relationship between an individual's marginal benefits and marginal costs is unaffected by group size. Finally, Frohlich and Oppenheimer (1970) reject Olson's overall conclusion that group size predicts the amount of the good that will be supplied voluntarily. The ability of individuals to supply themselves with a public good depends, instead, on some sort of mechanism to coordinate their expectations regarding the probable actions of others to contribute. In the absence of such a mechanism, Frohlich and Oppenheimer conclude that the differences between small and large groups do not produce different levels of public goods.

The conflicting nature of these conclusions presumably results from the use of different assumptions in the respective theories of group formation. In order to clarify the source of the disagreement between various authors on the effects of group size, the decision-making components used in the literature are listed. The basic variable conditions are as follows: (1) the availability of either positive or negative incentives beyond the indivisible benefits of the public goods, (2) the size of the group, (3) the extent to which the public good is indivisible and/or nonexcludability prevails, (4) the level of information an individual has about the decisions and actions of others, (5) the degree of independence between the actions of individuals, i.e., does an individual take the effects of his actions on the actions of others into account when making his decisions? (6) the income elasticity of demand for the public good, (7) the degree of similarity across individual preference orderings (utility functions) for public goods, and (8) the form (linearity v. nonlinearity) of both individual utility functions and production functions.

Given this broad range of variable conditions, it is not surprising that Olson, Frohlic and Oppenheimer, and Chamberlin reach different conclusions concerning the effects of group size. In fact, efforts have been made to demonstrate the way in which different assumptions about the nature of the conditions lead to quite different conclusions (Richelson, 1973; Chamberlin, 1974; Frohlich, Hunt, Oppenheimer and Wagner, 1975). Yet, no researcher has yet been able to convince the rest of the analysts working in this area of the most appropriate assumptions to make. Moreover, no one has been able to develop a model that is sufficiently general to accommodate all of the conditions.[8] As a result, the interrelated effects of all of the conditions remain unknown.

(B) Leadership

Mancur Olson's conclusions concerning the supply of public goods apply to situations involving an undifferentiated mass public. While this type of setting is politically relevant, it leaves out the basic political separation of roles between leaders and non-leaders. Following in the wake of Olson's analysis of the problems inhibiting the supply of public goods by a mass public, Frohlic, Oppenheimer and Young (1971), hereinafter referred to as Frohlich et al. propose a model in which leaders (or entrepreneurs) exist who somehow find it profitable to work toward the supply of public goods.[9]

Basically, the model consists of two expected utility equations. The first one, listed below, applies to the individual citizen. The citizen obtains a public good in exchange for payments, such as, donations and taxes. The satisfaction that the citizen derives from this exchange is a function of the benefits of the good times, the probability that the good will actually be provided; his share of the contracts awarded by the leader to the individual for production of the good; and costs in the form of taxes and donations. This relationship is captured in the following expression:

$$Uj\,(L_A) = Uj\,(X_A)\,Pj\,(X_A) + fj(A)r\,(C(0_A) + C(X_A)) - Dj\,(A) - Tj\,(A)$$

Where Uj is the utility of non-leader aj

L_A is the leadership role occupied by individual A
X_A is the public good supplied by A
$Pj\,(X_A)$ is the probability assigned by j that the good will be provided
$fj\,(A)$ is the fraction of the contracts let by A to aj
r is the prevailing profit rate for contracts in a social structure
$C(0_A)$ is the organizational costs incurred by A
$C(X_A)$ is the cost of producing the good
$Dj\,(A)$ is aj's donation to A
$Tj\,(A)$ is aj's tax payment to A

A non-leader will contribute some payment to the leader as long as its marginal utility is positive. In terms of the model, if $dUj\,(L_A)\,/\,d\,Dj\,(A) > 0$, contributions will be made. The utility that a non-leader receives is determined by differentiating the first term of the expected utility equation. This yields the following:

$$\frac{d\,(Uj\,(X_A)\,Pj\,(X_A))}{d\,Dj} = \frac{d\,Uj\,(X_A)}{d\,Dj}\,Pj + \frac{d\,Pj\,(X_A)}{d\,Dj}\,U_a(X_A)$$

This expression means that the utility that a non-leader obtains from his contributions are determined by (1) increases in the probability that the good will be supplied and/or (2) increases in the amount of the public good provided.

The second expected utility equation applies to the leader. It includes the same benefit and cost terms as used in the non-leader's calculus. A leader's utility is his own benefits of the public good as well as the donations and taxes received from the non-leaders. The leader's costs are those incurred in establishing the group and those of producing the good. Finally, Frohlich et al. include a benefit term to reflect the utility that a leader receives from occupying a leadership role. They assume that this factor, represented by the symbol b_A, is directly proportional to the organizational and production costs of supplying the good. The leader's expected utility equation is thus:

$$U_A\,(L_A) = U_A\,(X_A) + Dj\,(A) + Tj\,A - (1 - b_A)\,(y\,(0_A) + C\,(X_A))$$

While this equation is the model developed by Frohlich et al. it yields few non-obvious, deductive truths. The equation contains terms that represent certain factors affecting the non-leader's calculations. Yet, there is virtually no manipulation of these terms in order to predict a leader's actions.[10] Hence, despite the abstract nature of the model, very little axiomatic knowledge is gained.[11]

(C) Local Government Organization

V. Ostrom, Bish, and others have developed at least three key propositions about the relationship between local units of government and the supply of public goods. First, the coercive capacity of government is necessary to deal with the problems of free riders and holdouts (E. Ostrom and V. Ostrom, 1976: 15-19; Bish and V. Ostrom, 1973: 19). Second, the demand for public goods and services can be more easily articulated and aggregated in communities where the political tastes are homogeneous (E. Ostrom and V. Ostrom, 1976: 18; Bish, 1971: 46-53; Bish and Ostrom, 1973: 22-26). Since increases in the size of political units tend to lead to a diversity of citizen preferences, attempts to consolidate governmental authority make it more difficult for citizens to choose a community that fits their preference schedules for public goods. Efforts at governmental integration are likely to induce a supply of public goods that does not meet demands (Bish, 1971: 100-03, 148-56; Bish and V. Ostrom, 1973: 89-90; Olson, 1969). Third, common municipal services may be supplied more efficiently by non-municipal corporations. That is, while municipal governments may operate as providers of public goods and services, there may be more efficient processes than the governmental bureaucracy (V. Ostrom, Tiebout, and Warren, 1961: 834, 837-40; E. Ostrom and V. Ostrom, 1976: 19-24; V. Ostrom and Bish, 1971: 26-31; E. Ostrom, 1971: 467-69).

The efforts of V. Ostrom, Bish, and others have contributed to urban policy analysis by challenging conventional wisdom and traditional normative arguments. And these ideas are valuable because they suggest productive areas of hypothesis testing. Yet, the available evidence suggests that the theoretical posture being advanced by V. Ostrom, Bish, and others requires some clarification and refinement. This is seen by comparing the results of relevant empirical studies with the three previously mentioned propositions.

The evidence concerning the relative efficiency of private firms producing public goods on a contractual basis with local units of government is mixed and sketchy. One of the few studies cited by V. Ostrom et al. is a comparative analysis of the private supply of fire protection services in Scottsdale, Arizona with the public supply of fire services in the Seattle, Washington area

(Ahlbrandt, 1973, 1974). While the reported findings suggest a definite cost savings with the private production alternative, there are some problems of inference.[12] In addition, there is some evidence that the private production of public goods may not always be more efficient and that it may induce certain unanticipated consequences.[13]

The information concerning the relationship between the size of political communities and level of citizen satisfaction with public goods is not entirely supportive of the second proposition.[14] Initially, studies of citizen evaluation of police performance were seen as providing confirmatory evidence. Simply stated, the earlier studies revealed an inverse relationship between community size and citizen satisfaction (E. Ostrom, Parks, Whitaker, 1973; E. Ostrom and Parks, 1973; E. Ostrom and Smith, 1976). Yet, other research reveals that size does not appear to have strong, independent, negative effects on citizen evaluations. When the socioeconomic characteristics of cities are treated as control variables, the relationship between size and satisfaction is actually a positive one (Pachon and Lovrich, 1975). Hence, it is premature to conclude the perspective provided by the second proposition is guiding research in the right direction.[15]

The first proposition is difficult to resolve on the basis of empirical evidence. However, there is at least one opposing theoretical outlook. Even if a good has the properties of a public good, it may provide, in some way, sufficient reward to motivate private producers to effect its supply (Demsetz, 1970). If this is the case, then neither government coercion is needed to collect taxes or user's fees nor is a contractual arrangement necessary between private producers and units of government.

On the basis of the preceding combination of empirical and theoretical studies, several questions must be asked of the line of inquiry undertaken by V. Ostrom, Bish, and others. What is the range of public goods in metropolitan communities? Of these goods, which ones possess some private goods type attribute that permits them to be supplied without government intervention? Which public goods are most susceptible to crowding effects? Is it possible to limit the scale of the public production of public goods in order to minimize crowding effects?

2. HYPOTHESIS-TESTING

If, as Friedman (1953) says, the validity of assumptions is the ability to make accurate predictions, it is essential to confront theories of public goods with test data. It is clear that theories of public goods are based on a series of assumptions about rationality and calculations. Hence, let us consider the two primary areas where hypotheses based on theories of public goods have been verified.

(A) The Exploitation Hypothesis

Although Olson's basic claim about small groups is that the amount of a public good that is provided voluntarily will generally be suboptimal, he also advances a proposition about the sharing of costs and benefits among small-sized groups. If the good is not a superior good (if a good is a superior good, then expenditures for it increase by as much or more than available income increases) the distribution of the costs of supplying a public good will not be proportional to the distribution of the benefits of the good. How will they be distributed? Olson's answer is as follows (Olson, 1965: 35):

> The suboptimality or inefficiency will be somewhat less serious in groups composed of members of greatly different size or interest in the collective good. In such unequal groups, on the other hand, there is the tendency toward an arbitrary sharing of the burden of providing the collective good. The largest member, the member who would on his own provide the largest amount of the collective good, bears a disproportionate share of the burden of providing the collective good. The smaller member by definition gets a smaller fraction of the benefit of any amount of the collective good he provides than a larger member, and therefore has less incentive to provide additional amounts of the good. Once a smaller member has the amount of the collective good he gets free from the largest member, he has more than he would have purchased for himself, and has no incentive to obtain any of the collective good at his own expense. In small groups with common interests there is accordingly a *surprising tendency for "exploitation" of the great by the small.*

The critical assumption that Olson makes here is that the larger member (in terms of size) has a greater absolute value for the public good than the smaller member. In fact, the absolute value is assumed to be directly proportional to the size of the member. The exploitation hypothesis, then, asserts that the size of the member is inversely related to the member's share of the costs of supplying the good.

Attempts to verify the exploitation hypothesis have been conducted in the context of alliances, such as, the North Atlantic Treaty Organization (NATO). Olson and Zeckhauser (1966: 267) claim that NATO's objective of "deterring aggression" is a public good. Hence, they expect to find that the alliance members that place greater valuation on the defensive objective will bear a disproportionate share of the alliance's costs. This idea is verified in a test of five related hypotheses. According to Olson and Zeckhauser, "all of the empirical evidence tended to confirm the model." While all the measures of association used to test the hypotheses produced results that are in the predicted direction, their conclusion is too sweeping. First, it must be recognized that the exploitation hypothesis as originally formulated by Olson (1965) and as applied by Olson and Zeckhauser (1966) in the specific contexts of alliances rests on the auxiliary and empirical assumption that absolute size is directly proportional to the absolute value that an individual or group of individuals places on a public good. It is auxiliary in the sense that it has not been shown that it follows from higher order axioms in either the theory of public goods or in Olson's principle of the effects of group size on voluntary contributions. Unless it is established through some sort of deductive process, its truth must rest on empirical observations. As a result, the testing of the exploitation hypothesis provides no gains in verifying Olson's general model because it is logically independent of the model.

Viewed in this light, the explanatory value of the exploitation hypothesis hinges on the accuracy of the empirical assumption, which in turn hinges on the validity and reliability of the measurements. Here it is important to note that Olson and Zeckhauser provide no argument why it is reasonable to assume that absolute size is directly proportional to the absolute value for a public good.[16] At least in the context of military defense alliances, it is likely that relationships between absolute size and absolute value are affected by factors that promote military rivalries, such as, intra-country differences in language, religion, race, and social class. Unless these contaminating factors are screened out, the assumption in the case of NATO is not convincing (because of the empirical nature of the assumption other factors would have to be controlled for in other decision-making contexts). The problems in determining the absolute value that an individual member places on defense (and the relationship of absolute valuation to observables, e.g. size) apply afortiori to the claims of disproportionality. Disproportionality of cost sharing requires information on every member's marginal valuation and marginal costs. That is, over-contributions occur when a member's marginal costs exceed erase its marginal benefits.

Yet, it is difficult to see how marginal valuation can be determined when the basis for estimating absolute valuation has not yet been established. Moreover, the apportioning of marginal costs in light of marginal benefits makes the task of knowing when exploitation occurs even more problematic. Olson discusses the method of making these apportionments through "marginal cost sharing." Yet, as Loehr (1973) says, "marginal cost sharing is not an operational concept since it requires a knowledge of both the community welfare functions and the production possibilities relationships of members. While the latter is simply difficult to obtain, the former is impossible."

Moreover, even if the problems of measuring a member's absolute valuation are overlooked, the observed relationship in the case of NATO is not high. Olson and Zeckhauser correlate the size of a NATO member's GNP with the percentage of GNP allocated to defense and expect to find a positive rank order correlation. While the observed correlation is in the predicted direction, it has only a moderate value (+.49). Hence, for all of these reasons, the theoretical gains from Olson and Zeckhauser's empirical investigation is somewhat limited.

Despite these limitations, the effort by Olson and Zeckhauser should have encouraged other scholars to improve upon their earlier study. It is not clear, however, that subsequent works (Russett, 1970; Russett and Sullivan, 1971; Starr, 1974) overcome any of the difficulties confronting Olson and Zeckhauser. In fact, the later studies appear to follow the *modus operandi* established by them. Hence, the exact relationship between absolute size and absolute value remains unknown.

B. The Public Goods Character of Public Expenditures

The supply of public goods by local units of government has been a perennial problem since the classic remarks of Tiebout (1956). Charles Tiebout argues that an optimal supply of public goods may be achieved by individuals revealing their preferences through the selection of alternative communities in which to reside. Under certain conditions, if cities compete for residents, it is reasonable to expect that each community will contain a slightly different set of residents that share tastes for public goods.[17] As a result, the homogeneity of intra-community preferences means that all of the residents can agree on a supply of public goods that is consistent with every community member's marginal valuations of benefits and costs.

The basic thrust of Tiebout's theory has been extended by V. Ostrom and others in two related political arguments. First, they claim that efforts to reform the structures of local government by an integration of smaller units into larger units works against the positive effects of homogeneous intracommunity preference patterns. Second, in order to achieve the benefits of competition in the supply of public goods, e.g. lower costs, they argue for an expansion of private firm contracting with units of government to produce public goods along the lines of the Lakewood Plan in Los Angeles.

If the theoretical work of Tiebout is to be used in the manner of Ostrom and Bish, it is important to know if public goods are actually being provided by existing units of government. While there is some value in developing a pure theory of local public expenditures, the application of this theory requires that a basic condition, namely, that local government expenditures are public goods for some community, be fulfilled. If this condition is not met, the political argument against governmental consolidation cannot be based on the assumption that consolidation disrupts the demand structure for public goods.

Despite the obvious importance of knowing where actual public expenditures fit on the dimension of public versus private goods, few studies have adduced relevant evidence. There are, however, results from two recent econometric studies that bear upon this question. First, Bergstrom and Goodman (1973) examine the nature of demands for municipal expenditures in 826 municipalities with populations between 10,000 and 150,000, that are located in ten states. They determine the divisible nature of public goods by examining the relationship between the size of a community and expenditure demands. Here they consider two theoretically relevant effects of size on demand.

First, they argue that, if public expenditures are like Samuelson's pure public goods, the size of a city would only affect the quantity of services indirectly by affecting individual tax shares which, in turn, would affect the quantity of expenditures demanded. That is, the larger the size of the city, the smaller each individual's tax share. As the size of the tax shares decreases, individuals demand more public expenditures.

Second, if public expenditures are pure public goods, increases in city size are accompanied by only negligible crowding effects (or congestion costs). This means that because an increase in the size of a city does not diminish seriously the quantity and quality of the services provided by the municipal government, population increases will not be associated with a decline in the demand for public expenditures.

Given these two relationships, Bergstrom and Goodman estimate the public goods nature of city expenditures through a crowding parameter. The crowding parameter represented by γ is equal to the following ratio, $\alpha/(1 + \delta)$, where α and δ are the estimated elasticities of expenditure with respect to population size and the tax share of the person with the median income. If the γ is zero, Bergstrom and Goodman interpret this as evidence that the expenditures exhibit properties like Samuelson's pure public goods. However, if γ is one, they interpret this as evidence that the expenditures are more like private goods.

Interestingly, the estimates of γ for general expenditures (excluding education and welfare), police, and parks and recreation are seldom less than one. This means that as the size of the cities increases, the gains of sharing tax costs of public services are outweighed by the congestion costs of additional citizens using the public services. As a result, this set of findings suggests that the expected economies of scale that one expects to observe with public goods are not present. Hence, this finding casts doubt on the proposition that the public expenditures are public goods. Instead, it supports the opposite conclusion that the public expenditures exhibit the properties of private goods.

The results of Bergstrom and Goodman are supported by similar results produced by Borcherding and Deacon (1972). Borcherding and Deacon examine the nature of demands for state government expenditures in the eight categories of local education, higher education, highways, health and hospitals, police, fire, sewers and sanitation, and parks and recreation. One of the demand factors in their analysis is a "capturability" parameter, which indicates the degree of divisibility in the expenditure. It is represented by α which is equal to $1 + \theta / (\eta + 1)$, where θ and η are estimates of expenditure elasticity to population and price, respectively. If α equals zero, Borcherding and Deacon interpret this to mean that the expenditure category is like a public good. And, if α equals one, they interpret this to mean that the expenditure category is like a private good.

The statistical results show that α closely approximates unity, which means that the expenditures reflect the features of private rather than those of public goods. Consequently, these findings on the state level parallel those found by Bergstrom and Goodman on the municipal level. Hence, they bear upon the theory of local expenditures, at least indirectly, by being consistent with the more direct evidence of Bergstrom and Goodman.

The importance of these two empirical studies is in the new theoretical question that they raise for the study of public goods in local political communities. Assuming that there is a reasonable degree of validity and reliability in the statistical estimates of "crowding" and "capturability," the results have uncovered information about public expenditures which the research tradition begun by Tiebout has not fully addressed. That is, why would political decision-making processes be used to allocate resources for private goods when such goods are, theoretically at least, more efficiently allocated in private decision-making? Similarly, although these results do not torpedo the efforts of V. Ostrom and Bish to determine the most efficient way for local units of government to supply public goods, they suggest a possible theoretical puzzle that Ostrom, Bish, and others have not yet addressed.

III. WHITHER THE POLITICAL STUDY OF PUBLIC GOODS?

Despite the relatively short period of time in which political analysts have focused on the theory of public goods, it is remarkable how the work has advanced. Yet, it is equally clear that further work will need to address several unresolved questions before a coherent body of cumulative theoretical propositions, refined by appropriate hypothesis tests can emerge. While it is impossible to enumerate all of the further research possibilities, future studies are likely to consider the following sorts of questions:

(1) Under what set of interrelated conditions does the size of a group

make a difference in the amount of the public good that is provided?

(2) What are the comparative advantages of having public goods produced privately?

(3) In what contexts, other than alliances, is it appropriate to test aspects of Olson's model of group behavior?

(4) How can the basic model of leadership be extended?

(5) How and why do governmental units produce private goods?

It is beyond the scope of this paper to consider all of these questions in depth. Instead, an attempt is made to touch upon the last two questions in order to illustrate what needs to be done. They are selected because it is possible to show that these are fruitful areas of research. Some studies have already begun to construct models on topics revolving around these questions.

1. ELABORATION OF FROHLICH, OPPENHEIMER, AND YOUNG'S BASIC LEADERSHIP MODEL

An extension of Frohlich et al.'s model is not only possible, it is essential. They present the relations of the model in their simplest forms and leave it to further research to describe the explicit characteristics of their equations. One area of inquiry has already been suggested by Riker and Ordeshook (1973: 75-7). They offer descriptions of the type of person who will become a leader. This important question suggests how Frohlich et al.'s model may be used and refined.

Riker and Ordeshook's first claim is that a leader will be a risk taker. An extension of Frohlich et al.'s model is consistent with Riker and Ordeshook's observation. In fact, Frohlich et al. indicate that a member of a group in assessing his possibilities as leader, faces three outcomes: he may become leader (L) with probability $P(L)$; he may become a political opponent (L') with probability $P(L')$; or he may remain outside the political competition (E) with probability $P(E)$. So a leader hopes to maximize

$$U(L)P(L) + U(L')P(L') + U(E)P(E)$$

Included in the $U(L)$ and $U(L')$ terms is an estimation of the individual's profits in the role of leader or opponent; in fact the utility function which takes the form of benefits minus costs, is the exact expression for profits. In addition, it seems reasonable to include a term that reflects the probability that an individual will in fact make the profit that he estimates for each role.

This term can be expressed by P(U(L)) and P(U(L')). Hence, a leader would hope to maximize

$$P(U(L))U(L)P(L) + P(U(L'))U(L')P(L') + P(U(E))U(E)P(E)$$

Since the member is currently outside the field of political competition (he is occupying role E), he is certain of the profits he is making as a member of the group; if he were to remain outside the field of political competition he would continue to make this profit, and P(U(E)) is therefore equal to one. In addition, if the individual remained outside of competition, the probability of his continuing as a member of the group is one (P(E) = 1). Unless he enters the political competition, the individual is assured a utility of U(E) as a simple member of the group. But the utility he assigns to the leadership role is reduced by the probability that he will make a profit as a leader and by the probability that he will become the leader; these probabilities are generally less than one. The same is true of the utility he assigns to the role of political opponent. The outcome of entering the political arena is therefore risky, while the status quo (simple membership in the group) is certain, and only those willing to take risks will venture from the security of simple membership to the uncertainty of political leadership. It is a simple extension of this reasoning to predict that leaders will be risk takers.

Second, Riker and Ordeshook claim that leaders are more future oriented than others. This is apparent from the nature of the leader's utility function: the costs (organizational and productive) are immediate while the benefits (taxes, donations) are not. If a person discounts heavily for time, the utilities gained in the future are reduced, but the costs are not.

The third observation put forward is that potential leaders have relative freedom from constraints on resources. This is true to the extent that the leader must have access to financial resources in order to cover the initial organizational and production costs. But these need not be personal resources; there is no reason to assume that a leader can't build a political organization from nothing, just like the proverbial private entrepreneur. Informational resources are a more significant consideration. Riker and Ordeshook claim that the leader has access to more information than the ordinary member—a more realistic statement than that made by Frohlich, Oppenheimer and Young in their assumption that everyone has access to information. This might be a severe criticism of the leadership model were it not for the fact that this assumption isn't central to the analysis, and it is even relaxed in the section on politicization.

One final element of leadership proposed by Riker and Ordeshook is "the ability to get others to make choices they otherwise would not make." This suggests that the successful leader is able to influence, or alter, individual utility functions for members of the social group. Frohlich and Oppenheimer (1974) touch on this point, and since their work gives an illuminating example of the possible elaboration of the basic leadership model, it merits some discussion.

Recognizing that "nothing is certain except death and taxes," Frohlich and Oppenheimer examine in detail how the rational leader would make use of the latter. The analysis begins by dividing the collective good into two types: one that is excludable (X) and one that is non-excludable (Y). The utility of the individual in paying his taxes is

$$U(X) + U(Y) - T,$$

but if he does not pay taxes, his utility is

$$U(Y) + U(X)(1-P) + U(S)P,$$

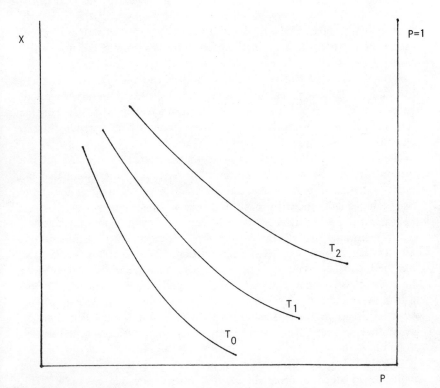

Figure 1: Iso-tax curves

where S is a sanction and P is the probability that the individual will receive the sanction. In other words, the delinquent taxpayer will get caught and suffer with probability P, or he will go free and continue to enjoy U(X) with probability (1−P). An important step then follows: the revenue-maximizing taxer will give the taxpayer an inducement to pay his taxes but will make it as small as possible by raising T (and therefore his tax revenue) so that in the limit the utility to the group member of paying taxes minus his utility of not paying taxes goes to zero. By combining the above two equations representing these utilities, in the limit

$$T = (U(X) - U(S))P$$

Using this relation, the assumption that U(X) exhibits consistently positive but decreasing marginal utility (a reasonable assumption) and the properties of differential calculus, Frohlich and Oppenheimer come up with iso-tax curves describing the optimal mixes of X and P (carrot and stick) for a given value of S. These curves are displayed in Figure 1.

A conclusion that can be immediately drawn is that as sanctions are decreased, the iso-tax lines descend less steeply, and all the lines have positive

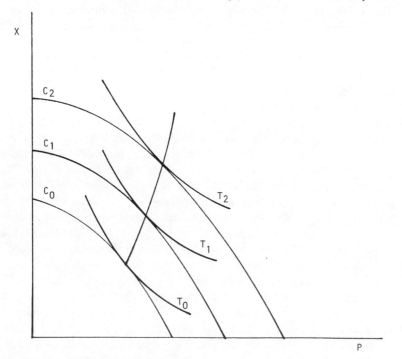

Figure 2: Iso-tax and Iso-cost curves

curvature, meaning that at small values of P it takes a large increase in the supply of the collective good to compensate for small decreases in the probability of conviction. These are intuitively acceptable results but they are also non-trivial: without this sort of analysis it would be impossible to state with certainty what the optimal mix of carrot and stick really is.

Frohlich and Oppenheimer then proceed to discover the shape of the iso-cost curves. Again they use P as the independent variable, and there is good reason for doing so: it is the discovery and conviction of tax offenders that costs; once the offender is caught, different degrees of S, as between making the offender pay a fine or cutting off his fingers, have a negligible effect on cost. These curves have negative curvature, and it turns out that the cheapest mix of X and P for a given optimal tax level is at the points of tangency between the iso-tax and iso-cost curves. The locus of these points is a curve of positive and increasing slope. This is displayed in Figure 2.

The last function examined is the "loyalty function," the line that forms the boundary between the region where the taxpayer receives positive utility in his relation with the taxer and the region where, whether he pays the tax or not, he is getting a bad deal. The horizontal distance between the optimal tax expansion line and the "loyalty" line is the net gains or losses that the citizen will receive at a given level of taxation. The authors show that until the tax level is identically equal to $U(X)$, the taxpayer will be disloyal. In other words, for small amounts of X, both the amount of the collective good and the tax must be raised if the taxer wants a loyal taxpayer. this is a surprising result, since it says that regardless of the functional forms of utilities and cost, there is a minimum level of operations that the political entrepreneur must maintain if the taxpayer is to have a net gain in utility.

The conclusions of the article are that the political entrepreneur will not tend to specialize in the provision of a collective good or in coercion but will supply some mixture of the two (as evidenced by the optimal tax expansion line); that as the taxer expands his scale of expenditure he will increase both the efficacy of enforcement and the scale of the positively valued programs; and that there is more than one equilibrium mix of coercion and positive benefits for the profit-oriented taxer. A final conclusion is that non-excludable collective goods have no effect on the tax revenue. These goods do affect the taxpayer's support of the leader, so he will provide them only if he is trying to undercut opposition, or when they are produced as externalities and the cost of excluding evaders from the benefits is prohibitive.

The importance of this model for political analysis is that it represents one of the few efforts to construct a rational choice model that includes the factor of coercion. Virtually all other theories posit a placid setting in which uncertainty is the most severe political constraint. As a result, it is vital to affirm the course of theoretical research that Frohlich and Oppenheimer have charted.

2. EXPLAINING THE COLLECTIVIZATION OF PRIVATE GOODS

The empirical discovery that some public expenditures are being consumed as private, rather than public goods, has been treated in a recent theoretical essay (Spann, 1974). A model of collective decision-making is posed in which the quantity of the good provided is the quantity demanded by the median voter in an electoral process governed by majority rule. It is shown that under certain conditions the collective consumption of private goods will yield gains to a decisive combination of voters. Simply stated, Spann claims that the collective consumption of private goods transfers income to at least one half of the voting population, i.e., those with incomes equal to or less than the median income, if the distribution of income is not skewed to the right and the income elasticity of demand is greater than price elasticity. As Spann (1974) observes these conditions were satisfied in earlier empirical studies and actual public policies were found to be like private goods (Borcherding and Deacon, 1972; Bergstrom and Goodman, 1973).

Despite the correspondence between these theoretical conclusions and the empirical estimates, information is missing on how political actions affect the collective consumption of private goods. The model does not yield specific predictions on the processes through which individuals exploit a collective decision-making situation to their advantage. Future research will need to address the following sorts of questions before a complete explanation of the collective consumption of private goods is established: Do coalitions of lower and middle-income persons dominate the adoption of private goods? How do higher income groups seek to block or defeat the policy alternatives favored by a coalition of lower income groups? At what point does the collectivization of private goods motivate higher income groups to leave the community? And what is the range of public policies that are like private goods and, hence, within the scope of the theory?

In summary, the economic theory of public goods has not radicalized contemporary political analysis. It appeared, at least initially, that public goods theory was a source of non-obvious propositions about the relationships between political choice mechanisms and decisional outcomes. A review of the literature reveals, however, that analysts have not identified the complete and correct set of conditions that govern these relationships. For example, the sweeping quality initially attributed to Olson's principle of collective action has been reduced considerably, and perhaps overturned, by subsequent studies. Hence, it is virtually impossible to point out an area of inquiry where the theory of public goods has contributed toward the establishment of a cumulative body of propositions.

Despite the fact that the positive expectations built around the earlier studies failed to materialize, subsequent studies have uncovered new questions. For example, how and why will private goods be consumed collectively when there is a net welfare loss associated with such consumption? What mixture of negative sanctions and positive inducements will produce the optimal supply of public goods? The future of public goods theory is in conducting inquiries along these lines.

NOTES

1. Some analysts see an important connection between Olson's problem of the group provision of public goods and classical political theory. The link is that both Olson's problem and the questions confronting theorists such as Hobbes are seen as n-prisoners' dilemma games. Hence, Olson's analysis involves the application of modern tools to one of the critical questions of political theory (Orbell and Wilson, 1975).

2. A striking feature of the existing applications of public goods theory is the lack of a comparative perspective. Yet, it may be possible to compare the types of organizational structures that provide for the supply of public goods across a range of performance criteria, such as, efficiency and responsiveness (V. Ostrom and Hennessey, 1974). Presumably, these evaluations can be conducted between national or subnational political cal units both within and between different countries.

3. The political analysts who have applied the theory of public goods are already committed to the proposition that the concept of public goods is a fruitful one. Some see it as a desirable alternative to more traditional views of politics. Vincent Ostrom (1974: 4-5, 17-20) goes so far as to say that the adoption of a public goods framework may ultimately contribute to an improvement of public policy. As Ostrom sees it, the area of public administration has been the source of inadequate policy advice because it has been based on misconceived principles of organizations and public services. Because the theory of public goods, along with other public choice concepts, promises to be the source of more valid principles, it may improve the nature of policy recommendations.

4. It is important to note that economists have not agreed on the essence of indivisibility. It has been interpreted by economists such as Buchanan (1968) to mean jointness of supply. However, Samuelson (1969) does not consider jointness of supply to be equivalent to the indivisible nature of pure public goods. Samuelson's separation of jointness of supply from the meaning of public goods has been criticized by Demsetz (1970), who claims to show that Samuelson's distinction is a false one.

5. For example, whereas deterrent services are pure public goods, purely defensive services are impure public goods. One potential value of this distinction is that the impure nature of defensive services suggests that problems of congestion (congestion refers to the decline in the quantity and quality of the good as new users of the service are added) are likely to occur for nation-states that seek to form defensive alliances. The congestion costs, in turn, highlight the need for members of the alliance to assess some sort of charge for new members whose presence creates the congestion (Sandler and Cauley, 1975).

6. Olson's model of the effects of group size is as follows:

Sg denotes the size of the group.

T denotes the amount of the public good that is supplied.

Vg denotes the group benefit.

Vi denotes the ith individual's gain

Fi denotes the proportion (fractional amount) of the group gain consumed by the ith the individual

C denotes the ith individual's cost of supplying (or purchasing) the public good.

Olson posits Vg equal to Sg times T and Fi equal to the ratio of Vi to Vg. From her he identifies the condition under which an individual maximizes his net utility by purchasing some amount of the public good. That condition exists when

$$dVi/dT - \alpha C/dT = 0 \qquad\qquad (1)$$

Since Fi = Vi/Vg, equation (1) becomes

$$Fi\,(dVg/dT) - dC/dT = 0 \qquad\qquad (2)$$

Olson argues that because Fi decreases with increase in Sg, the supply of the public good becomes smaller and more suboptimal.

7. Chamberlin explicitly distinguishes two types of public goods in a manner originally set forth by Olson. An inclusive public good is one that is perfectly indivisible, i.e., one individual's valuation of the good is not affected by the number of persons who consume the good. And an exclusive good is one which is divisible, but there is non-excludability. Here the satisfaction that an individual receives from the good decreases as the number of persons consuming the good increases, and it is not feasible to restrict persons from enjoying the benefits.

8. Attempts have been made to cast Olson's problem of collective action into a different analytical framework from the one principally set forth by Olson. One analysis views the problem as an n-prisoners' dilemma game. Here it is proposed that there is a joint cooperative strategy that will prevail (Hardin, 1971). The process by which cooperation is achieved is the subject of a second study (Schofield, 1975). Basically, the process is one of coalition formation, which culminates in the establishment of an inclusive coalition of all individual players. The potential advantage of these translations is that they bring Olson's problem into a well-established analytical framework. Hence, it may facilitate the development of a general model of the group supply of public goods.

9. Prior to the work of Frohlich, Oppenheimer, and Young, there were two efforts made to extend Olson's model by adding the component of leader (or entrepreneur) (Salisbury, 1969; Wagner, 1966).

10. While the study ends with a recapitulation of forty propositions that have appeared earlier in the text, only a handful seem to follow from the model. Approximately thirty-four of the propositions are based on insight and wisdom rather than strict mathematical proof.

11. Despite the limiting features of the expected utility equations. Frohlich et al. advance the level of theoretical knowledge about leadership and public goods by raising several theoretical issues. It is appropriate to assess the ideas that Frolich et al generate by forcing themselves to state explicitly the considerations taken into account by a leader. Here there are both gains and losses. For example, the donation and tax terms actually incorporate four types of receipts. Frohlich et al. construct a typology by classifying receipts along two dichotomous scales; one scale divides receipts in terms of whether or not they were either positively or negatively induced and the other scale

divides receipts in terms of whether they were derived from the provision of either public or private goods. Consequently, the receipts are as follows: (1) donations (positive, public), (2) taxes (negative, private), (3) purchases (positive, private), and (4) extortions (negative, public).

Compared to other studies, this typology provides a more extensive list of relevant receipts. And Frohlich et al. are right in giving explicit attention to the seamy side of leadership through the incorporation of purchases and extortions. Yet, there is a lack of conceptual clarity between donations and taxes. If, for example, an individual contributes a donation because he wants to avoid the social sanctions placed on him if he is seen by others as a free-rider, has he really made a positive contribution? When do social sanctions become negative inducements? In fact, does the possibility of social sanctions reduce donations to the empty set? The point here is that it may be more profitable to construct a typology that classifies receipts according to various types of coercion depending on the nature (magnitude, duration, intensity) of the negative sanction.

A second basic theoretical idea is the introduction of the concept of the personal satisfaction that leaders derive from being a leader. Frohlich et al. use it to describe the behavior of leaders. For example, a leader can have zero (or negative) utility for the good that he is providing and still make a profit (all that is required is that donations, taxes, and personal satisfaction outweigh costs). Higher profits will be made by those with a high b; if b is greater than one, the leader will be making a profit on his costs, and Frohlich et al. say that he is aptly described as a populist demagogue.

While be serves to enrich the descriptive qualities of the model, is it measurable? The subjective and quixotic nature of this intangible factor may make efforts to estimate it somewhat difficult. In building an abstract model of leadership, it seems counterproductive to posit factors that reflect the vagaries of political life. Instead, it is more productive to posit other factors that lead to propositions that can account for a wide range of behavior including that of populist demagogues.

12. In Ahlbrandt's study of public versus private production of fire services, the type of production mechanism is a residual, unmeasured category. As a result, the study does not demonstrate that the production category accounts for the alleged cost savings. Hence, the causal mechanism that may account for costs per capita remains unknown.

13. The apparent failure of a private firm to fulfill a performance contract for the public school system of Gary, Indiana indicates that private producers may not be more effective than public producers. Moreover, the profit motive seems to have led the firm into an allocation of resources of questionable merit. For example, because the firm was likely to show the greatest change in students who possessed neither low level learning abilities nor high level learning abilities, the firm distributed fewer resources to these children and focused a disproportionate amount of effort on those students who would be most likely to increase their performance levels (Peterson, 1974).

14. There is some disagreement concerning the relationship between size and another measure of efficiency, namely, costs per capita. Some analysts have adduced evidence of an inverse relationship between these two variables (E. Ostrom and Parks, 1973; E. Ostrom and Smith, 1976). However, other analysts claim that the effects of contaminating factors, e.g., greater demands on larger-sized jurisdictions and positive spillovers from larger jurisdictions to smaller ones, have not been screened out in studies that purport to show a relationship between size and per capita costs. When these extraneous factors are taken into account, the original inverse relationship may be weakened and perhaps reversed (Pachon and Lovrich, 1977: 39-40).

15. The relationship between community size and the quality of the public good of police protection depends, in part, on how police services are measured. If police

protection is measured in terms of the conversion of crimes to arrests, then some evidence suggests that the agencies with the larger per capita manpower resources are more effective than those with fewer resources (Skogan, 1976: 283).

16. In subsequent essays, Olson and Zeckhauser (1967) and Olson (1971) do not justify this assumption.

17. There is very little convincing evidence on the monopolistic versus competitive nature of actual local governments. Some findings have been interpreted as in support of the proposition that governments are monopolistic suppliers of public goods (Wagner and Weber, 1975). Yet, these results have been criticized on conceptual and methodological grounds (Rothenberg, 1975). However, V. Ostrom (1975) believes that these results do not weaken his claim that cities, acting as collective consumption units, may enjoy the benefits of competition among private producers of public goods. As a result, the extent to which there is actual competition among the suppliers of public goods remains unknown.

BIBLIOGRAPHY

AHLBRANDT, R. (1973) "Efficiency in the Provision of Fire Services." Public Choice 16(Fall): 1-16.
––– (1974) "Implications of Contracting for a Public Service." Urban Affairs Quarterly 9(March): 337-358.
BERGSTROM, T. and R. P. GOODMAN (1973) "Private Demands for Public Goods." American Economic Review 63(June): 280-296.
BISH, R. L. (1971) The Public Economy of Metropolitan Areas. Chicago: Rand McNally/Markham.
BISH, R. L. and V. OSTROM (1973) Understanding Urban Government. Washington, D.C.: American Enterprise.
BISH, R. L. and R. WARREN (1972) "Scale and Monopoly in Urban Government Services." Urban Affairs Quarterly 8(September): 97-110.
BORCHERDING, T. E. and R. T. DEACON (1972) "The Demand for the Services of Non-federal Governments." American Economic Review 62(December): 891-901.
BRETON, A. (1974) The Economic Theory of Representative Government. Chicago: Aldine.
BUCHANAN, J. (1968) The Demand and Supply of Public Goods. Chicago: Rand McNally.
BURGESS, P. M. and J. A. ROBINSON (1969) "Alliances and the Theory of Collective Action." The Midwest Journal of Political Science 13(May): 194-218.
CHAMBERLIN, J. (1974) "Provision of Collective Goods as a Function of Group Size." American Political Science Review 68(June): 707-716.
DEMSETZ, H. (1970) "The Private Production of Public Goods." The Journal of Law and Economics 8(October): 293-306.
FEELEY, M. (1970) "Coercion and Compliance." Law and Society Review 4(May): 505-520.
FRIEDMAN, M. (1953) Essays in Positive Economics. Chicago: University of Chicago Press.
FROHLICH, N., T. HUNT, J. A. OPPENHEIMER, and R. H. WAGNER (1975) "Individual Contributions for Public Goods." The Journal of Conflict Resolution 9(June): 310-329.

FROHLICH, N. and J. A. OPPENHEIMER (1970) "I Get by With a Little Help from my Friends." World Politics 23(October): 104-120.
——— (1974) "The Carrot and the Stick." Public Choice 9(Fall): 43-62.
FROHLICH, N., J. A. OPPENHEIMER, and O. R. YOUNG (1971) Political Leadership and Collective Goods. Princeton: Princeton University Press.
HARDIN, R. (1971) "Collective Action as an Agreeable N-prisoners' Dilemma." Behavioral Science 16(September/October): 472-481.
HEAD, J.G. (1962) "Public Goods and Public Policy." Public Finance 17, No. 3: 197-219.
HEAD, J. G. and C. S. SHOUP (1969) "Public Goods, Private Goods, and Ambiguous Goods." The Economic Journal 79(September): 567-572.
KRAMER, G. H. and J. HERTZBERG (1975) "Formal Theory." In F. Greenstein and N. Polsby (eds.) Handbook of Political Science, 7. Reading, Massachusetts: Addison-Wesley.
LOEHR, W. (1973) "Collective Goods and International Cooperation: Comments." International Organization 27(Summer): 421-430.
MARGOLIS, J. (1955) "A Comment on the Pure Theory of Public Expenditure." Review of Economics and Statistics 37(November): 347-349.
OLSON, M. (1965) The Logic of Collective Action. Cambridge: Harvard University Press.
——— (1969) "The Principle of 'Fiscal Equivalence'." The American Economic Review 59(May): 479-487.
——— (1971) "Increasing the Incentives for International Cooperation." International Organization 25(Autumn): 866-874.
OLSON, M. and R. ZECKHAUSER (1966) "An Economic Theory of Alliances." Review of Economics and Statistics 48(August): 266-279.
——— (1967) "Collective Goods, Comparative Advantage, and Alliance Efficiency." Pp. 25-48 in R. N. McKean (ed.) Issues in Defense Economics. New York: Columbia University Press.
ORBELL, J. M. and L. A. WILSON (1975) "Institutional Solutions to the N-prisoners' Dilemma." Working Paper Number Three, Institute for Social Science Research, University of Oregon.
OSTROM, E. (1971) "Institutional Arrangements and the Measurement of Policy Consequences." Urban Affairs Quarterly 6(March): 447-475.
——— (1972) "Metropolitan Reform." Social Science Quarterly 53(December): 474-493.
OSTROM, E. and R. B. PARKS (1973) "Suburban Police Departments." Pp. 367-402 in L. H. Masotti and J. K. Hadden (eds.) The Urbanization of the Suburbs, 7, Urban Affairs Annual Reviews, Beverly Hills, California: Sage.
OSTROM, E., R. B. PARKS, and G. P. WHITAKER (1973) "Do We Really Want to Consolidate Urban Police Forces?" Public Administration Review 33(September/October): 423-433.
OSTROM, E. and D. C. SMITH (1976) "On the Fate of 'Lilliputs' in Metropolitan Policing." Public Administration Review 36(March/April): 192-200.
OSTROM, V. (1974) The Intellectual Crisis in American Public Administration. University of Alabama: University of Alabama Press.
——— (1975) "Comment." The Journal of Law and Economics 18(December): 691-694.
OSTROM, V. and E. OSTROM (1976) "Public Choice in Public Agencies," Workshop in Political Theory and Policy Analysis, Indiana University.
OSTROM, V. and T. M. HENNESSEY (1974) "Institutional Structures. Territoriality and Development Perspectives." Paper prepared for the Eighth World Congress of

Sociology, Toronto, Canada, August 21.

OSTROM, V., C. M. TIEBOUT, and R. WARREN (1961) "The Organization of Government in Metropolitan Areas." American Political Science Review 55(December): 831-842.

PACHON, H. P. and N. P. LOVRICH (1977) "The Consolidation of Urban Public Services." Public Administration Review 37(January/February): 38-45.

PETERSON, G. E. (1974) "The Distributional Impact of Performance Contracting in Schools." Pp. 115-135 in H. M. Hochman and G. E. Peterson (eds.) Redistribution through Public Choice. New York: Columbia University Press.

RICHELSON, J. (1973) "A Note on Collective Goods and the Theory of Political Entrepreneurship." Public Choice 16(Fall): 73-76.

RIKER, W. N. and P. C. ORDESHOOK (1973) An Introduction to Positive Political Theory. Englewood Cliffs, New Jersey: Prentice-Hall.

ROTTENBERG, J. (1975) "Comment." The Journal of Law and Economics 18(December): 685-690.

RUSSETT, B. M. (1970) What Price Vigilance? New Haven: Yale University Press.

RUSSETT, B. M. and J. D. SULLIVAN (1971) "Collective Goods and International Organization." International Organization 25(Autumn): 845-865.

SALISBURY, R. H. (1969) "An Exchange Theory of Interest Groups." Midwest Journal of Political Science 13(February): 1-32.

SAMUELSON, P. A. (1954) "The Pure Theory of Public Expenditure." The Review of Economics and Statistics 36(November): 387-389.

––– (1955) "Diagrammatic Exposition of a Theory of Public Expenditure." The Review of Economics and Statistics 48(November): 350-356.

––– (1958) "Aspects of Public Expenditure Theories." The Review of Economics and Statistics 40(November): 332-336.

––– (1969) "Contrast Between Welfare Conditions for Joint Supply and for Public Goods." The Review of Economics and Statistics 51(February): 26-39.

SANDLER, T. and J. CAULEY (1975) "On the Economic Theory of Alliances." The Journal of Conflict Resolution 19(June): 330-348.

SCHOFIELD, N. (1975) "A Game Theoretic Analysis of Olson's Game of Collective Action." The Journal of Conflict Resolution 19(September): 441-461.

SHEPSLE, K. A. (1974) "Theories of Collective Decision-making." Pp. 4-77 in C. P. Cotter (ed.) Political Science Annual, V, Indianapolis: Bobbs-Merrill.

SKOGAN, W. G. (1976) "Efficiency and Effectiveness in Big City Police Departments." Public Administration Review 36(May/June): 278-286.

SPANN, R. M. (1974) "Collective Consumption of Private Goods." Public Choice 29(Winter): 62-81.

STARR, H. (1974) "A Collective Goods Analysis of the Warsaw Pact after Czechoslovakia." International Organization 28(Summer): 521-532.

TAYLOR, M. (1975) "The Theory of Collective Choice." In F. Greenstein and N. W. Polsby (eds.) Handbook of Political Science. Reading, Massachusetts: Addison-Wesley.

TIEBOUT, C. M. (1956) "A Pure Theory of Local Expenditure." Journal of Political Economy 44(October): 416-424.

WAGNER, R. E. (1966) "Pressure Groups and Political Entrepreneurs." Papers on Non-Market Decision-Making, 1, Charlottesville, Virginia: University of Virginia.

WAGNER, R. E. and W. E. WEBER (1975) "Competition, Monopoly, and the Organization of Government in Metropolitan Areas." The Journal of Law and Economics 18(December): 661-684.

WARREN, R. O. (1964) "A Municipal Services Model of Metropolitan Organization." Journal of the American Institute of Planners 30(August): 193-204.

PART II

SUPERNATIONAL INSTITUTIONS

Chapter 4

THE ECONOMICS OF THE OLYMPIC GAMES:
AN APPLICATION OF THE ECONOMIC THEORY OF CLUBS

ALLAN C. DeSERPA
Arizona State University

STEPHEN K. HAPPEL
Arizona State University

I. INTRODUCTION

The Olympic Games of the Twentieth Century represent a degree of international cooperation not often matched in recent history. The characteristics of competition, sportsmanship, excellence, and brotherhood create an environment that enables individuals and states of diverse goals and politics to set aside their differences and participate in, literally, a "meeting of the world" every four years. That the Games do indeed have a strong worldwide appeal can be evidenced by a number of economic and social signals: (1) the fact that cities and television networks bid large sums of money for the "rights" to the Games;[1] (2) the length of the planning period and the level of resource expenditures by participating nations and the host city; (3) the awesome training costs incurred by athletes in preparation for the competition; and (4) the repeated political conflicts undertaken in order to capitalize on the attention directed at the Games. Perhaps the best known of these political incidents was Hitler's attempt to exploit the 1936 Games for Nazi propaganda purposes. The most serious recent incident was the massacre of eleven Israeli athletes by Palestinian extremists in Munich in 1972. Other examples of lesser magnitude include the United States opposition to Soviet Union participation in the 1952 Games, the withdrawal by some of the Arab nations in 1956 in response to the Suez crisis, the exclusion of South Africa

AUTHORS' NOTE: The Olympics are sports at the summit . . . Yet the Olympics go beyond sports. They approach art . . . They offer competition, with the animal excitement of physical combat, strength matched against strength, style against style, stamina against stamina, courage against courage. And above all, they offer a singular spirit of a camaraderie born of shared victories, an understanding born of shared defeats [Schaap, 1967: ix].

and Rhodesia from participation on grounds of their apartheid policies, and the de facto exclusion of Taiwan in 1976 because of its insistence on bearing the flag of the Republic of China.[2]

The purpose of this paper is to examine this unique multinational alliance of athletes and polities using the economic theory of clubs as the vehicle for analysis. The main body of the paper is divided into four sections. In the first section a summary of the theory of clubs is presented. Next, the Olympic Games are cast into this theoretical framework. Specifically, the interdependent questions of the selection of athletes and the membership of nations are discussed. Then, the issue of whether the observed behavior of the governing body, the International Olympic Committee (IOC), over the past eighty years is consistent with the propositions of the theory of clubs is examined. In particular, the discussion delves into the success of the Olympic Games—why it has been a very "efficient" club throughout this century. Finally, the last section confronts a number of areas that are quite likely to influence the future success of the Games.

II. THE ECONOMIC THEORY OF CLUBS: AN OVERVIEW

In order to put the economic theory of clubs into perspective, it is necessary to begin with the Samuelson (1954, 1955) "pure public good-pure private good" dichotomy. A pure public good is defined to be indivisible, nonexcludable, and nonrival, where indivisibility means that the good cannot be consumed in parts, nonexcludability indicates that denying anyone the benefits associated with the good is either not possible or prohibitively expensive, and nonrivalry implies that one person's consumption of the good does not prevent someone else from using it. Since these features are seldom observed simultaneously in one good, for instance because congestion often develops, there are very few examples of pure public goods.[3]

Similarly, there are very few goods which possess the divisibility, excludability, and rivalry characteristics of pure private goods. For example, nearly all goods are capable of being shared to some extent and, consequently, exhibit properties associated with public goods. Thus, pure public and pure private goods are polar cases on the goods spectrum, with the vast majority of commodities falling between these two theoretical extremes. The economic theory of clubs, initially formulated by Buchanan,[4] examines non-pure cases where sharing arrangements and congestion problems are of major concern.

Buchanan's major contribution, besides introducing the problem and, therefore, providing a "theory of classification," is the idea that it is possible to identify an optimal size of the good to be shared (X) and an optimal number of members to share it (N). Moreover, as argued by Buchanan and shown in Figure 1, membership size and the size of the good (facility) itself are interdependent.

According to Buchanan, for a given size of the good and holding socio-economic factors such as tastes, incomes, and customs constant, expanding the size of the membership exerts important external effects upon established members. With a very low membership, expanding numbers might lead to external benefits in the form of more people with whom to socialize or compete if games are involved. However, as these benefits become exhausted, additional membership comes to be viewed as an external cost. (It is possible that this external cost of increased numbers may be partially offset by lower club dues per member of total operating costs are fixed with respect to membership size.[5]) Thus, for each level of provision (X), there exists an optimal membership size which is, in general, an increasing function of the level of provision. In Figure 1, the N_{opt} curve depicts this notion. By analogous reasoning, the optimal level of provision is likely to be an increasing function of membership, as indicated by X_{opt} in Figure 1.

At point A, given the low provision rate X_A, N_A is the optimal membership size. This does not imply, however, that X_A is the optimal provision rate for a membership size of N_A. As Figure 1 is constructed, X_A is too small, indicating that expansion to some point B is called for. But at point B the membership size is too small relative to the corresponding provision rate. Hence, ultimately an optimal club must satisfy two conditions simultaneously: (1) membership size must be optimal relative to the provision rate; and

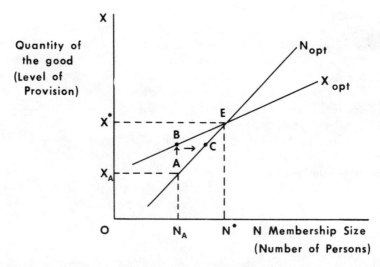

Figure 1: Optimal Club Membership and Provision

(2) the size of the good must be optimal relative to the size of membership. In Figure 1, these two conditions are satisfied only at point E since there is no incentive to move in either direction.[6]

As stated above, in the interest of isolating this idea, Buchanan held constant a number of important variables. For one thing, all members were assumed to have identical preferences. Yet obviously in reality there may be disagreement among members as to the optimal values of X and N. If so, the optimal solution will vary as different weights are attached to the preferences of the different individuals involved. These weights, in turn, depend upon both static and dynamic factors such as income distribution, location, the initial composition of membership, and the nature of the group decision making process.

For another, since the theory of clubs involves the problem of inclusion or exclusion, the question of discrimination may be important. The nature of sharing arrangements is subject to considerable variation, ranging from the purely impersonal (e.g., the mere sharing of expenses on such commodities as fire hydrants and traffic signals) to the very intimate (e.g., joint usage of shoes, bathtubs, and swimming pools). Only in rare circumstances would each and every member be indifferent to the identity and attributes of those with whom they are sharing the good. Clearly the more intimate the good in question, the more important such matters become. In the context of the Olympic Games, the number of athletes participating in a given event may be an important variable, but the skills of the participants may be at least as important.

Finally, and closely related to these first two problems, the issue of financing was not detailed by Buchanan. Yet the more diverse the preferences and characteristics of the members, the more difficult it becomes to form and then maintain a viable organization. Consequently, the financing arrangements underlying the organization may be critical. Those members who are more needed or wanted may bear a disproportionately low share of the costs, perhaps even to the point of receiving a subsidy, whereas those with a strong desire for the good may be willing to pay more than their proportionate share. In this type of environment one would expect gamesmanship, freeridership, threats of withdrawal, and other means of securing membership at the lowest possible individual costs to be employed rather extensively. As the above factors have been analyzed and incorporated into the club methodology, considerable evolution and refinement has taken place.[7]

III. THE OLYMPIC GAMES AS A CLUB

A. CONCEPTUALIZING THE PROBLEM

In many respects the applicability of the theory of clubs to the Olympic Games is obvious: the Games are an expensive extravaganza shared by a large group of individuals and nations. On the one hand, the facilities where the Games are held is a public good which must be shared by the athletes and spectators alike if they are directly to consume the "Olympic Spirit." On the other hand, via television, radio, and newspaper, the Games create spillover benefits to individuals and nations who are not actually present. For example, those athletes who attempt to qualify for the Games derive benefits from the training and competition whether they experience the "thrill of victory" or the "agony of defeat." Also, it has been argued that sports competition among nations is a surrogate for military conflict.[8] To the extent that this argument is valid, any reduction in the likelihood of war is a positive externality to much of the world. While exclusion from the global spillovers may be very difficult, if not virtually impossible, to achieve under present technology, the direct benefits to the participants are clearly excludable. Moreover, as our overview of the theory of clubs implies, the inclusion or exclusion of athletes and nations—membership decisions—are among the most important associated with the Games for a number of reasons.

First, as Buchanan argued membership decisions interact with provision (facility) decisions. With respect to the Olympic Games, the cities willing to submit bids and the size and dimensions of these bids depend upon both the number of individual competitions and the number of nations participating. Clearly the facilities for staging the events and housing the athletes are planned with an eye toward the number of competitors. Also, certain cities will not enter the bidding process if certain nations are excluded, i.e., Eastern European cities if the Soviet Union is barred.

Second, along similar lines, contributions by individual nations, an important component in the overall financing of the Games, are also a function of membership decisions. Nations are obviously going to be unwilling to contribute funds if they are not allowed to participate. Furthermore, the countries that do provide substantial contributions do so because membership decisions are compatible with their national objectives.

Finally and most importantly, as the theory of clubs stresses, membership decisions play the major role in determining the quality of and the interest in the Games. Since the Olympic Games are based on international cooperation and brotherhood, it is difficult to imagine the Games ever being congested with respect to the number of countries. Exclusion of countries takes place on an individual basis and, at least in principle, only for drastic reasons. On the other hand, congestion of athletes is a distinct possibility. Assuming competitors in each country are selected on the basis of skills, each additional participant from a given country in a given event tends to be less skilled than the preceding one and, therefore, reduces the average skill level of the group. Hence, while some minimum number of participants is necessary to stage competitive and exciting events, it is undesirable to expand the group of athletes indefinitely. The optimal number of athletes, in turn, depends primarily on the set of events and the national identities and specializations of the athletes included.

Figure 2 is a hypothetical "membership matrix," the elements of which, n_{ij}, denote the number of athletes representing the ith country in the jth event. For example, Country 1 sends on athlete to the first event, three to the second, and so forth for a total of ten, whereas Country 4 sends one athlete to the third event and participates in none of the other events.

The disaggregate elements of the "membership matrix" are important because they convey extensive information on quality of the Games. The high level of skills necessary to be an Olympic athlete requires that participants become highly specialized. As a result, there are very few substitution possibilities in the short run: swimmers do not become sprinters; high jumpers do not become shot putters, and so on. Accordingly, the numerical variables specify the identities and skills of the participating athletes. Moreover, these relative skills as reflected by the n_{ij}'s tend to determine the outcomes of the events. To the extent that national decisionmakers are motivated by the distribution of medals, even for events in which they do not participate or have a chance to win, the interest in the Games is determined. For example, while the United States might place greater weight on the outcome of the basketball competition than the equestrian competition, it nevertheless prefers a British victory to a Russian victory in the latter.[9]

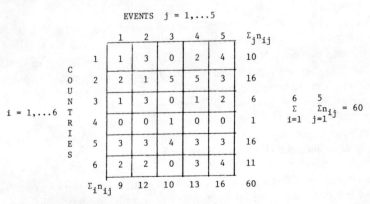

Figure 2: Hypothetical Membership Matrix

The n_{ij}'s, in addition to being important in their own right, determine all the aggregate membership variables. These include the number of athletes representing each country (obtained by summing horizontally across events), the number of athletes participating in each event (obtained by summing vertically across countries), and the total number of athletes participating in the Games (obtained by double summation). Including or excluding any country alters the number of athletes in each event in which that country would have had participants, while sanctioning an event likewise affects the number of representatives from each country. As an example of the importance of these factors for the Games, consider the third event in Figure 2. On the one hand, it is relatively unbalanced internationally. Because imbalance of this type might be considered to de-emphasize the international flavor of the Games in favor of competition among a few dominant nations, this event might be dropped from the Games. On the other hand, this event keeps Country 4 in the Games, a potential benefit which might take precedence over the problem of imbalance and lead to retention. Obviously final decisions such as these affect worldwide preferences for the Games.

Thus to summarize, each country or decision making body within that country is not indifferent with respect to either the disaggregate or the aggregate composition of the "membership matrix." At one extreme, preferences might be derived solely from preferences regarding the final distribution of medals. At the other extreme, preferences might be derived simply from a desire to promote competition, sportsmanship, and excellence. Or a range of preferences might exist where countries might be interested in one of these factors while desiring to maximize the number of participating nations. The analytical framework to follow is sufficiently general to cover any of these possibilities.

B. A FORMAL MODEL

The foregoing discussion implies that the number of external benefits and costs arising out of each nation's participation decisions is quite large. In this section, we present a rigorous analytical framework within which to bound the problem to some degree. Drawing upon previous discussion, the major features of this framework are:

(1) The Olympic Games are a "package" of public goods, the most important of which are the spillover costs and benefits that each participant provides for all other participants;

(2) Each country or athlete, therefore, supplies and consumes (non-material) public goods through participation in the Games. Specifically, each athlete supplies two basic characteristics:

     a.   he is a representative of a particular country, and
     b.   he is a competitor of known skills in a particular event;
(3) The major decision making power on the selection of the actual individuals participating rests with the individual nations. Some person or committee (often a National Olympic Committee—NOC) has charge of funding, selecting athletes, etc., and has the power to withdraw the entire team from competition.

Within the broad framework suggested by these features it is possible to derive a set of efficiency rules (optimality conditions) describing an ideal situation. These conditions, in turn, are helpful for two reasons: (1) they provide a benchmark with which the actual situation might be compared; and (2) they provide a means of keeping track of, or enumerating, the full set of costs and benefits associated with each membership decision.

Because the preponderance of these costs and benefits are external to the decisionmaker, some means of internalizing these externalities is required for efficiency. This requirement provides a *raison d'etre* for the IOC. By establishing and enforcing rules, the IOC translates individual interest into common good. However, while the IOC may quite properly wish to ignore the more self-serving motives of some of the participating countries[10] (specifically the politically motivated desire to accumulate medals for a certain bloc of countries), these desires cannot be ignored entirely. To the extent that the IOC wishes to ensure large scale participation, it is necessary to make the Games appealing to large numbers of countries. As more nations identify with narrow self-serving goals, it becomes increasingly difficult to ignore their preferences.

1. Defining the Problem[11]

The formal problem statement involves the enumeration of the set of decision (membership and provision) variables and the set of equations defining the interrelationships among the variables and the objective. The decision variables include the provision of a set of physical facilities (X) shared by all participants, the number of athletes provided by each of M countries to each of R events (n_{ij}, $i = 1, \ldots M; j = 1, \ldots, R$), membership for each of the M countries (c_i, $i = 1, \ldots; M$), and the sanctioning of the R events (e_j, $j = 1, \ldots, R$). We assume the numbers of athletes, events, and countries to be sufficiently large so as to warrant being treated as continuous variables. However, since admitting countries and sanctioning events involve whole groups of numbers (e.g., admitting the *ith* country increases the number of athletes by $\Sigma_j^R n_{ij}$), they will be treated as discrete variables: c_i, $e_j \in (0,1)$,

$i = 1, \ldots, M; j = 1, \ldots, R$. Finally, we assume that the NOC's preferences are representable by the (concave, twice-differentiable) utility functions,

(1) $\quad U^k = U^k(c_k X, c_k n_{11}^*, \ldots, c_k n_{MR}^*, Y_k), k = 1, \ldots, M$.

Each of the Olympic variables are weighted by c_k, indicating that the country (and its athletes) would not "consume" them if $c_k = 0$, but that each Olympic variable is a public good for each participating country: $X^k = X$, 0 for $c_k = 2, 1$. Similarly, each n_{ij} must be weighted by c_i and e_j to indicate that n_{ij} would not be provided to any of the participating countries if either the ith country were excluded ($c_i = 0$) or the jth event were not sanctioned ($e_j = 0$). Accordingly, preferences are directed toward the matrix of n_{ij}^*'s where

(2) $\quad n_{ij}^* = c_i e_j n_{ij}, i = 1, \ldots, M, j = 1, \ldots, R$.

The final argument in each utility function is Y_k, the amount of the purely private numeraire (a composite of all other goods) consumed by the members of the kth country whether or not that country participates in the Games.

(3) $\quad Y = \Sigma_k^M Y_k$,

with Y denoting the total quantity produced worldwide.

In actuality, each country or NOC has a budget for expenditures on Olympic related activities. In order to model this expenditure, it would be necessary to describe an intricate web of subsidies, transfers, training expenditures, expenditures on related activities, and so forth. It would be virtually impossible to specify a budget equation for Olympic expenditures, for so many non-Olympic expenditures benefit the Olympic effort. For example, college and university athletic programs provide training facilities for Olympic athletes. Moreover, to the extent that athletes attend college in a foreign country, one country is subsidizing the Olympic program of another. Similarly, whenever one country sponsors an athletic event involving international competition, it is aiding the Olympic programs of all participating countries (perhaps, indirectly, even non-participating countries) as well as its own. It is thus reasonable to assume that individual athletes and possibly entire teams may be added to the Games at negligible direct incremental costs.[12] Indirectly, more athletes tend to require more facilities and additional countries may result in additional events, but athletes *per se* require little more than transportation expenditures, which we shall assume to be negligible.

The direct real costs of providing facilities and organizing events in an economic sense may generally be accounted for by means of the (convex, twice differentiable) transformation function

(4) $F(X, R^*, Y) = 0,$

where $R^* \equiv \Sigma_j^R e_j$ denotes the number of events included in the Olympic program. This merely indicates that the Olympic Games are provided at an opportunity cost of foregone world production. It does not indicate how these costs are apportioned to participating (and non-participating) countries. While this is an interesting economic question, let it suffice to repeat that some of the financing comes from voluntary contributions by participating nations. As stated previously, those nations who are more affluent, who derive relatively large amounts of consumptive value (economic surplus) from the Games, or perhaps whose participation is not highly valued by others, tend to make large contributions relative to their proportionate share of the costs. The United States, for example, provides substantial indirect financial support for other nations' Olympic programs. To complete the model, it is useful to note that the total number of athletes (N) participating in the games may be counted either by events or countries:

(5) $N \equiv \Sigma_i n_{ij}^* \equiv \Sigma_j n_{ij}^*.$

2. Pareto Optimality Conditions

The necessary conditions for Pareto optimality are as follows:[13]

(6) $\sum_k V_x^k = MC(X)$, $k \epsilon M^*$

(7) $\sum_j^{E^*} \int_0^1 \left\{ \left[XV_x^r + \sum_i^{M^*} n_{ij} V_{n_{ij}}^r \right] + \left[\sum_i^{M^*} n_{rj} V_{n_{rj}}^i \right] \right\} dc_r \geqslant \sigma M_r$, for all $r \epsilon M^*$

(8) $\sum_r^{M^*} \int_0^1 \left[\sum_i^{M^*} n_{ih} V_{n_{ih}}^r \right] de_h - MC(E) \geqslant \gamma E_h$, for all $h \epsilon E^*$

(9) $\sum_k^{M^*} V_{n_{rh}}^k = \sigma + \gamma$, for all $r \epsilon M^*, h \epsilon E^*$

(10) $\sigma + \gamma = 0$,

where M_r denotes the total number of athletes representing the rth country and E_h the number of athletes from all countries competing in the hth event; σ and γ are shadow prices associated with adding athletes, the former relating to addition by country, the latter relating to addition by event. The V terms represent marginal valuations (marginal rates of substitution); superscripts identify evaluator, while subscripts identify what is being evaluated. For example, V_{nij}^k denotes the kth nation's marginal evaluation of the number of country i's athletes participating in the jth event. These conditions establish rules for: (1) provision of the public facilities, (2) national membership, (3) sanctioning of events, (4) membership of athletes by country and event, and (5) total membership of athletes, respectively.

As in the elementary theory of clubs in which the provision and membership conditions are interrelated (see Figure 1), all five sets of conditions derived here are interrelated. In general, some events will be excluded and some countries will not participate, either by choice (the typical reason for non-participation) or by involuntary exclusion. These events and countries are not explicitly represented in the marginal efficiency conditions. The relevant sets of countries and events are $M^* = (c_i \mid c_i = 1)$ and $E^* = (e_i \mid e_i = 1)$, M^* and E^* denoting the sets of participating countries and sanctioned events, respectively.

Equation (6) is the familiar Samuelson-Lindahl condition for public good provision, requiring that the vertical summation of all participating countries marginal valuation curves be set equal to the marginal cost of provision. Just as optimal provision in the theory of clubs depends upon the number of members, the marginal functions of (6) will shift up or down, depending on the size and composition of Olympic membership. For example, adding one more nation to the Games will tend to increase the total number of athletes and create more demand for facilities. Similarly, a new event may ultimately be sanctioned which conforms to the preferences or the comparative athletic skills of the new country. The new event tends to increase the demand for facilities, particularly if one of the original events is not eliminated from the program. However, since the provision question is unimportant relative to membership, we will concentrate on equations (7) through (10), which describe the interrelationships among the various membership conditions. Rather than to interpret each element of each equation, we describe the full system of equations in Figures 3 through 8.

Figures 3, 4, and 5 deal primarily with the determination of the number of athletes representing a given country (say, country r) in a given event (say, event h)—hence n_{rh}. Like all of the other membership variables, n_{rh} is a public good and thus the valuation curve (V_{rh}) in Figure 4 is the vertical summation of each country's marginal valuation curve $(V_1 + V_2 + \ldots)$. Inasmuch as athletes may be added to the games without any direct cost, country r's membership in event h should be expanded up to the point where $V_{rh} = 0$, at n^*_{rh} . This condition, represented by equations (9) and (10) should hold for each event and each country included in the Games. The two elements of the right hand side of (9), σ and γ, represent the contributions of the last athlete of this group to the net benefits attributable to country r's participation and event h's inclusion in the Games, respectively. The former, σ, is represented by the hatched region in Figure 3. The area beneath the gross marginal benefit curve represents the total benefits attributable to country r's participation in this particular event, which include those enjoyed directly by country r (private benefits) and those conferred upon others by r's participation (external benefits). The marginal athlete's contribution to these benefits (σ) should be the same for all participating countries and events.[14] The γ term is represented in Figure 5 as the diminution of that portion of country r's total benefits attributable to the sanctioning of event h.[15]

The conditions for aggregate membership must be consistent with those for individual membership. Figure 6 illustrates the conditions for inclusion of countries. The basic requirement is that the total benefits per athlete must be

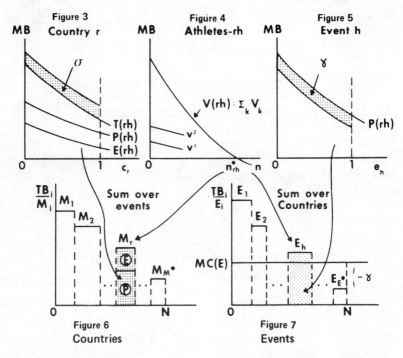

Figures 3-7: Membership Conditions

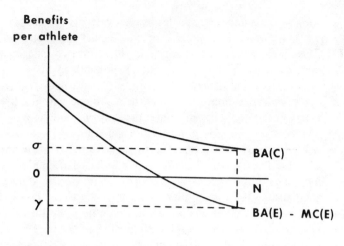

Figure 8: Aggregate Membership — Olympics

no less than that which a marginal athlete of some other country would contribute. Otherwise, the group would be better off adding athletes to the teams of countries already included than to admit a new team. Specifically, the benefits per athlete for the rth country may be determined by aggregating the area under the gross marginal benefit curve in Figure 3 and analogous areas for other events, plus those benefits attributable to that country's membership per se. Only in very rare circumstances would one expect entire teams to be excluded if the numbers of athletes representing that country in various events satisfied the optimality conditions. As stated earlier, the first athlete representing each country is apt to provide very high marginal benefits to other countries. Thus a team of some size is likely admissible for any country, although an excessively large team might be undesirable on balance. In practice, exclusion takes place for other reasons as well. Figure 7 illustrates the analogous conditions for sanctioning events. The negative total net benefits attributable to the marginal event is consistent with the negative marginal benefits of adding athletes to individual events. Finally, Figure 8 represents the optimality condition for the total number of athletes and is analogous to Figure 4 relating to athletes in specific categories. Since an additional athlete represents an increment both to some country's team and to some event, events may become crowded in the interest of reaping the benefits associated with expanding national membership per se. On balance, the net marginal benefits of athletes should be zero.

In summary, the model emphasizes the following conditions:

(1) Each athlete represents both a country and an event. For opti-

mality, the number of athletes in each category (country/event) is expanded up to the point of zero marginal net benefits.

(2) This implies that if the marginal athlete in each category has a beneficial impact on the benefits attributable to the country he represents, he must have a negative effect upon the benefits his country derives from his event. These positive and negative marginal effects should be uniform across countries and events.

(3) Membership conditions for countries and events must be consistent with those for individuals. The total net benefits attributable to any country (event) per athlete representing that country (event) must be no less than the benefits that could be gained by adding another athlete to some other country's team (some other event).

(4) The country will be willing to contribute no more than the total *private* net economic surplus (P in Figure 5) it derives from participation. If that sum is negative, that country might still be subsidized by others if its participation provides sufficient net external benefits (E in Figure 5) to other countries.

IV. THE OLYMPIC GAMES AS A SUCCESSFUL CLUB

A. THE PAST

Clearly the Modern Olympic Games have been an extremely successful undertaking. Beginning with their inception in 1896, their popularity and worldwide appeal have continued to grow over time, whereas interest in other well known sporting events such as the World Series or the Davis Cup has waxed and waned during the same time period. As Bill Henry (1976:3) aptly noted:

> [The Games] are in their modern revival no passing fancy, for in over a half century of renewed existence they have survived the life and death of nations, spanned devastating depressions, and lived through two world wars ... [the Games are a] source of astonishing vitality.

But why have the Modern Olympic Games been an "efficient" club; in particular, what has the IOC done in accordance with the theoretical constructs of the club methodology that has helped create and perpetuate this success?

In order to answer this question, it is necessary to begin by examining the basic principles as laid down primarily by Pierre de Coubertin, the founder of the Modern Games. To use Lancaster-Muth terminology,[16] these provide the characteristics which define the (public) good from the IOC's perspective and, in turn, are the basis for attracting members into the club. Specifically, five characteristics, at times reinforcing and at other times conflicting, stand out:

(1) The emphasis is on participation. As Coubertin argued:

> The important thing in the Olympic games is not to win but to take part, the important thing in life is not the triumph but the struggle. The essential thing is not to have conquered but to have fought well. To spread these precepts is to build up a stronger and more valiant and, above all, more scrupulous and more generous humanity (Henry, 1976:ix).

(2) Closely related to this emphasis on participation is the ideal of competition. The Games, like all sporting events, are based on the human desire to compete within a well-defined context and use athletics as the "universal language."

(3) The Modern Olympic Games stress the individual rather than nations, states, or regions. Coubertin felt that native French schools at the end of the nineteenth century were too regulated and mass exercise oriented, and he tried to model the Games after the individualism and independence of Rugby under Thomas Arnold as headmaster (Henry 1976:3-9). In fact, Coubertin did not even want team sports in the Games.

(4) The IOC is constantly demanding excellence in all phases of the Games, with its model being "Citius, Altius, Fortius" ("Faster, Higher, Stronger").

(5) The Games are to be a "reflection of life." As Coubertin (1908:7) wrote, he wanted the Games to encompass "all the important facets of modern life—the intermingling, the associations, the vote, the press, the opinion, the elective hierarchy which functions in a methodic and orderly manner."

Historically, the IOC has been virtually a model of inflexibility in its rigid adherence to these principles, particularly the first four.[17] It is noteworthy that this inflexibility has been maintained in spite of rapidly changing societal attitudes toward sports and in spite of significant changes in Olympic membership. In an economic environment one might be led to expect marginal adjustments as societal and member preferences change. The reason why these principles have not been compromised, we believe, is not that the IOC is "irrational" or refuses to reflect the preferences of member countries. Instead, by stressing adherence by individual participants, the wealth of external benefits to other participants is maintained. In other words, the Olympic ideals provide a means of protecting the interests of the group from the self-serving behavior of individual members. As noted earlier, the mutual benefits provided by common adherence to these principles are the product of the Games. To yield even slightly might induce each participating country to seek some additional concession. In the aggregate, the effect of this process could spell disaster for the continuation of the Games.[18]

In an effort to introduce the requisite flexibility with respect to changing times and changing membership while attempting to achieve its objectives, the IOC has employed a series of strategies. For one, the Games are held every four years. Obviously, the tradition and custom of the Ancient Games, with their thousand years of success, are exerting an influence here. However, economic arguments are also involved. First, the time lag facilitates careful planning through which orderly, deliberate changes can take place. Most notably perhaps, new events can be sanctioned and old ones discarded as membership changes or member preferences change. Secondly, preferences for sporting events like commodities, are subject to satiation. In this regard, the Olympic Games may be viewed by many as a refreshing contrast to the tedium of professional sports schedules. Finally, the four year period can be given a quality interpretation: a repeat gold medal winner can truly be labelled a superb performer.

A second strategy adopted by the IOC has been to award the site of the Games to a city, rather than a nation, through a competitive bidding process. This partially reflects the individualism and international flavor Coubertin so ardently wanted the Games to convey. But in terms of the theory of clubs, this can be seen as the way the IOC avoids the complex detailed financing problems inherent in a club environment due to freeridership and alliances. Moreover, this is a way of accommodating, to some extent, the preferences of participating countries.[19] Each Olympiad reflects the unique character and charm of the host city and occasionally permanent changes are effected through this process.

Along similar lines, the IOC minimizes coalition difficulties and withdrawal threats by placing emphasis on the individual rather than the team and not allowing the athletes to control the Games. No official team scores are kept (see notes 10 and 17). Members of the IOC are considered to be . . .

'trustees' of the Olympic idea. They would be selected for their knowledge of sport and their national standing, since according to Coubertin's principle of a 'delegation in reverse,' an IOC member is an ambassador from the Committee to his own country and not an ambassador of his country to the IOC (Berlioux, 1976:12).

Finally, and most importantly, since the number who share the facilities affects performances, the IOC has made various membership decisions. In general, the IOC has tried to maximize potential worldwide participation, thereby stimulating demand, by offering a variety of events rather than just one event, as was the situation in the first Games in 776 B.C. The Summer Games entail running and jumping events, swimming, different team sports, cycling, gymnastics, boxing, fencing, weight-lifting and rowing. Also, since 1924 there have also been the Winter Games with, once again, a range of events. Moreover, the city awarded the Games has the privilege to add an event and if successful, as basketball in the 1936 Games or volleyball in the 1964 Games, have them incorporated permanently, hence allowing for changes in preferences. Thus, by allowing division and specialization of labor, individuals and nations have the opportunity for comparative advantage and the gains from trade are increased. In terms of Figures 6 and 7, apparently low quality events may be sanctioned to accommodate the preferences of a new or marginally participating country. At the same time, the IOC has not neglected congestion problems with respect to membership. Countries may enter at most three competitors in individual events and one team in team events. Furthermore, minimum standards are established in most events to avoid crowding and quality deterioration.[20]

B. THE FUTURE

The above arguments may be interpreted to mean that the IOC has explicitly recognized the economic dimensions of the Games, or at least behaved as though it did, and therefore, has acted "rationally." We recognize that this can be interpreted as an *ex post* argument, but we feel that they consistency of the IOC and the success of the Games during the past eighty years leave no alternative explanation. We believe that the Games are simply the best example of a viable worldwide club. But what about the future?

Lord Killanin, the current head of the IOC, has pointed out four major problem areas when he wrote:

> We shall always have our problems. Among these are the immense growth of the Games; amateurism and eligibility; political interference; and the use of scientific advances in medicine (Killanin, 1976:11).

In terms of the model presented earlier, each of these factors affect membership and participation decisions, implying that each will be associated with a myriad of costs and benefits. However, *ex ante* expectations can be formulated in light of the model.

The question of amateurism is a recurring theme. It is, of course, possible that members' demand for changes in rules regulating participation has reached the point where the IOC must respond. Yet the current popularity of the Games simply does not bear this out. Similarly, the use of drugs by athletes will probably not be a burning issue. Just as technological advances in equipment have received slow and sometimes inconsistent approval by the IOC, medical advances have and will continue to receive similar treatment. Rulings made by the IOC will be criticized by some, acclaimed by others, abided by all. In the final analysis, the resolution of both the question of amateurism and the question of medical advances must require arbitrary rules. While these rules will necessarily be controversial, the growth of the Games and their continuing popular appeal will doubtless overshadow the controversies.

Growth and popularity, on the other hand, will make political activities more and more attractive to those individuals and nations who wish to exploit the Games at the expense of all others concerned. In our opinion, this is the greatest danger of all. It strikes at the essence of the economic benefits derived from the Games—the mutual spillovers benefits provided by each participant. It strikes at the weakness common to all public goods, the need for all individuals to strive for the collective's benefit of all. Because the "product" of the Games is such a valuable one and the potential harm from large scale politicization so great, the penalties for such activities need to be made more severe and more certain. Those responsible must be made to bear the costs of their actions. This, however, is no small task. The imposition of penalties must be consistent and have virtually unanimous support of member countries. Expulsions and suspensions in response to political activity are, unfortunately, political activities. Should they elicit retaliation, the "meeting of the world" could become an ever more fragile alliance.

NOTES

1. For some interesting accounts of this process, see Johnson (1977) or "They Got It by Salesmanship," *Economist* 253 (October 25, 1974):42-47.

2. For an interesting and more complete discussion of these and other such incidents, see Kieran and Daley (1969), especially pp. 153-181, 219-232, and 365-381. See also Schaap (1967).

3. The problem of congestion and the nonexistence of *pure* public goods was first brought out by Margolis (1955) in a comment on Samuelson's (1954) paper. Olsen and Zeckhauser (1966, especially note 22) analyzed some of the impurities of defense expenditures in the context of alliances. Oakland (1972) formally incorporated the generic concept of congestion into the theory of public goods and applied his model to such problems as highway congestion, allocationally neutral financing, and exclusion. Subsequent applications and extensions of Oakland's model may be found in Sandler's analyses of interregional spillovers (1975b) and alliances (1975a, 1977) and James' (1974) analysis of interregional pollution. A broad interpretation of Oakland's model might view it as encompassing the theory of clubs as a special case. There are, however, important distinctions. See DeSerpa (1976).

4. In the interest of simplicity, Buchanan ignored the social aspects of group formation and interaction in his formal model. Individuals are implicitly assumed to exhibit identical preferences with no tastes for discrimination.

5. In the context of Pareto optimality, this aspect of expanding membership would be an irrelevant income transfer. However, since Buchanan implicitly assumed that all individuals exhibit identical preferences, the existence of a viable club implies that each member will have some economic surplus left after contributing to the provision costs. Hence, it does no harm to impose this financing arrangement on the problem.

6. Figure 1 is essentially reproduced from Buchanan's (1965, p. 10) Figure 3. The N_{opt} and X_{opt} curves are formally derived in Buchanan's Figures 1 and 2.

7. Ng (1973, 1974) developed the more general conditions of Pareto optimality where preferences are non-homogeneous and emphasized the possible desirability of taxes or subsidies to internalize external effects of membership. Pauly (1967, 1970) addressed the problem of actual formation of the club and establishment of rules necessary to ensure a stable coalition. While Pauly touched on the question of discrimination, discriminatory clubs were not formally analyzed prior to the work of Tollison (1972). Tollison applied the model, with a discrimination factor, to the analysis of various anti-discrimination laws and the effect of discrimination upon optimal club size. Tollison and Ng (1973) showed that the direction of this effect could not be determined *a priori*. DeSerpa (1977) viewed discrimination as directed not toward individuals but toward characteristics of individuals. A particularly interesting application of clubs theory to the question of optimal city size, as well as some interesting theoretical extensions, may be found in McGuire (1974).

8. See Natan (1958), cited in Ball (1972:188).

9. It has been suggested (Edelman, 1964; Ball, 1972) that the Olympics provide an opportunity for nations to establish superiority over others. To the extent that this political game may be extended to blocs, preferences with respect to outcomes of various events may be quite intense, even for nations not directly participating in the event in question. An additional reason for interest in the distribution of athletes over events would be the mere interest in preserving close competition, an obviously desirable attribute of the Games. For an attempt to model this feature in the context of team sports, see Canes (1974) or Quirk and El Hodiri (1971).

10. The "hard line" policies often associated with Avery Brundage are typified by Brundage's statement that:

> The Games are not, and must not become, a contest between nations which would be entirely contrary to the spirit of the Olympic Movement and would surely lead to disaster. For this reason there is no official score of nations and tables of points are really misinformation because they are entirely inaccurate. To be correct they would have to be weighted since it is certainly unfair to give the winner of the marathon or decathlon, a winning gymnast, pistol shooter or yachtsman, and a winning football soccer or basketball team the same score. Moreover, the factor of population should be considered . . .
> . . . Neither the Olympic Games nor any sport contest can be said to indicate the superiority of one political system over another, of one country over another . . . The IOC resents attempts to use the Games as a political instrument or to pit one country against another. We trust that you will do everything in your power to discourage the publication of scoring tables, which are quite worthless . . . (Brundage, 1956: 35), cited in Ball (1972: 188).

11. This subsection and the subsequent one dealing with the Pareto optimality conditions represent an extension of the models developed by Ng (1973) and DeSerpa

(1977). While the analysis of these subsections provides a theoretical base for subsequent policy discussions, it might be avoided without serious loss of continuity.

12. This is consistent with the treatment of membership in other models in the clubs literature, wherein number of members does not enter the transformation function. The only direct costs of expanding membership are the psychic costs of congestion and crowding. The indirect costs are illustrated in Figure 1. To the extent that the optimal size of the public good (X_{opt}) increases with membership, there is a real cost associated with expanding membership.

13. These conditions are formally derived in the mathematical appendix.

14. Ignoring the initial summation sign and the XV_x^r term, the left side of equation (7) is represented in Figure 3. The integral denotes areas under the curves, the first summation term denotes private benefits to country r (superscript r on V terms), and the second summation term denotes external benefits to other countries (superscript i on V terms).

15. The areas under the "Private (rh)" curves in Figures 3 and 5 must be equal, for they merely represent two different ways of counting country r's benefits from event h. This follows from the fact that the bracketed term in (8) is identical to the summation term inside the left-hand squared bracket in (7). This means that the amount the last athlete adds to total benefits in Figure 3 should equal the amount by which he reduces total benefits in Figure 5. As a result, the marginal athlete's membership must increase (reduce) external benefits by exactly twice that it reduces (increases) private benefits.

16. See Lancaster (1966) and Muth (1966). In the interest of generality, we avoided references to specific characteristics in building the formal model in the preceding section. The characteristics of participation, competition, individual excellence, etc. may be derived from individual participation rates. In this regard, the Lancaster-Muth notion of consumption technology provides a convenient theoretical linkage between these final two sections.

17. The only exception might be the sanctioning of team events, but the emphasis on individuality is underscored both by the IOC's refusal to tally total medals by country and by the fact that even in team competition, medals are individually awarded to each team member.

18. The reader might consider the analogy between this process and the plight of the Catholic Church after that institution implemented the somewhat modest liberalizations of Vatican II.

19. Nevertheless, this practice has on occasion generated direct conflict between the host city and the IOC on matters of principle. The exclusion of Taiwan, noted in the introduction, is one example.

20. However, each country is allowed one participant even if it has no athletes who can meet the minimum standards. In other words, universal representation and the maintenance of international flavor remain extremely important and take precedence over considerations of congestion.

MATHEMATICAL APPENDIX

The formal problem is to maximize the Lagrangian function,

$$L = \Sigma_k^M \lambda_k (U_k - \bar{U}_k) + \mu F(X, R^*, Y) + \kappa(Y - \Sigma_k Y_k) + \bar{\sigma} (N - \Sigma_i^M n_{ij}^*) + \bar{\gamma}(N - \Sigma_j^R n_{ij}^*),$$

Where $U_k = U_k\,(c_k X, c_k n^*_{11}, \ldots, c_k n^*_{MR}, Y_k)$, for all k

$n^*_{ij} = c_i e_j n_{ij}$, for all i, j

$c_i \epsilon\,(0, 1)$, for all i

$e_j \epsilon\,(0, 1)$, for all j

$R^* = \Sigma^R_j\,e_j$.

The first order partial derivatives of L with respect to X, Y, N, the Y'_ks, and the $n^{*'}_{ij}$s must be set equal to zero. In addition, since the c_i's and the e_j's are discrete, their partial derivatives integrated over the interval zero to unity must be nonnegative if their optimal value is unity. These conditions are as follows.

(A.1) $L_X = \Sigma_k \gamma_k c_k \partial U_k / \partial X_k + \mu F_X = 0$

(A.2) $L_Y = \mu F_Y + K = 0$

(A.3) $L_{Y_k} = \lambda_k \partial U_k / \partial Y_k - K = 0$, K = 1, ..., M

(A.4) $L_{n^*_{ij}} + \Sigma_k \lambda_k c_k \partial U_k / \partial n^*_{ij} - (\bar{\sigma} + \bar{\gamma}) = 0$, i = 1, ..., M
$\qquad\qquad\qquad\qquad\qquad\qquad\qquad\qquad\qquad$ j = 1, ..., R

(A.5) $L_N = \bar{\sigma} + \bar{\gamma} = 0$

(A.6) $\displaystyle\int_0^1 L_{c_r} dc_r = \int_0^1 \left\{ \lambda_r \left[X\,\partial U_r / \partial X_r + \Sigma^M_i \Sigma^R_j \partial U_r / \partial n^*_{ij} \right] + \right.$

$\qquad\qquad\qquad \left. \left[\Sigma^M_i \Sigma^E_j \lambda_i c_i \partial U_i / \partial n^*_{rj} \right] \right\} dc_r \geqslant \bar{\sigma} M_r$, $r \epsilon M^* \equiv (c_r \mid c_r = 10$

(A.7) $\displaystyle\int_0^1 L_{e_h} de_h = \int_0^1 \left[\Sigma^M_r \Sigma^M_i n^*_{ih} \partial U_r / \partial n^*_{ih} \right] de_h + \mu F_{R^*} \geqslant \bar{\gamma} E_h$,

$\qquad\qquad\qquad\qquad\qquad\qquad\qquad\qquad h \epsilon E^* = (e_h \mid e_h = 1)$

From (A.2) and (A.3), $\lambda_k \partial U_k / \partial Y_k = \mu F_Y$, for all k. Hence the λ's and μ's may be eliminated by substituting this relation into (A.1), (A.4), (A.6), and (A.7). Marginal utility terms are replaced by marginal rates of substitution or marginal value terms [e.g., $V^k_X \equiv (\partial U_k / \partial X_k)/(\partial U_k / \partial Y_k)$]. Wherever μ appears we divide through by μF_Y, replacing partial derivatives of $F(\cdot)$ with marginal rates of transformation in numeraire units, or marginal costs [e.g., $-F_X / F_Y \equiv MC(X)$ and $-F_{R^*}/F_Y \equiv MC(E)$]. Finally, the shadow prices of athletes, σ and γ are also converted into numeraire units: $\bar{\sigma} \equiv \sigma/\kappa$ and $\bar{\gamma} \equiv \gamma/\kappa$. Thus (A.1), (A.6), (A.7), (A.4), and (A.5) respectively reduce to (6) through (10) in the text.

BIBLIOGRAPHY

BALL, DONALD W. (1972) "Olympic Games Competition: Structural Correlates of National Success." International Journal of Comparative Sociology 13(September): 186-200.

BERLIOUX, MONIQUE (1976) "The History of the International Olympic Committee." In Lord Killanin and John Rodda (eds.) The Olympic Games. New York: Macmillan.

BRUNDAGE, AVERY (1956) "President's Statement." Bulletin du Comité International Olympique 55(February): 35.

BUCHANAN, JAMES M. (1965) "An Economic Theory of Clubs." Economica 32(February): 1-14.

CANES, MICHAEL E. (1974) "The Social Benefits of Restrictions on Team Quality." Pp. 81-91 in Roger G. Noll (ed.) Government and the Sports Business. Washington, D.C.: Brookings.

COUBERTIN, PIERRE de (1908) Une Campagne de Vingt-et-un Ans. Paris: Librairie de l'Education Physique.

DeSERPA, ALLAN C. (1976) "Multidimensional Public Goods." Arizona State University Department of Economics Working Paper #76-72.

--- (1977) "A Theory of Discriminatory Clubs." Scottish Journal of Political Economy 24(February): 33-41.

EDELMAN, MURRY (1964) The Symbolic Use of Politics. Urbana: University of Illinois Press.

HENRY, BILL (1976) An Approved History of the Olympic Games. New York: G. P. Putnam's Sons.

JAMES, ESTELLE (1974) "Optimal Pollution Control and Trade in Collective Goods." Journal of Public Economics 3(August): 203-216.

JOHNSON, WILLIAM O. (1977) "A Contract with the Kremlin." Sports Illustrated 46(February 21): 14-19.

KIERAN, JOHN and ARTHUR DALEY (1969) The Story of the Olympic Games: 776 B.C. to 1968. Philadelphia: J. B. Lippincott, 7th ed.

KILLANIN, LORD and JOHN RODDA (1976) The Olympic Games. New York: Macmillan.

LANCASTER, KELVIN (1966) "A New Approach to Consumer Theory." Journal of Political Economy 74(April): 132-157.

MARGOLIS, JULIUS (1955) "A Comment on the Pure Theory of Public Expenditure." Review of Economics and Statistics 37(February): 347-349.

McGUIRE, MARTIN (1974) "Group Segregation and Optimal Jurisdictions." Journal of Political Economy 82(January/February): 112-132.

MUTH, RICHARD (1966) "Household Production and Consumer Demand Functions." Econometrica 34(July): 699-708.

NATAN, ALEX (1958) Sports and Society. London: Bowes and Bowes.

NG, Y.K. (1973) "The Economic Theory of Clubs: Pareto Optimality Conditions." Economica 40(August): 291-298.

––– (1974) "The Economic Theory of Clubs: Optimal Tax/Subsidy." Economica 41(August): 308-321.

––– and ROBERT TOLLISON (1974) "A Note on Consumption Sharing and Non-Exclusion Rules." Economica 40(November): 446-450.

OAKLAND, WILLIAM H. (1972) "Congestion, Public Goods, and Welfare." Journal of Public Economics 1(November): 339-57.

OLSEN, MANCUR and RICHARD ZECKHAUSER (1966) "An Economic Theory of Alliances." Review of Economics and Statistics 48(August): 266-79.

PAULY, MARK (1967) "Clubs, Commonality, and the Core." Economica 34: 314-324.

––– (1970) "Cores and Clubs." Public Choice 16(Fall): 53-65.

QUIRK, JAMES and MOHAMED EL HODIRI (1974) "An Economic Model of a Professional Sports League" in Roger G. Noll (ed.) Government and the Sports Business. Washington, D.C.: Brookings.

SAMUELSON, PAUL A. (1954) "The Pure Theory of Public Expenditures." Review of Economics and Statistics 36(November): 387-389.

––– (1955) "A Diagrammatic Exposition of a Theory of Public Expenditure." Review of Economics and Statistics 37(November): 550-566.

SANDLER, TODD (1975a) "The Economic Theory of Alliances: Realigned," in C. Liske, W. Loehr, and J. McCamant (eds.), Comparative Public Policy: Issues, Theories and Methods. New York: Wiley, 223239.

––– (1975b) "Pareto Optimality, Pure Public Goods, Impure Public Goods, and Multiregional Spillovers." Scottish Journal of Political Economy 22(February): 25-38.

––– (1977) "Impurity of Defense: An Application to the Economics of Alliances." Kyklos 30 (Fasc. 3): 443-460.

SCHAAP, RICHARD (1967) An Illustrated History of the Olympics. Toronto: Random House, Inc., 2nd ed.

TOLLISON, ROBERT D. (1972) "Consumption Sharing and Non-Exclusion Rules." Economica 39(August): 276-291.

Chapter 5

CATASTROPHE THEORY, TAX EXPORTATION, AND PUBLIC GOOD SPILLOVERS

123-44

E L S I E K N O E R
Arizona State University

INTRODUCTION

As economics has strived to become an exact science, the search for mathematical models to describe, explain, and hopefully predict economic phenomena has been deemed of paramount importance. For behavior which is a smooth and differentiable function of a number of variables, the differential calculus was an ideal method for stating a complex model in a straightforward manner as a system of differential equations; analytic geometry, which combines algebra and calculus with geometry, then allowed us to pass to the geometric properties of the system. The existence of canonical forms meant that we could study a few simple curves, learn their properties, and use the results in models that may be reduced to the same form by changing coordinates; moreover, the limited number of canonical forms bounds our search for the one relevant to our model. Thus the behavior of continuous processes could readily be understood.

There has been no equally effective mathematical tool for explaining and predicting the occurrence of discontinuous phenomena. In economics, as in many social sciences, well behaved systems are the exception rather than the rule. Even in the hard sciences, particularly physics, many important phenomena have resisted analysis because behavior changes radically with small parameter shifts or because the time path of the controls influences the behavior variable.

A new branch of topology known as Catastrophe Theory has unexpectedly provided a conceptually elegant way of visualizing and categorizing certain discontinuous phenomena when behavior is determined by optimizing some function of the behavior variable. Thus it appears that much of the indeterminacy of the "soft" sciences may have been due to the lack of adequate

AUTHOR'S NOTE: The author is extremely grateful to Todd Sandler for numerous comments, suggestions, and criticisms on earlier drafts of this paper. Any remaining errors are entirely my own.

mathematical theory. And most conveniently, catastrophe theory provides us with simple canonical forms with which to categorize certain classes of discontinuous models.[1]

It is the object of this paper to provide an introduction to catastrophe theory and to present some original results based on catastrophe models. Section I gives a simple exposition of the general theory and briefly describes the two lowest order catastrophes. Section II consists of three models of public goods production under conditions of benefit spillover and tax exportation. Section III applies catastrophe theory to a problem of supranational design. Each section is self-contained.

I. A BRIEF INTRODUCTION TO CATASTROPHE THEORY

The central theorem of catastrophe theory is the Classification Theorem. Briefly stated, it says that 1) if a process is determined by optimizing some function, then whenever a continuously changing parameter causes abruptly changing behavior, that process must be described by a catastrophe model, and 2) given the number of control parameters and the number of behavior variables, there are a limited number of catastrophes that can occur.

Suppose that a behavior variable x is given as a function of an exogenous control parameter y. A "catastrophe" occurs when smooth changes in y cause abrupt changes in x, from one behavior mode to a radically different one. (Note that catastrophe is not synonymous with disaster.) The essence of catastrophe theory is that under certain conditions, x(y) may be represented geometrically as a smooth behavior surface in multidimensional Euclidean space, and the critical points identified.

The condition that allows such a representation is that, for y fixed, x must be chosen to optimize (maximize or minimize) some function $f(x,y)$. Suppose we wish to minimize $f(x,y)$ over x subject to y fixed. It will be remembered (we hope) from calculus that a necessary condition is that $f_x(x,y)=0$, where f_x is the first derivative of f with respect to x. This condition is not sufficient, since it is satisfied for x such that $f(x,y)$ is a maximum or an inflection point, as well as those x for which $f(x,y)$ is minimized. To categorize those x for which $f_x(x,y)=0$ into maxima, minima, and inflection points we must examine $f_{xx}(x,y)$, the second derivative of f with respect to x. We recall that only the minima have $f_{xx} > 0$; the maxima are characterized by $f_{xx} < 0$; if $f_{xx}(x,y)=0$, x is an inflection point.

The general model may be derived as follows. Assume that a behavior variable x is chosen as a function of a continuous (vector-valued) control parameter y to minimize some function $f(x,y)$; i.e.,

$$x(y) = \left\{ \bar{x} \mid f(\bar{x},y) \leqslant f(x,y) \right\} .$$

Then define the behavior surface by $G = \left\{ (x,y) \mid f_x = 0 \right\}$. As noted above, the surface will contain minima, maxima, and inflection points. (It is the inclusion of the maxima in the graph that allows behavior to be represented by one smooth hypersurface.) The dynamic of the system (i.e., choosing x to minimize $f(x,y)$) implies that minimum points represent stable behavior and maxima unstable, while inflection points are points of (possibly) discontinuous behavior.[2]

To motivate the designation of optima as stable, consider a problem in consumer theory. Let x be the commodity bundle chosen by a rational consumer who regards prices as fixed and wishes to minimize expenditure while maintaining a given level of utility. If she first chooses a bundle which maximizes expenditure, that position is behaviorly unstable, since she will certainly discover a slightly different bundle which yields the same utility but costs less. Conversely, a correct decision—a bundle which minimizes expenditure—is a stable position; as long as prices remain constant and desired utility does not change, the consumer will tend to maintain (or reestablish) that level of consumption.

We are using "stable" in a physical—or behavioral—rather than a mathematical sense. If behavior is chosen "correctly," only stable (optimal) points occur. In physical models, unstable positions are totally unattainable without some force acting against the dynamic of the system. In economics we shall see that since we are optimizing specific quantities, unstable behavior represents least efficient use of resources within the limits of the problem.

In catastrophe models, as parameters change behavior may exhibit discontinuities. That such discontinuities may occur only at inflection points is a direct result of the Implicit Function Theorem and the fact that the optima are characterized by non-zero second derivatives f_{xx}. The set of inflection points in G is found by setting f_{xx} equal to zero. Combining the two equations to eliminate the behavior variable gives the bifurcation subset. the projection into parameter space of the inflection points on the behavior surface; i.e.,

$$B = \left\{ (x,y) \mid f_x = f_{xx} = 0 \right\}.$$

The bifurcation subset is so named because here the stable sheets of the behavior surface may bifurcate, or fork into two (or more) branches. Hence in catastrophe models behavior may no longer be a single-valued function—with two parameters there are regions of bimodality (two stable positions); with four parameters there are regions of trimodality, and so on.

The bifurcation subset not only defines the critical parameter points; it precisely divides parameter space into distinct regions with characteristic behavior. Because behavior need not be everywhere unimodal, it is not in general the case that behavior can be predicted on the basis of the parameters alone; the time path is crucially important. However, a catastrophe model is completely determinate given knowledge of recent events. Knowing the characteristic behavior of regions of the parameter space allows the results of a time path to be predicted without explicit reference to the behavior surface. This is fortunate considering the dimensionality of the surface.

Canonical forms for catastrophes have been derived; any catastrophe which occurs must be similar to one of these simple models. The Classification Theorem states that the number of possible catastrophes is limited by the dimensionality of the problem. The power of the theorem lies in the fact that the number is very small indeed, so that the canonical forms can be described and mastered for relatively low dimensions. Although catastrophes have been classified up to twenty-five dimensions, the main emphasis has been on the "seven elementary catastrophes" generated by four-dimensional control and two-dimensional behavior space. An important aspect of the canonical models is that every catastrophe contains all lower degree catastrophes as transverse sections; conversely, higher degree catastrophes can be constructed by composing all lower order catastrophes and adding one new singularity[3] at the origin. Clearly the number of catastrophes which can occur is strictly increasing with dimensionality.

The simplest catastrophe model is the fold catastrophe which occurs when there is only one control parameter and one behavior parameter. The canonical model is derived by minimizing $f = 1/3 \ x^3 - ax$ over the real line. The control space is the line $\{a \geqslant 0\}$. The behavior surface, given by $G = \{(a,x) \mid x^2 - a = 0\}$ is the parabola shown in Figure 1. One arm represents stable states, the other unstable. Taking the second derivative of f with respect to x gives $f_{xx}(x,a) = 2x$. Hence it is the upper arm of G which is stable; the lower is unstable. The two segments are joined at the fold point. The bifurcation set is the single point $B = \{a = 0\}$, the parameter associated with the fold point.

Since behavior is never observed on the unstable portion of a behavior surface, no true catastrophe (i.e., abrupt change in x with smooth change in a) can occur. And since in two dimensions, the fold represents the most complicated thing that can occur in the graph, no situation which can be correctly modelled as an optimization problem in two dimensions will exhibit discontinuities. Conversely, we can conclude that whenever catastrophes occur in a one parameter model in which the behavior variable is determined by optimization, the problem is modelled incorrectly—there is clearly at least one more parameter effecting behavior, an understanding of which is crucial to explaining and predicting behavior.

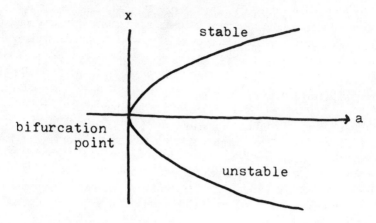

Figure 1: The Fold Catastrophe

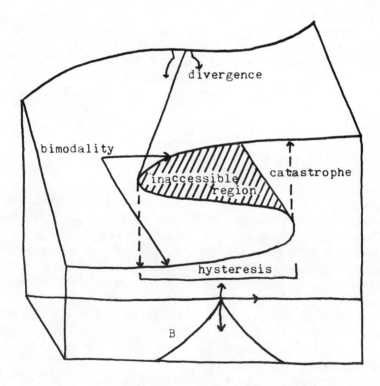

Figure 2: The Cusp Catastrophe

If the control space is made two dimensional while behavior remains one dimensional, the new singularity which appears at the origin is the cusp catastrophe, whose canonical model is derived by minimizing $f=1/4x^4 - ax - 1/2bx^2$ over the real line. The control space is the plane $\{(a,b) \mid b \geqslant 0\}$. The behavior surface, shown in Figure 2, is given by $G=\{(a,b,x) \mid x^3 - a - bx = 0\}$. In two dimensions the behavior surface was folded at a point; in three dimensions it is folded along curves. The projection of these curves into parameter space is the bifurcation subset, $B=\{(a,b) \mid 27a^2 = 4b^3\}$. As can be seen from the graph, the bifurcation subset has a cusp at the origin; it is from this that the name derives. The second derivative is $f_{xx}(a,b,x) = 3x^2 - b$; hence the stable points are those for which the absolute value of x is large relative to b. Thus it is clearly the middle sheet (shaded in the graph) which represents unstable positions. Points on the middle sheet of the graph are inaccessible from any path.

The cusp catastrophe has several features which make it completely distinct from models based on differential calculus. First, as is clearly seen from the graph, there are two sheets of stable behavior above the region bounded by B; i.e., the cusp catastrophe exhibits bimodality. However, this does not make the model indeterminate. Rather, we can predict that behavior continues on the sheet which it has inhabited recently until the control passes through the boundary into a region where that sheet ceases to be defined— then catastrophe is inevitable. This demonstrates the second distinctive feature of the cusp (and higher order) catastrophe models—sudden changes in behavior mode. If we retrace our steps through parameter space, we notice a third significant characteristic, hysteresis; i.e., transition from the top sheet to the bottom does not occur at the same point as that from bottom to top.

The last important feature, divergence, is grasped most easily if we remember that a transverse section of the cusp is a fold; i.e., a parabola. Hence the two stable sheets must be getting farther apart as b increases. This means that two paths, $a \equiv -\epsilon$ and $a \equiv \epsilon$ result in dramatically different behavior as b increases, no matter how small $\epsilon \neq 0$. When the axes are oriented as in the model shown above, the parameters are named in an obvious way for their roles; b, whose axis bisects the cusp, is called the splitting factor since increasing b increases the divergence between stable sheets of the surface; a, whose axis is perpendicular to that of b, is called the normal factor since at b=0 behavior is a continuous function of a.

An important variant of the canonical cusp model detailed here is one in which the control axes diverge on either side of the cusp. This construction enables us to describe how two competing factors can interrelate and interfere with each other in influencing behavior.

Space limitations prohibit us from discussing further canonical models, but the interested reader is encouraged to develop behavior graphs for the next simplest elementary catastrophes by minimizing $f = 1/n \ x^n - \sum_{i=1}^{n-2} 1/i \ y_i x^i$ over the real line. When $n=5$, the new singularity is the swallowtail catastrophe, whose behavior graph is folded along entire surfaces. $n=6$ gives the butterfly catastrophe, the lowest order model to exhibit trimodality.

II. PUBLIC GOOD PRODUCTION UNDER CONDITIONS OF BENEFIT SPILLOVER AND TAX EXPORTATION

There has been much discussion in the literature of late on the influence of benefit spillovers on public good production, and speculation as to whether a condition of tax exportation would offset inefficiencies introduced by such spillovers. (For a summary see Sandler and Shelton (1972).) This discussion has depended mainly on analysis of "reaction" curves, a tool not really adequate to the task. We shall use catastrophe theory to examine each effect separately, drawing heavily on the results of other authors, then try to develop a comprehensive model which takes both effects into account.

A. BENEFIT SPILLOVERS

Interesting examples of fold catastrophes arise when we consider patterns of nations engaged in the production of public goods with interregional spillovers. Consider a public good A produced in Region I, which cannot be produced in Region II but may spill out into that region.[4] In addition, suppose A is purely private between regions, so that spillout to Region II is seen as loss in consumption to Region I.[5] Let total regional incomes be $I_1 = I_2$. The total marginal willingness-to-pay for good A is constant in each region for given income, namely $c_1 I_1$ in Region I and $c_2 I_2$ in Region II. Also, let $c_2 > c_1$, so that at all income levels Region II places a higher valuation on good A than does Region I. The amount of A produced is centrally determined in Region I to maximize social welfare.[6]

To find the amount of A that Region I will produce under various conditions of spillout, we must distinguish between the solutions of independent equilibrium and equilibrium under interregional cooperation. Assume that tax exportation, if any, is at a constant level. Let b be percent spillout of A from I to II. In the case of independent adjustment, Region I selects optimal output A_b by equating $(1-b)c_1 I_1$ to MC_A.[7] Let marginal cost be an increasing function of output with a point of inflection where $c_1 I_1 = MC_A$; i.e., at the historical point of production before spillout. Ceteris paribus, as b increases, A_b decreases at a decreasing rate, from $A_b(0)$ to $A_b(1) = 0$. In contrast, under total cooperation, Region I is induced to equate $(1-b)c_1 I_1 + bc_2 I_2$ to MC_A. Because of our assumption on c_1, c_2 the left-hand side of the

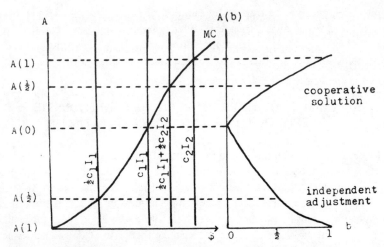

Figure 3: The Effect of Spillout on Public Good Production

equation is everywhere greater than $c_1 I_1$. With the assumption on MC_A, we have A_b increasing at a decreasing rate as b goes from 0 to 1.

The analysis and the output graph of $A(b)$ are shown in Figure 3. The graph is double valued because the condition of cooperation effects the production decision. Since $A(b)$ is determined by maximizing a welfare function, the model is clearly a fold catastrophe—hence one arm must be unstable; in point of fact, it is the bottom arm, representing points that are not Pareto optimal. Sandler (1975: pp. 28-29) notes: "it is a naive assumption to presuppose that the regions would not discover that it is in their mutual interest to cooperate in determining public good production." Catastrophe theory reinforces this observation; the fact that the process may be modeled as a fold catastrophe indicates that reaction curve analysis is inappropriate for determining behavior.

The bifurcation subset consists of the single point b=0, at which the absence of spillovers implies that independent equilibrium is Pareto optimal. The exact location of the stable arm depends on the extent to which Region II is forced to compensate Region I for its improvement in welfare due to consumption of A. This will depend on the relative strength of the two regions in terms of bargaining power and cannot be predicted on the basis of economic factors alone. However, $A(0)$ remains the same and the shape of the graph is not altered.

B. TAX EXPORTATION

Let us assume that benefit spillout is constant at rate b, $0 \leqslant b < 1$, and examine the effects on public good production of introducing tax exportation from Region I to Region II. Again the marginal cost curve has a kink at the historical point of production; i.e., where $(1-b)c_1 I_1 = MC_A$. Suppose an excise tax is imposed on a private good X, consumed in both regions. In Region II X is a normal good whose consumption increases at a decreasing rate with income. Say the tax yields total revenue of T_x and t is the percent of T_x paid into Region I from Region II because of tax exportation. T_x is redistributed to the residents of Region I.

The tax has two effects on residents of Region I. First, they see aggregate regional income increasing by tT_x. This shifts the marginal willingness-to-pay curve upward by $c_1 tT_x$. Second, the existence of the tax on good X raises its price, shifting demand away from X and toward other goods, including A. Hence, price distortions are created which rotate the marginal cost curve downward to MC', so that the amount of A demanded is greater at all income levels. This price distortion is independent of t. If T_x is large and regional government is responsive to individual choices, the distortion may be significant. Under conditions of independent adjustment, $A_t(t|b)$ increases at a decreasing rate with t, and it increases more than warranted by the increase in regional income alone.

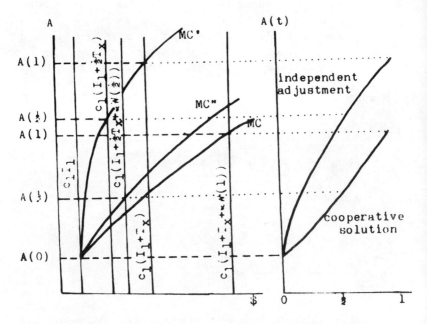

Figure 4: Effect of Tax Exportation on Public Good Production

This situation is unstable as pointed out by Loehr (1974). If Region II consumes goods besides A and X, such as another public good B, the distortion caused by an excise tax when $t>0$ creates welfare cost $W(t)=-1/2tT_x\triangle X$ above and beyond the loss of income tT_x. By the assumption on tastes for good X in Region II, we know that $W(t)$ increases at an increasing rate with t. Thus Region II could pay Region I an amount exceeding tT_x to reduce T_x. Clearly there is an incentive for cooperation, increasing as t becomes larger. Conversely, as $t \rightarrow 0$, Region II's incentive for and ability to influence I decreases to zero, so that the cooperative solution converges to A_t $(0|b)$.

If a cooperative (tax harmonization) solution is chosen, Region I sees its income increase with t by $tT_x+\alpha W(t)$, where $0\leqslant\alpha\leqslant 1$ is determined by noneconomic factors. The marginal cost curve shifts back toward MC_A by an amount determined by the reduction in T_x. (We assume that the greater the α, the greater the shift.) The relatively lower price of X means that a smaller share of this marginal income is spent on A as compared with the noncooperative solution. For T_x sufficiently large, the effect of increasing income swamps the effect of increasing marginal cost and A $(t|b)$ increases at an increasing rate. Figure 4 shows the effect of t on A under both adjustments. Here we assume b=0; as b increases, the arms of the curve are compressed proportionally and become a single straight line along the t axis for b=1. (Note that we are assuming that the cooperative solution changes only T_x and does not imply adjustment for spillovers.) The bottom arm of the graph represents the Pareto optimal tax harmonization. The exact position of this arm will be influenced by the relative bargaining strength of Regions I and II. As noted above the cooperative solution is identical with independent equilibrium at the bifurcation point t=0.

C. TWO EQUAL AND OPPOSITE FORCES?

It is well known that higher dimension catastrophes are just "stacks" of lower order models with a new singularity. Since both of our fold models above have the same behavior variable, we are emboldened to try our tools on the problem of production of a public good in a system with both benefit spillovers and tax exportation. If we place our earlier graphs at right angles to each other, we see that they have a common singularity at 0; i.e., $A_t(0|0)=A_b(0)$. Moreover, as we move through the A, t plane (Figure 5) $A_b(0)$ moves up along the unstable arm of $A_t(t|b)$. Conversely, as b increases, $A_t(0|b)$ collapses to a straight line, $A_t(t|0)=0$. A cross section of the behavior surface looks like Figure 6.

How can we interpret Figure 6? Clearly the surface is a cusp model with the bifurcation subset equal to the parameter axes. This means that behavior changes can occur only when one control is missing. This is reasonable when we consider the economic meaning of the branches. All stable points on the surface are Pareto optimal points; bimodality can occur because Pareto optimal solutions are not unique, but rather depend on income distribution. The higher branch represents a maintenance of initial distribution $I_1 = I_2$; the lower comes from the redistribution effected by transfers of $tT_x + \alpha W(t)$ from Region II to Region I; $I_1' = I_1 + tT_x + \alpha W(t)$, $I_2' = I_2 - (tT_x + \alpha W(t))$. Since Region II places the higher valuation on good A, their reduction in demand more than offsets the increase from Region I due to higher income. The middle sheet here has an economic meaning: it is the set of independent adjustment equilibria and represents the least likely behavior under the possibility of cooperation. Thus, we cannot expect tax exportation to offset the effects of benefit spillovers sufficiently to make the noncooperative solution stable. The

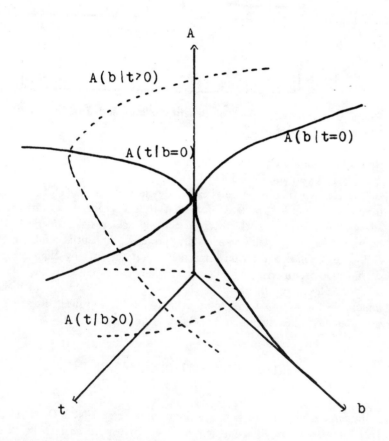

Figure 5: Tax exportation combined with public good spillout

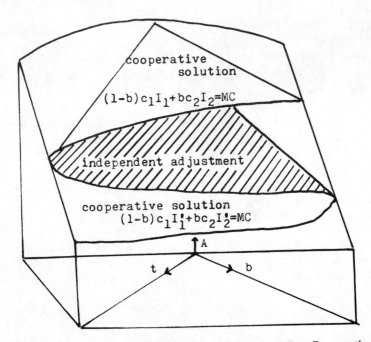

Figure 6: Combined Effect of Benefit Spillout and Tax Exportation on Public Good Production

results here are closely allied to the analysis of cooperation and learning in a duopoly by Cyert and DeGroot (1973).

The element of divergence is especially clear in this model. Benefit spillovers work to the advantage of Region II; tax exportation works to the advantage of Region I. Which region actually achieves the superior relative position depends crucially on bargaining power under neutral conditions, i.e., at the cusp. Once one region gains the advantage, only by eliminating the detrimental factor can the other region hope to move to the superior position. Hence on the bottom sheet, Region II should try to make it impossible for Region I to export its taxes; on the top sheet, Region I will seek a method of excluding Region II from consumption of A.

III. A MODEL OF PARTICIPATION IN
SUPRANATIONAL ORGANIZATIONS

In this century, supranational organizations (e.g., UNESCO, NATO, the U.N.) have become common and the trend is toward an increase in such structures. Hence efficient design has become an important political and economic concern. In their recent paper, Sandler and Cauley (1977) discuss the occurrence of supranational design decisions which, although optimal for the set of states under consideration, are not implemented, some states apparently not finding the union to their advantage. They attribute this to a low probability of initial formation and suggest that the difficulty could be circumvented by an optimal path of formation. How this paradox could occur, and that an optimal path is indeed the solution, is readily seen in the context of a cusp catastrophe model.

Suppose the decision involves one transnational public good and N countries with L_n persons in country n. For each country the decision to participate is responsive to public opinion and is determined by a simple majority.[8] At each point in time γ, each person possesses a unique function $B_\gamma^i(t)$ describing in monetary units the net benefits flow to herself deriving from her country's membership in a supranational organization of tightness t. The tightness of the cooperative link may vary from 0 for independent national action for all, to t for total cooperation. t is defined continuously over the interval $[0,\bar{t}]$ and $B_\gamma^i(\bar{t})$ achieves a unique maximum on the interval. Since individuals vary, $B_\gamma^i(\cdot)$ is different for persons; however, within a country n, the $B_\gamma^i(\cdot)$'s are distributed normally around a mean function $B_\gamma^n(\cdot)$. Over time, increasing spillover effects cause $B_\gamma^n(\cdot)$ to shift upward and to the right and likewise cause the individual functions $B_\gamma^i(\cdot)$ to cluster more tightly around $B_\gamma^n(\cdot)$.

The costs to the nation from the supranational union are of two types: $C(t)$ is the cost flow at time γ due to maintaining membership if the organization operates at tightness t. $C(t)$ is independent of time and increases monotonically with t. $\bar{C}$ is the cost of joining the organization; i.e., the cost of setting up the apparatus for cooperation. $\bar{C}$ is independent of the level of tightness and is constant over time. If at some later point in time γ_q the nation leaves the organization, some of the resources should be recoverable. We assume that this "resell" value (denoted by $R_q(\gamma)$) is independent of time of joining but decreases with γ_q.

Both $C(t)$ and $\bar{C}$ are distributed among the residents of the country. Denote by $C^i(t)$ and $\bar{C}^i$ the membership and joining costs faced by individual i. Likewise $R_q^i(\gamma)$ is the individual's share of $R_q(\gamma)$. We assume that $\bar{C}$ and $R_q(\gamma)$ are distributed identically and that $\bar{C}^i - R_q^i(\gamma) > 0$, for $\gamma > 0$, for all i.

We assume further that the good is considered a necessity by each country and will be provided independently at some level if the state chooses not to join the organization.[9] D^n represents the cost to the state of establishing an independent facility to produce the public good. D^n is also constant over time. An independent country which later opts for linkage can recover some of its investment, namely $R_j(\gamma)$ which decreases with γ, with $R_j(0)=D^n$ and $R_j(T)=0$. Yearly costs of running the independent facility are included in the net benefit functions $B_\gamma^i(t)$. Implicit in the statement of costs is that a unique optimal level of independent action is being compared, regardless of the time period under consideration. The cost D^n and resell value $R_j(\gamma)$ share the same distribution over persons in country n and these shares are represented by D_i^n and $R_j^i(\gamma)$. Again, we assume that $D_i^n - R_j^i(\gamma) > 0, \gamma > 0$. This distribution need not—in fact probably will not—coincide with that of $\bar{C}$ and $R_q(\gamma)$.

Let γ_0 be the first time period in which the organization is to exist (it may be at level 0). The analysis here is uncomplicated; each person examines the function $\beta_o^i(t) = B_o^i(t) - C^i(t)$ to determine the range of t over which $\beta_o^i(t) \geqslant C^i - D_i^n$. As t increases, more and more persons find that benefits outweigh costs and hence favor union. Beyond some level t, the percentage of persons favoring membership decreases. The opinion graph for the country looks like Figure 7. J is the percentage of people favoring membership. The values for t for which the country actually joins or quits the organization are those such that J(t)=.5; the points are the same for t increasing and decreasing.

At some later point in time $\hat{\gamma} > \gamma_0$, the picture is complicated by the difference in analysis between persons in a country already a member and those in an independent nation. Because we assume positive costs for joining and leaving the union, the individual must consider her present position. At γ_0, the change in decision occurred where $\beta_o^i(t) \geqslant \bar{C}^i - D_i^n$. At $\hat{\gamma} > \gamma_0$, if the nation is already a member, the resident evaluates the cost of remaining in the union as $C^i(t)$ while costs for leaving are $D_i^n - R_q^i(\hat{\gamma})$. Since the state may change position vis à vis the alliance in succeeding time periods, the individual behaves as though decision costs must be recovered at $\hat{\gamma}$. ($\bar{C}^i$ is treated as a sunk cost and does not enter the analysis.) Hence a person in a member nation desires to remain in the union for values of t such that $-\beta_\gamma^i(t) = -(B_\gamma^i(t) - C^i(t)) \leqslant D_i^n - R_q^i(\hat{\gamma})$; i.e., she will suffer a small loss due to membership as long as it does not exceed the net cost (to her) of establishing

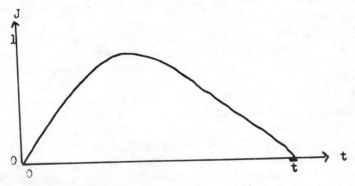

Figure 7: Opinion graph for Country n at ζ_0

independent facilities. Only if $-\beta_\gamma^j(t) > D_i^n - R_q^i(\hat\gamma)$ does the individual desire to quit.

Asymmetrically, a resident of a nonmember nation would face costs of $C^i(t) + \bar{C}^i - R_j^i(\hat\gamma)$ to participate. And since D_i^n is treated as a sunk cost, remaining independent would be costless. Hence the citizen of the nonmember nation would require that $\beta_\gamma^j(t) > \bar{C}^i - R_j^i(\gamma)$ before wanting to join.

(Throughout we assume a naive approach in which the individual takes account only of costs and benefits accruing in the time period under consideration. This is done for reasons of simplicity and does not affect the nature of the important result of this section; namely, that positive costs for joining

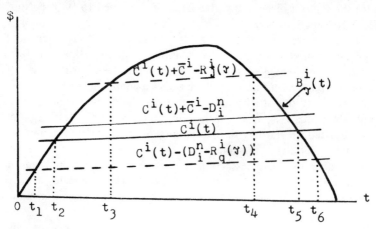

Figure 8: Individual Cost-benefit Analysis

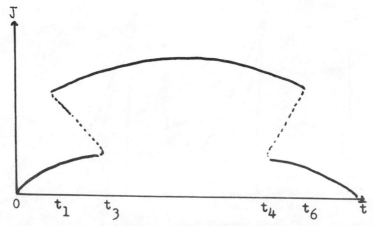

Figure 9: Opinion graph at time $\gamma > \gamma_0$

and quitting cause intervals of t over which the individual's opinion depends crucially on the country's previous involvement. To make the analysis more sophisticated, let $\beta_\gamma^i = \int_{\hat\gamma}^T (B_\gamma^i(t) - C^i(t)\, d\gamma.)$

Graphically (see Figure 8), the individual's decision is determined by the points of t at which $B_\gamma(t)$ exceeds total cost. At γ_0 these costs are $C^i(t) + (C^i - D^n)$. At $\hat\gamma > \gamma_0$, the toal cost of belonging for a citizen of a member nation is represented by a line parallel to $C^i(t)$ but below it a vertical distance $D_i^n - R_q^i(\gamma) > D_i^n - \bar{C}^i$. This enlarges the interval of t over which membership is desirable to $[t_1, t_6]$. Similarly the resident of a nonmember nation faces a total cost curve located a vertical distance $\bar{C}^i - R_j^i(\gamma) > \bar{C}^i - D_i^n$ above $C^i(t)$; hence the interval of desired participation is shortened to $[t_3, t_4]$. Note that the t_i's are functions of γ.

The opinion graph at time $\hat\gamma > \gamma_0$ looks like Figure 9. As t increases from 0, public opinion gradually shifts in favor of joining. However, for most people, cost of joining continues to outweigh net benefits. Because $B_\gamma^j(t)$ is clustered around a central value, there comes a point where a large number of people suddenly find it advantageous to join. The decision is not precipitous for the individuals—$\beta_\gamma^i(t)$ was increasing smoothly—but the effect on public policy is a sudden startling shift to joining. Suppose Figure 8 represents the mean function $B_\gamma^n(t)$ in the country at time $\hat\gamma$. Then we have t_3 in Figure 9. corresponding to point t3 in Figure 8, where participation begins for t increasing. If t continues to increase, participation ends suddenly at t_6 where a majority of the population finds personal costs of enduring membership exceed costs of leaving.

By similar reasoning, as t decreases from $\bar{t}$, public opinion favors independence until t_4; opinion remains high over the interval (t_4, t_1) and suddenly

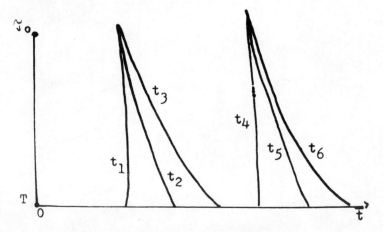

Figure 10: Time path of joining/nonjoining boundaries

decreases sharply at t_1. The important point is that in the intervals $[t_1, t_3]$ and $[t_4, t_6]$ we cannot predict what choice the state will make without a priori knowledge of its historical position. Also note that the points t_2, t_5 at which $\beta_\gamma^n(t) = 0$ are marked by no behavioral changes in Figure 9.

In general we can say that involvement in the supranational union is a function of time and tightness, and that at every point, $\gamma > \gamma_0$, there are regions of bimodal behavior. The intervals of bimodality must increase with γ because we have assumed an increase over time in decision costs. Because we assume that $B_\gamma^i(\cdot)$ clusters more tightly around $B_\gamma^n(\cdot)$ as γ increases, we also have an increase in the distance between the two sheets in the regions of bimodal behavior. Moreover, because of the assumption on the movement of $B_\gamma^n(\cdot)$ over time, the points t_i, i=1,2,. . .,6, are increasing functions of time. If we plot these $t_i(\gamma)$'s in the parameter space we have Figure 10.

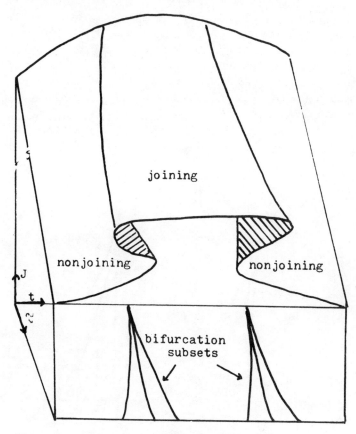

Figure 11: Opinion surface for Country n

Clearly the model is a simple variant of the cusp catastrophe with two folds;[10] t is the normal factor; for $\gamma=0$, $J(t)$ is a smoothly continuous curve; γ is the splitting factor, causing the sheets of the behavior graph to separate (because of our assumption that the variance of $B_\gamma^j(\cdot)$ decreases over time). Sudden changes in the behavior mode come because the government makes a discrete decision (to join or not to join). Bimodality and hysteresis result from the dependence of individual analysis on initial position. Divergence is created by freedom from historical restraints on decisions at γ_0 and from the inability to attain the middle sheet. The middle sheet is inaccessible; decisions based on these values of J would tend to minimize public acceptance and hence imply a short life for the party in power.

Now assume that the designers select t to maximize $\sum_{n=1}^{N} L_n \beta_{\hat\gamma}^n(t)$ at some $\hat\gamma$ subject to the constraint that $t \epsilon [t_2(\hat\gamma), t_5(\hat\gamma)]$ for all countries, without taking into account the variability of $B_\gamma^n(\cdot)$ over time. (If for some nation m the constraint is violated—i.e., $\beta_\gamma^m(t) < 0$—clearly that nation will refuse to participate.) Suppose that for some country m, $\hat{t} \epsilon [t_4(\hat\gamma), t_5(\hat\gamma))$. Then $\hat{t}$ was determined assuming a strictly positive value for $\beta_\gamma^m(\hat{t})$. If in fact this state chooses not to join, it is no longer apparent that $\hat{t}$ is optimal for the set of remaining states. Is it possible that such a country will refuse to join? If the intervals $[t_4(\hat\gamma), t_5(\hat\gamma)]$ are small for all nations, it is probable that several will refuse under certain assumptions on the time path of t.

Suppose that the link is proposed to be at tightness t from time γ_0 at least through $\hat\gamma$. For country m, whose upper bifurcation subset is depicted in Figure 12, the time path $t(\gamma) \equiv \hat{t}$ begins and remains on the lower, non-joining branch of the behavior surface, since the $t_4(\gamma)$ arm is never crossed. Although

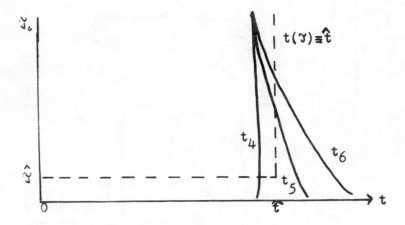

Figure 12: Non-participation in a Country for which Union is Beneficial

$\hat{t}$ is optimal for the set of states and beneficial to nation m, the desired linkage will not occur.

The policy implication is clear—if participation is desired at time $\hat{\gamma}$, $t(\gamma)$ must be below $t_4(\gamma)$ for some $\gamma \leqslant \hat{\gamma}$ and thereafter must remain below $t_6(\gamma)$. If full participation is required at all $\gamma \epsilon [\gamma_0, T]$, $t(0)$ must start in the interval $(t_2(0), t_5(0))$ and remain within $[t_1(\gamma), t_6(\gamma)]$. Figure 13 shows three paths in parameter space and their functional paths on the behavior surface. Path A is the same as Figure 12; path B allows non-participation initially; C is a path which yields participation at all points in time.

A path guaranteeing full participation is not necessarily an optimal path as defined by Sandler and Cauley; i.e., one for which $\sum_{n=1}^{N} L_n \beta_\gamma^n(t)$ is maximized

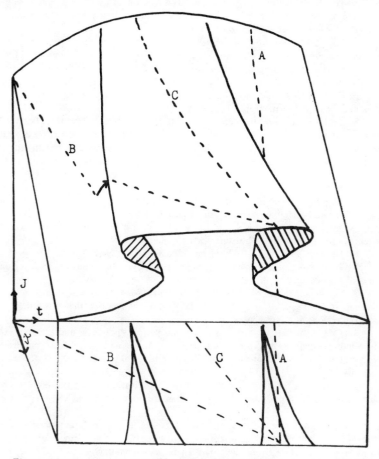

Figure 13: Participation Under Various Time Paths

at all γ. An optimal path is sufficient but not necessary to the solution of the problem as stated, since an optimal path lies within $[t_2(\gamma),t_5(\gamma)]$. Since exact knowledge of the relevant functions and boundaries is unlikely, it is worthwhile to know that a ballpark estimate of the optimal path carries with it assurance of desired participation.

NOTES

1. A word of warning is in order: Not all discontinuous phenomena are catastrophes; e.g., many step functions exhibit some properties of catastrophes. We must look closely at the underlying motivation to justify the use of catastrophe theory.

2. The prototype of catastrophe models is a potential energy function in which the dynamic of the system is to minimize potential energy. Stability characteristics of points on the behavior surface then become obvious.

3. For most points on the hypersurface G it will be true that for any control parameter there exists a neighborhood of the point on which x is a single-valued function of that parameter, holding the others constant. A singularity of the graph occurs at any point where for some parameter no such neighborhood exists. That every behavior surface G as herein defined has a singularity at the origin with respect to the new control parameter is basic to catastrophe theory.

The implicit function theorem tells us that $f_x(x,a,b,c,d)=0$ and $f_{xx}(x,a,b,c,d) \neq 0$ imply that for every control parameter there exists a neighborhood of (x,a,b,c,d) on which x may be written as a single-valued function of that parameter, holding the others constant. Hence singularities will only be found at points which project onto the bifurcation subset B.

4. Note that this assumption implies that there is no reciprocal spillin. To handle reciprocal spillovers would require a higher dimensional model. The author speculates that this could be accomplished by using a cusp catastrophe. Likewise, if tax exportation may go either direction, this would be modelled as a cusp. Combining the two sets of effects would then require a butterfly catastrophe model.

5. This type of public good has been discussed by Pauly (1970).

6. We postulate the existence of such social welfare functions for each region and maximizing behavior by the central authority.

7. This is our reaction curve. It differs from those found in the traditional analysis because we assume one-way spillover. Because of our assumption that A is purely private between regions, it is still a meaningful concept.

8. That is, we assume the government has perfect knowledge and acts to maximize the number of persons agreeing with its decisions. This would clearly be accomplished by joining (staying in) the organization if and only if this were optimal for a simple majority.

9. Hence benefits from belonging to the organization may be entirely from efficiency gains, scale economies, etc., rather than from an increase in consumption of the good.

10. This is not strictly accurate. More precisely, it is a cross section of a butterfly catastrophe with negative bias factor and zero butterfly factor. Using the more general formulation of a butterfly model would enable us to simultaneously study cases where spillovers decrease over time (implying a tendency to "overjoin").

BIBLIOGRAPHY

ABRAHAM, R. and J. ROBBIN (1967) Transversal Mappings and Flows. New York: Benjamin.

BOEHNE, EDWARD (1969) "The Partial Symmetry of Benefit and Cost Spillovers and Allocative Efficiency in a Federal System." Canadian Journal of Economics 2(3):461-462.

BRAINARD, WILLIAM and F. DOLBEAR, JR. (1967) "The Possibility of Oversupply of Local 'Public' Goods: A Critical Note." Journal of Political Economy 75(1):86-90.

BRETON, ALBERT (1970) "Public Goods and the Stability of Federalism." Kyklos 23(4):882-902.

CYERT, RICHARD and MORRIS DEGROOT (1973) "An Analysis of Cooperation and Learning in a Duopoly Context." American Economic Review 63(1):24-37.

DOLBEAR, F., L. LAVE, G. BOWMAN, A. LIEBERMAN, E. PRESCOTT, F. RUETER and R. SHERMAN (1968) "Collusion in Oligopoly: An Experiment on the Effect of Numbers and Information." Quarterly Journal of Economics 82(2):240-259.

GOLUBITSKY, M. and V. GUILLEMIN (1973) Stable Mappings and Their Singularities. New York: Springer-Verlag.

ISNARD, C. A. and E. C. ZEEMAN (1972) "Some Models from Catastrophe Theory in the Social Sciences," presented at Edinburgh Conference, July 1972.

JANICH, KLAUS (1974) "Caustics and Catastrophes." Mathematische Annalen 105:161-180.

LEVINE, H. I. (1971) "Singularities of Differential Mappings." Pp. 1-89 in C. T. C. Wall (ed.) Proceedings of Liverpool Singularities—Symposium I. Lecture Notes in Mathematics 192. New York: Springer-Verlag.

LOEHR, WILLIAM (1974) "Fiscal Federalism, Spillovers, and the Export of Taxes: An Extension." Kyklos 27(3):606-609.

MCLURE, CHARLES, JR. (1969) "The Interregional Incidence of General Regional Taxes." Public Finance 24(3):457-483.

MILNOR, J. (1965) Topology from the Differential Viewpoint. Charlottesville Virginia: University Press of Virginia.

NG, YEW-KWANG (1971) "Public Goods and the Stability of Federalism: An Extension." Kyklos 24(3):562-563.

OATES, WALLACE (1968) "The Theory of Public Finance in a Federal System." Canadian Journal of Economics 1(1):37-54.

OLSON, MANCUR, JR. and RICHARD ZECKHAUSER (1966) "An Economic Theory of Alliances." Review of Economics and Statistics 48(3):266-279.

PAULY, MARK (1970) "Optimality, 'Public' Goods, and Local Governments: A General Theoretical Analysis." Journal of Political Economy 78(3):572-585.

PORTEOUS, I. R. (1971) "Simple Singularities of Maps," pp. 286-307 in C. T. C. Wall (ed.) Proceedings of Liverpool Singularities—Symposium I. Lecture Notes in Mathematics 192. New York: Springer-Verlag.

SANDLER, TODD (1975) "Pareto Optimality, Pure Public Goods, Impure Public Goods and Multiregional Spillovers." Scottish Journal of Political Economy 22(1):25-38.

SANDLER, TODD and JON CAULEY (1977) "The Design of Supranational Structures: An Economic Perspective." International Studies Quarterly 21(2).

SANDLER, TODD and ROBERT B. SHELTON (1972) "Fiscal Federalism and the Export of Taxes." Kyklos 25(4):736-753.

THOM, RENE (1964) "Local Topological Properties of Differentiable Mappings." Pp. 191-202 in Bombay Colloquium on Differentiable Analysis. Oxford: Oxford University Press.

TIEBOUT, CHARLES (1956) "A Pure Theory of Local Expenditures." Journal of
    Political Economy 64(5):416-424.
WALL, C. T. C. (1971a) "Introduction to the Preparation Theorem." Pp. 90-96 in C. T.
    C. Wall (ed.) Proceedings of Liverpool Singularities—Symposium I. Lecture Notes in
    Mathematics 192. New York: Springer-Verlag.
——— (1971b) "Lectures on C-stability and Classification." Pp. 178-206 in C. T. C. Wall
    (ed.) Proceedings of Liverpool Singularities—Symposium I. Lecture Notes in Mathe-
    matics 192. New York: Springer-Verlag.
WILLIAMS, ALAN (1966) "The Optimal Provision of Public Goods in a System of
    Local Government." Journal of Political Economy 74(1):18-33.
——— (1967) "The Possibility of Oversupply of Public Goods: A Rejoinder." Journal of
    Political Economy 75(1):91-92.
WOODCOCK, A. and T. POSTON (1973) A Geometrical Study of the Elementary
    Catastrophes. Lecture Notes in Mathematics 373. New York: Springer-Verlag.

Chapter 6

ALLIANCE POLITICS:
A MODEL BASED ON DIVISIBILITY OF PAYOFFS

STEPHEN M. SHAFFER
The George Washington University

INTRODUCTION

Alliances can be studied from a variety of complementary perspectives, each focusing on different aspects of the processes leading to the formation of an alliance, its performance through time, and its effects on international politics. This paper focuses on the effects of the divisibility of payoffs provided by an alliance on the performance of the alliance across time.[1] More specifically, my concern is with the impact of supplying both public and private goods simultaneously as payoffs to alliance members on a nation's behavior toward its alliance partners.

Attention to the coalition literature has shed considerable theoretical light on alliances in world politics. But the bulk of the theorizing has been applied to the problems of why and how a particular coalition forms from among a set of potential coalition participants (Riker, 1962).[2] Determinants of strategies nations choose to interact with their alliance partners in an extant alliance, while a topic of considerable speculation and occasional empirical study, have not been frequent subjects of formal deductive theorizing.

Public goods is one theoretical framework that has been used to study alliances (Olson and Zeckhauser, 1966; Ypersele de Strihou, 1968; Russett, 1970; Burgess and Robinson, 1969; Beer, 1971). These studies are concerned chiefly with problems of optimality of supply of a public good and with determining whether burden sharing is proportional. This paper applies the concepts of public and private goods, and joint products, to international alliances by linking intra-alliance behavior to the amount and type of payoffs provided by the alliance. A model of alliance politics is developed based on assumptions and propositions from relevant literature in public goods, game theory, coalition theory and alliances. Implications are stated as empirically testable hypotheses.

AUTHOR'S NOTE: I wish to thank Bruce Bueno de Mesquita for our discussions concerning some of the ideas on alliances in this paper and William Loehr for his helpful comments on an earlier draft.

One important limiting condition is the restriction of the unit of analysis to a formal, defense-oriented alliance based on a principle of mutual defense. Any grouping of nations is not relevant to the model. The aligned nations must be signatories to a formal treaty establishing an alliance. Also, the aim of the alliance (as expressed in the treaty) must be to provide security for its members. Security is guaranteed through two types of defense pacts: collective security arrangements; and collective defense alliances. The former protects the members against aggression from within and without the organization and has no specific target. Collective defense alliances are intended to protect from aggression originating outside the alliance, and are usually created in response to a (potential) threat from an identified enemy (Wolfers, 1959: 52; Claude, 1962: 94-204).

NATIONAL STRATEGY IN ALLIANCES

National alliance strategy is the dependent variable in this study. Strategy refers to a series of actions directed toward achieving some goal. These actions in turn are influenced by the actions of other actors whose behavior likewise determines the outcome(s). Hence, the use of strategy corresponds to the use of the concept in game theory.

In considering the possible strategies a nation might follow vis-à-vis the alliance, three options are most likely: cooperative, competitive, and mixed cooperative-competitive strategies.

Cooperative and competitive strategies refer to the balance of benefits and costs borne by alliance members. To the extent that a nation used its alliance bonds to enjoy alliance benefits without footing its share of the costs required to achieve common alliance goals, it is pursuing a competitive strategy vis-a-vis an alliance. For instance, a common assumption in the alliance literature is that nations ally to supplement their capabilities. The relationship of members' capabilities is thought to be additive. Thus, from the standpoint of a particular nation, alliances are a means of increasing its capabilities. It is therefore reasonable to assume that nations might exploit the opportunities alliances afford to obtain benefits without paying commensurate costs. Such a competitive strategy is rational, however, only to the extent that other alliance members are willing to tolerate the behavior, that achievement of alliance goals is not impaired (which implies that the share of the costs of the noncooperative member must be made up by others), and so long as retaliation leading to loss of all benefits does not occur.[3]

The tolerance point for competitive behavior is not known, but once that point is reached, a competitive strategy has to be converted into a cooperative one. Adoption of both strategies over a period of time is a mixed strategy.

France's behavior toward NATO is perhaps the clearest illustration of a mixed cooperative-competitive strategy. From the outset of his presidency, De Gaulle lessened France's support of and commitment to NATO by disengaging from joint military commands. De Gaulle did not, however, sever his ties with the North Atlantic Alliance, insisting on a distinction between the organization and the alliance. He made it clear that he thought the Alliance was central to France's (and Western Europe's) security. While decreasing NATO commitments, a large portion of French defense expenditures were directed to the development of the "force de dissuasion," an independent nuclear force which De Gaulle used as a bargaining tool in his relations with NATO allies and non-allies alike. In a word, De Gaulle felt comfortable under the Alliance's security umbrella and relied on it to give him the opportunity to pursue France's national goals—prestige, regaining of national sovereignty (i.e., control over national defense), and increased military capabilities—at the expense of other NATO Allies.

The fundamental question is what determines whether a nation pursues a cooperative, competitive, or mixed strategy. The initial choice of one of these strategies and the change in strategy over time are hypothesized to be due primarily to the divisibility of alliance payoffs. The less divisible the payoffs, the greater the "temptation" to be competitive. If we assume that a principal goal of alliance members is to maximize their individual interests in the alliance rather than to maximize only the total alliance payoffs, our major hypothesis is:

> In payoff oriented, redistributive alliances where indivisible payoffs predominate, the probability that most members of the alliance will pursue mainly a competitive strategy toward the alliance over time increases; as the divisibility of payoffs increases, the likelihood of cooperative strategy choice increases.

This hypothesis is the major implication to grow out of formal theories of strategy choice and collective behavior. In the following section, the model and its implications are developed.

ALLIANCES IN INTERNATIONAL RELATIONS RESEARCH

By and large, alliances are viewed as almost exclusively cooperative ventures whose purpose is the achievement of some commonly shared purpose (Friedman, 1970; Wolfers, 1968; Liska, 1962; Morgenthau, 1967). Morgenthau (1967: 179) offers perhaps the clearest statement of this position: "A typical alliance attempts to transform a small fraction of the total interests of the contracting parties into common policies and measures . . . Whether and for how long [the alliance] will be operative depends upon the strength of the interests underlying it as over and against the strengths of the other interests of the nations concerned."[4]

The assumed primacy of shared goals is predicated in turn on the assumption that nations enter into alliances to pursue a goal which they cannot achieve in the absence of cooperative effort with other nations. Again, Morgenthau (1967: 175) argues that "a nation will shun alliances if it believes that it is strong enough to hold its own unaided." Liska (1962: 26) observes that "States enter into alliances with one another in order to supplement each other's capability." In effect; Liska argues that alliances are an important way for nations sharing a similar objective to reduce their individual costs of achieving that goal through joint efforts to supply a desired good such as security.

Yet not all alliances are seen as cooperative groups at all times. The aims or purposes of an alliance, for example, may exercise some influence over the actions of its members. In an offensive alliance a concern of all members is the distribution of the expected spoils of victory, and coalitions frequently split apart over the issue of who gets what percentage of the "take."[5] A different pattern might be expected in alliances created to combat a potential threat. In such a defensive situation, victory might be defined as blocking (deterring) the adversary, with minimal attention paid to more tangible payoffs such as control over additional territory and population.

A framework incorporating elements of this difference in alliance goals is discussed by Bueno de Mesquita and Singer (1973: 259-63). With respect to basic goals, they suggest alliances are of two types: (1) policy-oriented, fixed-capability alliances, and (2) payoff-oriented, redistributive alliances.

Balance of power alliances are examples of the fixed-capability variant. Balance of power models view alliances as a means of counteracting threats of preponderant power in the state system. Major actors are not eliminated from the system. The purpose of the alliance is to restore an equitable distribution of power by restoring the independent status of nations, not to redistribute capabilities altering the status quo ante (Gulick, 1955; Kissinger, 1957; Kaplan, 1957).

Redistributive alliances are characterized by some degree of competition among their members for shares of the payoffs or side payments distributed by the alliance (Liska, 1962: 26-7, 30). As Liska (1962: 72) notes, members of coalitions seek "simultaneously to maximize individual advantages and both maximize and share advantages procured jointly."[6] It is in the effort to maximize individual benefits while continuing to enjoy shared, collective benefits that competitive or mixed strategies emerge.

To summarize, it has been suggested by several scholars that whether a nation cooperates with its alliance partners is determined, at least in part, by whether a major purpose of the alliance is the redistribution of payoffs according to some explicit or implicit criteria such as contribution to alliance goals.[7] What are these criteria? To what extent does competition predominate over cooperation in an alliance?

This issue is considered most explicitly in the largely speculative literature dealing with alliance cohesion.[8] While the meaning of cohesion is frequently vague and ambiguous, the concept can best be thought of as implying the balance of cooperative to competitive behavior toward the alliance by its members.[9]

Four determinants of the cooperation to competition ratio in alliances identified in the international politics literature are: (1) the goals of an alliance; (2) shared characteristics of members; (3) distribution of capabilities within an alliance; and (4) the structure of the alliance.

ALLIANCE GOALS

The most frequently encountered theme in the literature is that alliance cohesion is strengthened by the presence of a common external threat (Liska, 1962; Kaplan, 1957; Morgenthau, 1967; Haas and Whiting, 1956; Holsti, 1976; Holsti, 1977; Wolfers, 1959). Liska (1962: 106) points out that the interests of alliance members are disparate when they are concerned with combatting different adversaries. Also, Liska sees the extent to which one or several conflicts predominate in the international system as an important factor influencing cohesion (pp. 16-19). As the magnitude of external threat declines, cohesion is reduced (Dinnerstein, 1965: 593; Wolfers, 1962: 28).

Guetzkow (1957: 65-66) places less emphasis on a common external threat, but stresses the importance of shared goals in hypothesizing that the more multifunctional a coalition, the greater its internal cohesion.

SHARED CHARACTERISTICS

Similarity of interests and attitudes is proposed as a major determinant of cooperation among alliance members in much of the literature. Liska (1962: 62) observes that "To facilitate coalescense, . . . [the alliance] will emphasize pressing common interests, while ignoring or minimizing divergent interests."

In their study of the Anglo-American alliance, Dawson and Rosecrance (1966) argue that ideological, cultural, and historical similarities facilitate cohesion (see esp. pp. 47-51). Russett's (1963) study of British-American relations draws heavily on Deutsch's (1957) study of community building, in which important variables include shared attitudes and beliefs, mutual attention, mutual responsiveness, and other aspects of communication theory.

Russett (1968) differentiates between peacetime and wartime alliances, suggesting that alliances operating in peaceful periods of history are more likely to be cohesive if based on non-utilitarian factors—e.g., mutually shared attitudes. Taking a different approach, Guetzkow (1957) postulates a form of learning model, noting that nations that are successful in past experiences of joint action are more likely to continue collaborative behavior.

CAPABILITY DISTRIBUTION

A third approach to alliance cohesion is concerned with both the initial distribution of national capabilities among alliance members and levels and rates of change in capability distribution. Small nations (in terms of their capabilities) have fewer options than major powers; a central concern of their foreign policy will be the preservation of some degree of independence and autonomy in the face of pressures pulling them to join alliances (Liska, 1962; Rothstein, 1968; Fox, 1959). In alliances dominated by a single power, Liska argues that alliance cohesion may be reduced (p. 89). He further notes that as a rule, alliance members with low capability profiles who seek resources from the alliance (as well as investing resources in it) will attempt to expand alliance functions in ·both depth and scope, often against the desires of the powerful members (pp. 76-77). Dinnerstein (1965: 598-99) takes the opposite view, arguing that hegemonic power in an alliance prevents challenges from less powerful nations for leadership roles.[10]

When we shift from hypotheses regarding initial capability distribution to changes in distribution, we find both absolute and relative capability shifts to be identified as important determinants of cohesion. Rapid shifts in capability distribution are viewed as potentially destabilizing, as are unequal gains (and losses) within the alliance (Liska, 1962). Liska writes that "The best thing for cohesion is an even and moderate rise in capability" (p. 90). Similarly, Haas and Whiting (1956) hypothesize that the greater the changes in power relations within an alliance, the greater the challenge to its maintenance.

These hypotheses receive some support from experimental evidence. Brody's (1963) man-machine simulation of the diffusion of nuclear weapons finds that with a nuclear differential (i.e., only one nation has a nuclear capability), intra-bloc cohesion is high. As nuclear parity is achieved, cohesion within a bloc is reduced.

ALLIANCE STRUCTURE

A final variable which might affect cooperation and competition in alliances is an alliance's formal or informal structure or hierarchy. There is an obvious link between structure and capability distribution; alliances organized

around a dominant power are more likely to be tightly hierarchically organized and controlled by the major power, while alliances characterized by a
more equitable power distribution will be less subject to the control of a
single member. The implications of this reasoning are considered by Holsti
and Sullivan (1969: 163-68), who propose that more monolithic alliances are
likely to have greater cohesion than pluralistic ones.[11] Liska (1962) focuses
on bargaining and consultation opportunities as a determinant of cohesion.
He proposes that "the scope of consultations bears on the degree to which
members practice solidarity" (p. 75).

It is apparent that there is no single answer to the earlier query: Under
what conditions would cooperative behavior predominate over competitive in
alliances? This outcome is particularly distressing because of the great diversity of variables suggested to have a bearing on the issue, the often-times
contradictory speculation in the literature, and the dearth of empirical
evidence. Nonetheless, as Bueno de Mesquita and Singer (1973) and others
have observed, calculations of the costs and benefits of alliance membership
affect the types of behavior found in alliances. My strategy is to develop the
link between the distribution of alliance payoffs and action strategies of
alliance members by using the concepts of public goods and joint products.

ALLIANCES AND PUBLIC GOODS

This section explores the implications for intra-alliance behavior derived
from attention to the characteristics of the payoffs alliances provide their
members. The utility of public goods theory will depend quite directly on the
extent to which certain kinds of alliances supply a public good. The common
defense is a mixed good or an impure public good having aspects of both
public and private goods; it falls somewhere between the polar extremes of
pure private and pure public goods.[12] A closer approximation to a pure
public good is the notion of deterrence or security.

Deterrence refers to the ability of an actor to convince another that hostile
behavior on the part of one will be met by a response in kind. The object is to
deter the adversary by a credible threat. Credibility is partly a consequence of
the strength of commitment to protect all relevant interests of the actor
(Russett, 1963). Thus, at the national level, deterrence appears to meet the
definitional criteria of pure public goods—jointness of supply and non-excludability. There is little doubt that an attack on one part of the United States
will be considered as an attack against all parts, for example. As Russett
(1970) notes, it would be difficult to exclude some particular state from
enjoyment of external security. And, of course, Washington's "consumption"
of security does not reduce the amount consumed by California.

The credibility of the deterrent threat is important. Security or deterrence is no longer a pure public good when a nation decides to weaken its commitment; there is less security for an ally to enjoy if a major power in the alliance weakens (or is perceived by others to weaken) its resoluteness to protect that ally. For instance, De Gaulle had serious doubts that the United States would risk nuclear attack on its territory to defend Europe, and used this fear as one rationale for the "force de dissuasion."

The amount of benefit derived from the provision of a public good such as security thus may vary across members of the alliance. In this sense, an equal amount of the public good is not available to all members. Security in an alliance is more properly referred to as a mixed good (Beer, 1971: 9-10; Ypersele de Strihou, 1968: 263-76; Wagner, 1973: 13-25; Sandler and Cauley, 1975: 333-43). Assigning security to a precise location along the private-public continuum is impossible, but it is quite likely that security retains aspects of a public good. Thus, security benefits are treated as indivisible payoffs in the alliance; it cannot be distributed in different amounts to different members.

An important characteristic of collective security or collective defense alliances is that they supply private benefits as well as public goods. Private goods include economic assistance of a military and non-military variety, as well as cultural, educational, trade, and status benefits. Some of the private goods are externalities resulting from the provision and/or consumption of the public good. For example, military expenditures for defense can generate qualitative and quantitative improvements in the armed forces of member nations in terms of training, weaponry, and so on. Certain benefits not related to defense may accrue to members as a result of the provision of the public good, such as domestic security and positive effects on the domestic economy (Olson and Zeckhauser, 1966; Russett, 1970). While the conceptual distinction between public and private benefits is analytically sharp, considerable blurring is likely when alliances are examined. Beer (1971: 11) concludes that "it is probably not possible to isolate areas where *only* common or private [benefits] are involved."

Since defense pacts supply two kinds of payoffs to their members—public and private—a model of collective behavior is needed based on the distinction between alliance benefits that are indivisible (public) and those that are divisible (private). Mancur Olson (1965) sets out a model that explains individual behavior in collective action situations as a function of the divisibility of the payoffs provided by the collectivity. Two propositions from Olson summarize his theory:

(1) [In an association intended to supply a public good,] "unless the number of individuals in a group is quite small, or unless there is

coercion or some other special device to make individuals act in their common interest, rational self-interested individuals will not act to achieve their common or group interests" (p. 36).[13]

(2) "Where small groups with common interests are concerned, then, there is a systematic tendency for 'exploitation' of the great by the small" (p. 29).

Two points are noted. First, Olson's theory suggests that despite their shared interests, members of groups which provide public goods, particularly small groups where no coercion is imposed, may act competitively toward their fellow members and toward the group as a whole.[14] Olson argues that while organizations pursuing a common goal traditionally have been viewed as totally cooperative ventures, temptations exist for the member to act competitively while continuing to share in the public good. The tendency to compete is a function of the nature of the collective payoff—viz., its indivisibility.

Second, Olson posits that the temptation to compete might be reduced either by coercion, or "selective incentives," i.e., private benefits. It is this latter category that is of greatest interest here. Selective incentives are functionally identical to side payments in coalitions; they are intended to "purchase" the support of potential or extant members of the coalition. Thus, competitive behavior might be reduced, and cooperative behavior (i.e., working to achieve group interest) increased, by the presence of more divisible payoffs.[15] To explore the logic of this argument, the concept of joint products is considered.

JOINT PRODUCTS AND STRATEGY CHOICE IN ALLIANCES

The case in which an alliance simultaneously produces both public goods and private goods as payoffs is interesting because it raises the issue of how divisible and indivisible payoffs interact to determine an alliance member's strategy choice. An area of the public goods literature heretofore ignored in the treatment of alliances which discusses public good-private good interaction is the concept of joint products. Joint production refers to situations where both a public good and a private good are produced simultaneously. Although a recent and not well developed area in economics, joint production models may be relevant to an understanding of the effects of payoff divisibility on members' strategy choice in alliances.[16] In particular, the concept of joint products suggests why the introduction of divisible payoffs leads to cooperative strategies for supplying the collective good.

As noted in the discussion of Olson's work, the core problem confronted by collectivities producing public goods is the competitive strategy of the free-rider. Due to the inability to vary quantities of public goods demanded at different prices, there is no market mechanism for revealing demand preferences.[17] For jointly produced private goods, on the other hand, variations in quantities demanded at different prices serve to reveal demand preferences. Thus, whenever exclusion from the benefits of production is feasible, partial or full preference revelation occurs.

An interesting case occurs in international alliances when the production and/or consumption of a public good such as security yields an externality which is an internalized private good from the point of view of any particular member nation. Three examples of jointly produced private goods in an alliance are: (1) new diplomatic channels for a nation to interact with other allies; (2) infrastructure such as airfields, radar bases, training facilities, and command and control facilities; and (3) command and staff headquarters. These jointly produced private goods in effect constitute payoffs or side-payments which are available to alliance members as a result of the alliance's production of military security. Exclusion from these divisible benefits is possible. Thus, to increase such jointly produced private goods, more of the public good must be supplied. Under these conditions, alliance members may choose to mask their true demand preferences for the private good and choose instead to be more cooperative by supplying more of the collective good, anticipating greater private goods as a by-product.[18]

It was suggested earlier that some allies may "bribe" others through side-payments to increase their colleagues' share in producing the public good. Bribery is one method of revealing preferences for greater public good production while remaining silent on the jointly produced private benefits the "briber" may expect from increased supply of the public good.

Thus, the addition to alliance payoffs of sizable divisible benefits in the form of jointly produced private externalities may force nations to reveal their demand preferences for the public good to a greater extent than would be expected when only indivisible payoffs are provided. Restated in terms of strategy choice, greater cooperative behavior would be expected.

The three examples of jointly produced private goods are found in NATO. NATO Infrastructure provides the public works facilities necessary to the production and supply of security in the Alliance. The construction and operation of these facilities produces domestic employment and a boost to the economy of the nation in whose territory the facilities are located. While NATO Infrastructure facilities are for the use of all NATO nations, and thus provide collective benefits, they also confer private benefits to the host nations (as well as some costs: the host nation must provide necessary land, roads, and utilities).[19] Infrastructure benefits are not perfectly divisible, however, since their distribution is dependent to some extent on factors of geographic location.[20]

NATO Headquarters offers additional jointly produced private benefits, although these private goods are much more lumpy than infrastructure benefits, and accrue to only one nation (Belgium). However, NATO Headquarters and the associated commands provide the bureaucratic structure and staffs to facilitate a variety of diplomatic and military interaction opportunities, including consultation and access to other nations' policy-makers. The emergence of a consulting group such as Eurogroup within NATO is an example of a diplomatic channel which from a European nation's point of view could be a private good.[21]

WEAKNESSES OF SOME PRIOR STUDIES

Four studies directly address the effect of type of payoff on the behavior of coalition members. One uses experimental or simulation methods (Burgess and Robinson, 1969), while the other three are empirical case studies of NATO (Olson and Zeckhauser, 1966; Beer, 1971; Shaffer, 1975).[22]

Olson and Zeckhauser attempt to test implications of Olson's economic theory of alliances. The model they develop posits that the defense expenditures of an alliance member are a function of the costs incurred, defense expenditures of allies,[23] and the value a nation places on defense. They treat deterrence as a pure public good in an alliance, and assume that defense is produced at constant costs for all alliance members. Also in determining contributions, alliance members do not take into account the reactions of other members to the strategy selected.

Olson and Zeckhauser show for NATO that the burden is not shared according to a proportionality criterion defined as the ratio of defense expenditures to Gross National Product (GNP). Their finding is evidence that several members of the NATO Alliance seem to be adopting a competitive approach. However, Olson and Zeckhauser find that this disproportionality can be reduced by altering the pattern of incentives in NATO—i.e., by providing more private benefits in the alliance.[24]

Beer (1971) criticizes a number of the assumptions and operational decisions of Olson and Zeckhauser, and replicates their analysis of NATO, using additional indicators and more appropriate statistical techniques. Two major criticisms are the treatment of the common defense as a pure public good, and the measurement of proportionality of burden sharing. Beer is led to place less emphasis on the nature of the payoffs in the alliance (i.e., whether they are public or private) and to focus on the presence or absence of institutionalization as the major causal agent in determining the behavior of members toward their alliance. Beer finds only moderate support for the findings of the Olson-Zeckhauser study. Perhaps most interesting is his conclusion that the institutionalization of a mechanism for supplying alliance goods replaces disproportionality of burden sharing with "countervailing disproportionality" in which members pay more than their fair share for some programs and less for others.

In a time-series study of national defense expenditures by NATO Allies during the period 1950-1969, I found no apparent substitutability of U.S. defense expenditures for the expenditures of other Allies, i.e., increases in spending by the U.S. were met by increases in defense spending by other Allies (Shaffer, 1975). The public goods model predicts the opposite, due to the presence of indivisible (collective) benefits; as U.S. expenditures increase, Allies' expenditures decrease. This study presents evidence on the importance of side-payments in NATO as incentives for increased defense spending by U.S. Allies.

Burgess and Robinson (1969) test two propositions: (1) coalition cohesion is affected by supplementing collective with private benefits; and (2) coalition effectiveness is affected by adding private benefits. They find that both cohesion and effectiveness are increased by the addition of private benefits to the coalition. Since Burgess and Robinson use the Inter-Nation Simulation, however, they are not able to isolate the main effects of private benefits from the extraneous variance introduced by the INS model itself. That is, the programmed constraints on the decision-makers might have interacted with the experimental conditions (private benefits) to produce the increase in alliance cohesion and effectiveness.

The review of this literature highlights several limitations. First, there has been surprisingly little attention to the effect of differences in the divisibility of payoffs on members' actions toward the alliance, and the empirical findings are equally sparse.

Second, many of the studies have been constrained by assumptions and limiting conditions which may do extreme violence to alliances. For example, Olson and Zeckhauser (1966) assume that defense is a pure public good, despite the serious weakness of this position.[25] Burgess and Robinson (1969) assert that their experimental coalitions face a common and constant threat; the effect is to control for external threat in their design. Further, several of the studies are cross-sectional (Olson and Zeckhauser, 1966; Burgess and Robinson, 1969), and the external validity (generalizability) of simulation work is open to serious doubt.

Perhaps the most troublesome and potentially damaging constraints are to be found in the treatment of the problem of proportionality and in the dichotomous definition of both alliance payoffs and alliance strategies. The meaning of proportionality of burden sharing has significant implications for the conceptual and operational treatment of collective benefits in alliances as well.

It seems quite clear in the theory of public goods that proportionality should be determined by a cost-benefit calculus. Olson (1965: 29) states that "since no one has an incentive to provide any more of the collective good, once the member with the largest [individual fraction of the total value of the collective good] . . . has obtained the amount he wants, it is also true that the distribution of the burden of providing the public good . . . will *not* be in proportion to the benefits conferred by the collective good." Olson and Zeckhauser (1966: 30) reaffirm this principle, noting that a member will pay a disproportionate share when "It will pay a share of the costs that is larger than its share of the benefits."[26] However, the empirical indicator of proportionality is ability-to-pay, and it is measured as a ratio of defense expenditures to GNP (Olson and Zeckhauser, 1966; Beer, 1971; Russett, 1970). The only exception is Ypersele de Strihou (1968) who discusses the benefit criterion and alternative operational approximations.

The benefit derived from a public good is determined by the utility function of the consumer.[27] The utility of the public good supplied by a military alliance may be a function of the level of external threat to security; the greater the perceived threat, the more valuable the collective good the alliance supplies. For example, Russett (1970: 115) states that the Warsaw Treaty Organization members may "set their own levels of contribution in accordance with their own perceptions of security needs."[28]

There are likely to be other benefits members derive from alliances that are less dependent on (or entirely independent of) the importance of security. Such benefits would be acquired as the result of providing the common good. These might include internal security, increases in trade or improvement of balance of payments, and a generally positive effect on the domestic economy (Russett, 1970: 127-156). Thus, it might be argued that the more positive the domestic economic effect of the alliance, the more valuable it is to be a member.

The mistake of believing that the weight given these or other factors in the calculation of alliance benefits will be the same for all alliance members should not be made. It is very likely that utility functions vary both across members and across time. To the extent that members' evaluations of the public good at the margin differ, the marginal cost they are willing to pay will also vary across members. Variable benefits derivable from a collective good also indicate that the commodity departs from a pure public good by the failure of one or both criteria of nonrivalness and nonexcludability to be met. The commodity may not be equally available to all members, for example, leading to reduced benefits for some.

A second limitation of the literature is introduced by the dichotomous definition of alliance payoffs and strategy. Payoffs are seen as either only collective or both collective and private. Nations' strategies toward an alliance are treated as cooperative or competitive. Some evidence suggests a link between the addition of private benefits in alliances and a reduction in competitive behavior within the alliance (Burgess and Robinson, 1969). But competitive behavior in an alliance may be increasing or decreasing due to the mix between collective and private benefits. For example, a variety of threshold effects might occur. An alliance member might pursue a more cooperative strategy only so long as the amount of private side-payments provided justified the costs of foregoing private good production in order to produce the public good. Similarly, a nation might choose to follow a mixed strategy toward an alliance, behaving in a cooperative way on some kinds of issues and in a competitive manner on others. Thus, the dichotomous definitions of payoffs and strategy should be seen as representing the polar extremes of two continua, with the most interesting cases for study lying somewhere between the end points on both dimensions.

PUBLIC GOODS INTERACTION AS A MIXED-MOTIVE GAME

One way to understand the logic behind the argument linking type of payoff (public or private) to the strategy of nations in an alliance is through the theory of mixed-motive games.

The theory of games is a prescriptive, structural theory of choice behavior under conditions of uncertainty which has as a principal purpose the explication of the logic of strategic choice. Mixed-motive games are those in which the interests of the players are not strictly opposed (Rapoport and Guyer, 1969). Thus, we would expect to find cooperative as well as competitive behavior among the players. Mixed-motive refers to the "ambivalence of [one player's] . . . relation to the other player—the mixture of mutual dependence and conflict, or partnership and competition" (Schelling, 1960: 89).[29] A mixed-motive game of interest is prisoner's dilemma.

Prisoner's dilemma is characterized by a choice dilemma for the players. If each chooses a strategy maximizing his individual gain, both will end up with fewer payoffs than if they had cooperated with each other. That is, there are motivations (in the form of rewards and punishments) for the players both to cooperate, so as to maximize joint gains, and to compete, so as to maximize individual gains.

In any single play of prisoner's dilemma, the competitive strategy dominates—i.e., if each player is rational, he will select the competitive (minimax) strategy.[30] However, as Rapoport (1966) makes clear, while the competitive strategy is rational in the individual sense, it is not rational for the collectivity—i.e., for all players. For had both players selected cooperative strategies, both would have been better off.

The possibility exists in this variety of a mixed-motive game to exploit a cooperative opponent by competing. In such a situation, the competitive player is winning his maximum gain compared to the cooperative player's minimum gain. So one player can increase his payoffs at the expense of an opponent.

While dominant in a single play, the competitive strategy is abandoned for the cooperative strategy by players in iterative (dynamic) games (Rapoport and Chammah, 1965; Rapoport and Guyer, 1969). Without reviewing the extensive literature on experimental dynamic games, two conclusions are singled out.

First, strategy choice in iterative games is very sensitive to changes in the game's payoffs (Rapoport and Guyer, 1969; Guyer, n.d.). Guyer notes that as rewards for cooperating increase, cooperative strategy choice increases, while increasing the reward for competing reduces cooperative choice. Also, as the costs of cooperating with a competitive partner increase, cooperative strategy choice drops off. Second, experimental results indicate that cooperative strategy choice in the face of a competitive opponent will persist only up to a point (where presumably the costs become too great), at which such unilateral responses (i.e., one player is cooperative while the other is competitive) will be replaced by mutually competitive responses (Guyer n.d.). This shift in the pattern of interaction occurs fairly early in the course of the iterated plays.

Evidence of an experimental character which appears to contradict the unilateral response findings summarized above is provided by Shure, Meeker, and Hansford (1965) in a study of the efficacy of pacifist bargaining strategies. A significant finding is that a pure pacifist strategy (which means always choosing a cooperative strategy no matter what action the opponent takes) has extremely low efficacy in converting adversaries in an experimental game to do likewise. In fact, a negative conversion process is observed, such that by the end of the game, a larger number of subjects play competitively than did so at the outset of the game.

One further result linking payoffs to strategy choice in the Shure et al. study is that the amount of payoffs a player would receive as a result of his (and his adversary's) strategy choices was varied. Two options were presented: low payoffs, certainly less risky in case the adversary decided to compete; and high payoffs, which would lead to maximum gain if the adversary chose to cooperate, but maximum loss if he chose to compete. As the experimental subjects became increasingly aware of their adversaries' refusal to compete, they pressed for greater exploitation and hence higher payoffs.

There are several limitations of the Shure et al. study. First, it deals with the "ethically motivated cooperator" who bases his strategy choice on moral grounds. A second type of pacifist identified but not explicated in the study—the "resolute or strategic cooperator"—might more closely correspond to the dominant nation in an alliance that is supplying most of a public good to its allies. What differences in results, if any, might occur if other varieties of pacifist behavior were examined is not known.[31]

A second limitation is that while the game involved several plays and was thus iterative in character, the number of iterations was quite small (fifteen). Experimental game theory research has shown that a large number of iterations is necessary for mutual cooperative strategy choice to occur.

Finally, a potentially confounding factor was the presence of considerable group pressure on the experimental subjects to play competitively against the pacifist opponent.

The relevance of mixed-motive games to public goods theory and thus to the present inquiry is quite direct; the logic which underlies strategy choice in a prisoner's dilemma game is very similar to that which determines the choice of cooperative or competitive responses to providing a public good.[32] At an intuitive level, consider Olson's (1965) conclusion that a rational strategy for an individual player is to compete against the collective—in other words, not to contribute to the provision of a public good. In almost all cases, he will be better off with a competitive strategy: if the collective good is provided by the collective, he shares in its benefits, while if there is no provision (or a very sub-optimal supply) of a collective good, his losses are minimized.

Choice logic of this kind can be illustrated by constructing a prisoner's dilemma game matrix. Suppose there are two actors, A and B for each of whom the benefit is 10 units and the cost of producing the good is 14 units.[33] Assume that A and B are identical with respect to taste and resources, i.e., they have equivalent utility functions. This assumption simplifies the task considerably.[34] The logic of strategy choice is, however, a direct function of the payoffs in any particular game, and hence strategy choice is ultimately determined by a utility calculus.

Public goods interaction between actors A and B is shown in Figure 1. A's payoffs are listed first in each cell. Inspecting the matrix, note that if both actors choose to provide the good, their net payoffs are 3 units (or total benefits minus the actor's share of the cost—7 units). If Actor B chooses to provide the good while Actor A does not, B bears the total cost of supplying the good, and thus receives a negative "payoff" which is the net benefit of 10 units of gross benefit minus the cost of 14 units.

The relationships of the payoffs show that the dominant strategy for both actors is not to provide the public good—the competitive strategy. An actor can always do better choosing not to produce regardless of what strategy the other actor follows. This can be seen more clearly in the two matrices in Figures 2 and 3. Figure 2 shows only the net payoffs for Actor A, while

Actor B

	Produce (Cooperative)	Not Produce (Competitive)
Produce (Cooperative)	3, 3	-4,10
Not Produce (Competitive)	10,-4	0, 0

Actor A (label at left)

Figure 1: Public Goods Interaction as a 2-Person Prisoner's Dilemma Game

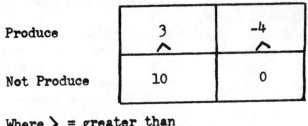

Produce	3	-4
Not Produce	10	0

Where $>$ = greater than

Figure 2: Actor A's Payoffs

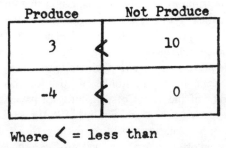

	Produce	Not Produce
	3	10
	-4	0

Where $<$ = less than

Figure 3: Actor B's Payoffs

Player 1
Provide

Player 2

Player 3	Provide	Not Provide
Provide	5,5,5	3,9,3
Not Provide	9,3,3	9,9,-3

Player 2
Not Provide

Player 2

Player 3	Provide	Not Provide
Provide	3,3,9	-3,9,9
Not Provide	9,-3,9	0,0,0

*Player 3's payoffs are listed first, followed by players 2 and 1.

Figure 4: Public Goods Interaction as an n-Person Prisoner's Dilemma Game

Actor B's net payoffs are given in Figure 3. In both matrices, the net payoffs for the competitive strategy are greater than those for the cooperative strategy.

Extending public goods interaction to an n-person game also shows that the logic of strategy choice is the same as that of the prisoner's dilemma. A three person game matrix is shown as Figure 4 where the total cost of the good is 12 units and the value is 9 units. Here again, the cell entries are net payoffs defined as gross benefits less the actor's share of costs. As in the two player case, the competitive strategy always dominates for all players. The stable equilibrium is the 0,0,0 cell—the intersection of the competitive strategies for all three players. Should one or even both of the other players cooperate, it is still more rational to compete.

It is unrealistic to specify only the pure strategies of provide/not provide public good as options for the players. Some payment is highly likely from all the players, although costs may not be shared in a proportionate manner. And some amount of public good, albeit sub-optimal for all players, is likely to be provided. As Buchanan (1967: 110) points out, expanding the two-strategy matrix into three strategy choices appears to eliminate a dominant solution, even in a single play of the game.

Despite these difficulties, it is the case that public goods interaction is logically identical to strategy choice in a prisoner's dilemma game. In addition to providing further support for Olson's conclusion that costs of alliance are not shared proportionately, there are two other implications relevant to the model developed here. First, indivisible collective alliance payoffs lead to the expectation of competitive behavior. Second, as the game is repeated over a period of time, the players may change their strategies.

Shifting from game theory to studies of coalition formation, there are experimental studies of the effect of divisibility of payoffs on strategies of choosing coalition partners. Nitz and Phillips (1969) experimentally test the hypothesis that decision rules of coalition partner choice depend upon the divisibility of the payoffs the coalition will provide. Their findings indicate that in the presence of highly divisible payoffs, the "anti-competitive" norm (Gamson, 1964) tends to be selected most frequently. That is, the decision rule is one which seeks to maximize intra-coalition cooperation. The major limitation of this research is its static quality; it provides no information about changes in strategy choice as the divisibility of payoffs varies.

A MODEL OF STRATEGY CHOICE IN ALLIANCES

I now summarize the theoretical work which is the foundation for the model and set out the model in the form of logically interconnected assumptions, limiting conditions, propositions, and hypotheses.

The model is based on the economic theory of alliances formulated by Olson (1965) and Olson and Zeckhauser (1966), but differs from it in several respects:

(1) Alliance payoffs are treated in terms of their divisibility and divisibility is a continuous variable, that is, the total payoffs provided by an alliance are divisible to a greater or lesser degree, while for Olson, payoffs are either divisible or indivisible.

(2) The value of an alliance to the members is dependent on the extent to which payoffs are divisible.

(3) The model seeks to explain the strategy choices of alliance members with respect to the alliance as a whole, over time, as a function of the divisibility of the alliance payoffs.

(4) Strategy choice also may be determined by a member's expectations regarding the strategy choices of other members of the alliance, where Olson explicitly does not allow for strategic behavior within the alliance.

(5) The potential applicability of the model is restricted to collective security and collective defense alliances which operate during periods characterized by the absence of major overt armed hostility between competing alliances.[35]

Having considered a sizable chunk of the literature in several different areas, it is helpful to review the major implications which determine our model.

Scholars in world politics propose a variety of factors which may influence the ratio of cooperative to competitive behavior in alliances. While there is little overall agreement (or evidence) on which factors are more important, it seems to be a very common assumption that the level of external threat in the alliance is important. The basic proposition of most of this work is that higher levels of threat produce greater internal cohesion in alliances. Reinterpreted in light of the concepts employed in this paper, external threat affects a nation's desire for security, which is a public good supplied by many international alliances. The value placed on this public good is thus determined by the amount of external threat.

The choice of an individual member's strategy toward the group is considered with greater rigor by Olson's (1965) theory of collective action. Cooperative action is viewed in terms of the member's evaluation of the utility of the public good at the margin, and the presence of selective incentives. Competitive behavior is the individually rational strategy of all group members, regardless of the potential gains from cooperating with each other.

This implication is strengthened when we recognize the similarity of choice logic underlying public goods interactions and prisoner's dilemma games. Alliances supplying collective goods thus have properties of mixed-motive situations in which there are pressures (in the form of payoffs) to cooperate as well as to compete. Although the competitive strategy is dominant in a single play of the game (assuming two possible strategies), a dominant solution may disappear if additional strategies are considered. And, to the extent that public goods interaction is a continuous (iterative) rather than episodic phenomenon, changes in the properties of the payoffs will have an effect on the ratio of cooperative to competitive strategy choices.

INDICATORS OF PRINCIPAL CONCEPTS

(1) Cooperative and competitive strategies: this does not refer to cooperation and conflict as these terms are used frequently in event/interaction models. Rather, a cooperative strategy is one in which the alliance member contributes a fair-share for the provision of the public good supplied by the alliance. A member following a competitive strategy contributes less than a fair-share, thus enjoying the benefits of the good at other members' expense. (2) Fair-share: this is a function of the benefits a member obtains from the alliance; the more benefits, the higher the contribution should be. (3) Value: this is the positive (or negative) effects of alliance membership in terms of economic, military, and political factors. Benefits are determined by subtracting the costs of supplying the good from the benefits. (4) Contributions: these are military expenditures. (5) Divisible and indivisible payoffs: an indivisible payoff is the public good supplied by the alliance—viz., security. Divisible payoffs are of two varieties: (a) unequally divisible payoffs—those which can be distributed across the alliance only in an unequal manner, e.g., infrastructure benefits which accrue to that member on whose territory airfields, radar locations, training institutions, and so on are located; (b) equally divisible payoffs—the distribution of these payoffs is not restricted or limited in any formal way, e.g., financial aid, technical assistance, and military training.

The following interrelated propositions lead to the model's principal hypothesis:

P_1:   A formal collective defense alliance is a voluntary association of relatively small size providing its members both public and private goods simultaneously.

P_2:   Interaction between the alliance members and the alliance as a whole directed toward the provision of these public and private benefits is an iterative process occurring through time.

P_3: The interactive process may be characterized as a mixed-motive situation, with a logic of strategy choice similar to that found in the prisoner's dilemma game.

P_4: There is a significant difference between the utility function of the dominant member of an alliance and those of the other smaller members.

P_5: The utility functions of alliance members are such that the members value benefits from the alliance in the amount of observable effect—i.e., a favorable impact of +1 is equal to +1 utiles, while a negative effect of -1 is equivalent to -1 utiles.

P_6: The value of the alliance derives from the provision of both public and private goods.

P_7: The benefits deriving from the public good are not necessarily dependent on the presence of private benefits, and vice-versa.

P_8: The public good can be defined in terms of production or supply units which are equally available to all alliance members, and thus can be held constant across members over time.

P_9: The benefits from the public good by and large will be the same at any given point in time for all the smaller members of an alliance. Thus, while the amount of benefit varies over time, the amount of benefit does not vary across members; thus the benefits of the public good may be held constant across members (controlled).

P_{10}: Across members, increments or decrements in benefits obtained from the alliance are a function of a decrease or increase in the amount of divisible payoffs in the alliance.

P_{11}: Alliance members behave as if they are rational actors, and they are capable of "learning" (through rewards and punishments) that cooperative behavior may increase the benefits from the alliance.

These propositions lead to the following major hypothesis, which is the statement of the major concepts and their interrelationships specified by the model:

When largely indivisible payoffs characterize an alliance, small member nations will tend to pursue a predominately competitive strategy toward the alliance; as the alliance introduces more divisible payoffs, these nations will tend to pursue a predominately cooperative strategy toward the alliance.

The model may be summarized by a simple mathematical function:

$$C_{it} = f(D_t, V_{it})$$

where: C_{it} = strategy choice for member i at time t
    D_t = the divisibility of payoffs in the alliance at time t
    V_{it} = the value of the alliance for member i at time t
and where: $V_{it} = g(P, M, E, S)$
with: g = some function
    P = political factors
    M = military factors
    E = economic factors
    S = security factors

Plausible alternative rival hypotheses include:

(1) A member's strategy choice is determined by expectations of the strategy choices of other members of the alliance regardless of the divisibility of payoffs.
(2) Strategy choice is a random process governed by stochastic factors.
(3) Strategy choice is a function of long-term trends in the economic prosperity of smaller nations; that is, as these nations increase their resources (wealth) their contributions to the provision of the public good may increase.
(4) Observed effects of payoff characteristics on strategy choice are specific to the measurement strategy and concepts employed in the study, and would disappear if other indicators or measures are employed.

To increase the tractability of the problem for empirical analysis, two additional simplifying assumptions are made which permit considering an alliance as approximating a closed system. The first assumption is that structural properties of the international system (e.g., bi-polarity, multi-polarity) do not interact with the hypothesized relationship between divisibility of payoffs and strategy choice. Second, extra-alliance inputs such as arms transfers are not confounding factors.

These assumptions do not suggest that we can ignore the fact that alliances interact with other alliances. Indeed, this factor is taken into account by linking the benefits obtained from the public good to the amount of threat felt by the alliance members from some internal or external enemy.

A further limiting condition is that alliances exist in an environment of uncertainty and risk. That is, misperceptions may occur; complete information is lacking.

CONCLUSION

This paper has explored the relevance of formal models of choice behavior to the functioning of international alliances through time. The result is a model of national strategy choice which predicts whether a nation will follow policies which result in either cooperation or competition with their allies.

The applicability of this model to alliances will be determined by its confrontation with empirical data. And here is found a major dilemma. A laboratory experimental design is one means of testing the model. In such a setting, rigorous experimental controls help insure internal validity; that is, extraneous confounding variance is controlled. Furthermore, the laboratory provides ample opportunities to formulate indicators and measures of major concepts such as payoffs, utilities, and value of the coalition. However, the generalizability (external validity) of experimental studies to international alliances is low, and one is confronted with findings that do not permit statements about the behavior of nations.

A quasi- or non-experimental design involving nations as units of analysis is the solution to the problem of external validity. But measurement of concepts such as utility rapidly leads one to despair of ready solutions.

It appears as if the scholar seeking to apply formal models of the kind developed in this paper to international alliances is impaled on the horns of a dilemma: internal and external validity cannot simultaneously be maximized. This dilemma accounts in part for the dearth of applications of formal theoretical approaches as explanatory models. Yet the parsimony and explanatory power of such approaches suggests more effort is needed to develop quasi- and non-experimental designs for investigating formal models.

NOTES

1. Divisibility of payoffs refers to the extent to which the payoffs can be disaggregated and distributed in different quantities to different recipients. In the language of public finance, perfectly divisible payoffs are private goods which can be consumed in varying amounts such that the consumption of the good by one consumer reduces the amount of the good available to another consumer. Perfectly indivisible payoffs are classed as public goods. Distribution of different amounts of the good to different consumers is impossible. As discussed later in the paper, divisible payoffs may be equally or unequally divisible.

2. An exception to this trend in the literature is the work of Bruce Bueno de Mesquita (1975). In a study of parliamentary coalitions, he develops a theory of coalition maintenance which predicts that in a certain kind of coalition competitive or mixed strategies will occur. In particular, see his discussion of determinants of coalition members' strategies (pp. 26-40). The theoretical formulation in this paper differs from

Bueno de Mesquita's by predicting strategy choice in alliances from the theory of public goods and joint products. See also Bueno de Mesquita and Singer (1973) and Holsti (1976).

3. For another statement of this argument, see Bueno de Mesquita (1975: 29-30).

4. Liska (1962: 28) makes a similar observation: "The chances of convergence are best when there are complexes of interests, encompassing identical, disparate, and even conflicting ones. Such complexes of interests are more likely to converge when actors rate disparate interests differently, preferably in an inverted hierarchy of importance. A certain amount of identical interests must, moreover, complement the conflicting ones and serve as a basis for adjusting them."

5. Liska (1962: 39) says that "offensive alliances tended to be uncommonly fragile. The best of allies do not easily maintain the singleness of positive purpose that is necessary if offensive action is to be effective. And the very success of an expansionist alliance tends to transform prior disparity of interests into conflict, most flagrantly when partners covet the same territory and seek equal gains."

6. See also Haas and Whiting (1956), and Russett (1968) for treatments of alliances as vehicles for increasing the capabilities of alliance members.

7. Liska (1962: 57), for example, says "In one way or another, intra-alliance conflicts bear on the gain-loss equation concerning policy aims and alliance strategy."

8. See, for example, Holsti, Hopmann, and Sullivan (1973) and Bueno de Mesquita and Singer (1973: 263-268).

9. A rigorous attempt to define cohesion in operational terms is undertaken by Holsti et al. (1973). They specify two indicators of alliance cohesion: (1) a behavioral component based on the ratio of cooperation and conflict in the interactions of alliance members; and (2) an attitudinal component which includes the degree of consensus about some external enemy (pp. 101-109).

10. The stability of preponderance of power in the structure of the international system is discussed by A. F. K. Organski (1968). Also see Deutsch et al. (1957) on the importance of a powerful and politically and economically developed core-area in promoting integration.

11. A difficulty with their paper is the vague and imprecise operationalization of cohesion as the presence or absence of behavior not conforming to "the alliance norm."

12. Discussions of public and private goods are found in, inter alia, Samuelson (1954; 1955; 1969), Head (1962), Steiner (1970), Buchanan (1968), and Burkhead and Miner (1971).

13. Size of group is regarded as an important factor determining members' behavior. Buchanan (1968) offers a clear treatment of group size. He notes that strategic behavior (i.e., one player's action influences the action of other players) is possible only in rather small groups. In large groups, the acts of a single member will have (and be perceived to have) no effect on the acts of any other player (cf. Olson, 1965: 44). Size is an imprecise concept, however, for one is never really clear on how large a large group is, and how small a small group should be. An alternative approach permits individual members of a group to estimate the impact on their behavior of the number of members by focusing on their subjective probability estimates of others' behavior (Buchanan, 1968; Frohlich and Oppenheimer, 1971).

14. By compete, I mean failing to pay a proportionate share of the burden of support for the alliance. Olson (1965: 29) specifically defines proportionality in terms of a cost-benefit analysis: "the distribution of the burden of providing the public good in a small group will not be in proportion to the benefits conferred by the collective good." See also pp. 33-52.

15. One logical but nonobvious implication of these two statements is that a decline in alliance "virtues" such as community of interest, may strengthen the effectiveness of an alliance by producing a high ratio of private to collective benefits (Olson and Zeckhauser, 1966: 36).

16. The concept of joint products is developed in Mishan (1969), Shibata (1972), and Samuelson (1969).

17. A Pareto optimal supply is achieved through adjustments in the price structure for the good rather than through adjustments in consumption since consumption of the good by one consumer does not reduce the amount available for consumption by others (Burkhead and Miner, 1971: 29).

18. This case is the opposite of the familiar case in the literature on joint products concerning the relevance of joint production to production externalities, where these externalities are collective economies or diseconomies resulting from production inter-dependence. In this case the classic free-rider problem exists because any single producer of a private good will find it rational (under certain conditions) to disguise demand preferences for the collective externality (Shibata, 1972: 30-32). The case developed in this paper concerns jointly produced collective goods yielding an externality that is a private good from the point of view of each producer. Under these circumstances, an impetus exists to reveal preferences for the collective good in order to maximize private benefits.

19. The NATO Infrastructure program is financed by the Alliance through voluntary contributions from the Allies based on an agreed-upon cost-sharing scheme. Data from the years 1963 and 1974 show that in general the NATO nations which enjoy the greater private benefits from the Infrastructure program exert much more effort in financing the program relative to national defense expenditures to help supply the Alliance's public good. The biggest contributor to NATO Infrastructure is the United States, whose 1974 contribution was almost thirty percent of the total. (These data are taken from Shaffer, 1975, and Office of the Secretary of Defense, International Security Affairs, the Pentagon, 1976.) The U.S. has no projects located on its territory. However, the United States may obtain primarily private benefits through its use of NATO facilities to pursue U.S. foreign policy goals, for example, by giving the United States a military presence in foreign territory, and through forward bases. The United States used NATO facilities to aid in its supply efforts to Israel in the 1973 mid-East war.

20. According to the Office of Secretary of Defense, International Security Affairs (OSD/ISA), West Germany and Turkey have been the primary beneficiaries of NATO Infrastructure since 1951, based on their percentage shares of programmed NATO Infrastructure work (18.7 and 13.7 percent respectively). (OSD/ISA, 1976: 8.)

21. The Eurogroup relies on the British mission to NATO to act as its secretariat.

22. Additional studies of alliances from the perspective of collective goods include Pryor (1968), Olson and Zeckhauser (1967), Russett (1970), Russett and Sullivan (1971), and Ypersele de Strihou (1968).

23. "... each ally's military spending provides an external economy to the other allies" (p. 45).

24. A critique of Olson and Zeckhauser's work is provided by William Loehr (1973).

25. Beer (1971) manages to ignore this thorny problem by focusing on institution-alization as the major variable.

26. See also Beer (1971).

27. See H. Aaron and M. McGuire (1970) for a demonstration of the high sensitivity of benefits from public goods expenditures to the utility function of the consumer.

28. Russett argues in a similar fashion for NATO members (Russett, 1970: 110-111). Burgess and Robinson (1969), by controlling threat, cannot isolate this effect.

29. Gamson defines a coalition as the "joint use of resources to determine the outcome of a decision in a mixed-motive situation involving more than two units." The coalition situation according to Gamson

is defined by mixed motive, n-person games. In such games, there is an element of conflict, since there exists no outcome which maximizes the payoffs to everybody. There is an element of coordination, since there exists for at least two of the players the possibility that they can do better by coordinating their resources than by acting alone.

See Gamson (1964: 85).

Other examples of collective goods interaction as a prisoner's dilemma are found in Russell Hardin (1971), Buchanan (1967), and Riker and Ordeshook (1973: 250-252). It has been suggested that deterrence alliances produce a collective good. The bargaining process involved in deterrence has been presented as a mixed-motive non-constant sum game. That is, there are both divergent and shared interests. The former constitute the arena of conflict between threatening party and the object of the threat. Shared interests include the mutual desire of both parties to avoid the threat being carried out. See Schelling (1960: 15, 89) and passim, Snyder (1971), and Rapoport (1967).

30. Prisoner's dilemma is based on the assumption that there is no communication between the players and complete information is lacking. Therefore, in selecting a strategy, each player assumes that the other is rational and (assuming similar preference schedules for players) will select the non-cooperative strategy. This process of adjustment to the adversary's anticipated behavior under imperfect information leads to the game's dilemma and the intersection of non-cooperative strategies for both players as the equilibrium solution. Conceptualizing collective goods interaction as a prisoner's dilemma game implies that these same assumptions apply to the interactions of group members in achieving the group's common goal.

31. Motivation of the behavior is important in the Shure et al. study because it is built into the context of the game situation—i.e., either the pacifist attempts to convince his adversary why he is taking the cooperative strategy, or the motivation is made clear by written communication.

32. Thus, in both the prisoner's dilemma game and collective goods interaction, each player takes into account how he thinks the other will behave. Whether or not a player assumes his behavior to be unimportant to the behavior of the other is immaterial, because in reality his behavior is taken into account by others. It therefore would not seem to be necessary to assume, as does Olson, that individuals have perfect information in order to arrive at the same conclusions regarding how the rational actor behaves.

33. The numbers selected to represent cost and benefit from the production of the public good are arbitrary; we could as easily have selected benefits of 1 unit and costs of .5 units per player. The only restriction imposed on the value of the numbers is that if each actor bears his equal share of the costs, benefits must outweigh costs for each player so that there is an initial incentive to produce the good. In calculating the payoffs to each player resulting from each of the possible strategies, two points should be noted. First, since the good produced is a public good, the total benefit is available to each player. Second, the payoff is defined as the value of the good minus its cost.

34. Should the preferences of the players differ significantly such that, for instance, one player places such a high utility on the provision of the good that he will provide it for himself regardless of how his partners behave, the non-cooperative strategy for the other players is still dominant. This is the case even if such information is not known. As information becomes available on utility schedules and it is clear that one partner will

(nearly) always be cooperative (this information assumption is a departure from the assumption of prisoner's dilemma games) the incentive for other players not to cooperate becomes even greater. If one player's preferences dictate he will pay for the good regardless of others' behavior, the 0,0,0 cell of n-prisoners' dilemma never occurs since some amount of the collective good is always provided. Such a situation is found in Olson's privileged group.

35. It would be an interesting extension of the model's generality to apply it to a war-time coalition such as the anti-Napoleonic coalition or the allied coalition of World War II, looking at the division of spoils as a variable.

BIBLIOGRAPHY

AARON, H. and M. MCGUIRE (1970) "Public Goods and Income Distribution." Econometrica 38(November): 907-920.

BEER, F. A. (1971) "The Political Economy of Alliances: Benefits, Costs and Institutions in NATO." Paper prepared for delivery at the 1971 Annual Meeting of the Amer. Pol. Sci. Assn. Chicago.

BRODY, R. (1963) "Some Systemic Effects of the Spread of Nuclear Weapons Technology." J. of Conflict Resolution VII (December): 663-753.

BUCHANAN, J. M. (1967) "Cooperation and Conflict in Public Goods Interaction." Western Economic Journal V (March): 109-121.

––– (1968) The Demand and Supply of Public Goods. Chicago: Rand McNally and Co.

BUENO DE MESQUITA, B. (1975) Strategy, Risk and Personality in Coalition Politics. Cambridge, Eng.: Cambridge Univ. Press.

––– and J. D. SINGER (1973) "Alliances, Capabilities, and War: A Review and Synthesis." In C. Cotter (ed.) Political Science Annual: An International Review. Vol. 4. Indianapolis, Ind.: Bobbs-Merrill.

BURGESS, P. and J. A. ROBINSON (1969) "Alliances and the Theory of Collective Action: A Simulation of Coalition Processes." In J. N. Rosenau (ed.) International Politics and Foreign Policy. New York: Free Press.

BURKHEAD, J. and J. MINER (1971) Public Expenditure. Chicago: Aldine Publishing Co.

CLAUDE, I. L. (1962) Power and International Relations. New York: Random House.

CROSS, J. G. (1967) "Some Theoretic Characteristics of Economic and Political Coalitions." J. of Conflict Resolution XI (June): 184-195.

DAWSON, R. and R. ROSECRANCE (1966) "Theory and Reality in the Anglo-American Alliance." World Politics XIX (October): 21-51.

DEUTSCH, K. W. et al. (1957) Political Community and the North Atlantic Area. Princeton: Princeton Univ. Press.

DINNERSTEIN, H. S. (1965) "The Transformation of Alliance Systems." Amer. Pol. Sci. Rev. 59(September): 589-601.

FOX, A. B. (1959) The Power of Small States. Chicago: Univ. of Chicago Press.

FRIEDMAN, J. R. (1970) "Alliances in International Politics." In J. R. Friedman, C. Bladen, and S. Rosen (eds.) Alliance in International Politics. Boston: Allyn and Bacon, Inc.

FROHLICH, N. and J. OPPENHEIMER (1972) "Entrepreneurial Politics and Foreign Policy." In R. Tanter and R. Ullman (eds.) Theory and Policy in International Relations. Princeton: Princeton Univ. Press.

GAMSON, W. A. (1964) "Experimental Studies of Coalition Formation." In L. Berko-
witz (ed.) Advances in Experimental Social Psychology. New York: Academic Press.

GUETZKOW, H. (1957) "Isolation and Collaboration: A Partial Theory of Internation
Relations." J. of Conflict Resolution I (March): 48-68.

GULICK, E. V. (1955) Europe's Classical Balance of Power. New York: W. W. Norton
and Co., Inc.

GUYER, M., "A Review of the Literature on Zero-sum and Non-zero-sum Games in the
Social Sciences." Univ. of Michigan, Mental Health Research Inst., mimeo.

HAAS, E. and A. WHITING (1956) Dynamics of International Politics. New York:
McGraw Hill.

HARDIN, R. (1971) "Collective Action as an Agreeable N-prisoners' Dilemma." Behavioral Science 16(September): 416-424.

HEAD, J. (1962) "Public Goods and Public Policy." Public Finance: 197-219.

HOLSTI, K. J. (1977) International Politics: A Framework for Analysis. (3rd ed.)
Englewood Cliffs, N.J.: Prentice-Hall, Inc.

HOLSTI, O. R. (1976) "Alliance and Coalition Diplomacy." In J. N. Rosenau, K. W.
Thompson, and G. Boyd (eds.) World Politics: An Introduction. New York: Free
Press.

——— and J. SULLIVAN (1969) "National-International Linkages: France and China as
Nonconforming Alliance Members." In J. N. Rosenau (ed.) Linkage Politics. New
York: Free Press.

KAPLAN, M. A. (1957) System and Process in International Politics. New York: John
Wiley and Sons, Inc.

KISSINGER, H. A. (1957) A World Restored: Metternich, Castlereagh and the Problems
of Peace 1812-1822. London: Weidenfeld and Nicholson.

LISKA, G. (1962) Nations in Alliance: The Limits of Interdependence. Baltimore: Johns
Hopkins Press.

LOEHR, W. (1973) "Collective Goods and International Cooperation: Comments."
International Organization 27(Summer): 421-430.

MISHAN, E. J. (1969) "The Relationship Between Joint Products, Collective Goods, and
External Effects." J. of Pol. Econ. 77(May): 329-348.

MORGENTHAU, H. J. (1967) Politics Among Nations. (4th ed.) New York: Alfred A.
Knopf.

NITZ, L. H. and J. PHILLIPS (1969) "The Effect of Divisibility of Payoff on Confed-
erate Behavior." J. of Conflict Resolution XIII (September): 381-387.

Office of the Secretary of Defense, International Security Affairs (1976) "NATO
Infrastructure Program." Mimeo (March).

OLSON, M. Jr. (1965) The Logic of Collective Action. New York: Schocken Books.

——— and R. ZECKHAUSER (1966) "An Economic Theory of Alliances." Review of
Economics and Statistics 48(August): 266-279.

——— (1967) "Collective goods, Comparative Advantage, and Alliance Efficiency." In R.
McKean, (ed.) Issues in Defense Economics. New York: Nat. Bur. of Economic
Research.

ORGANSKI, A.F.K. (1968) World Politics. (2nd ed.) New York: Alfred A. Knopf.

PRYOR, F. A. (1968) Public Expenditures in Communist and Capitalist Nations.
Homewood, Ill.: Richard D. Irwin, Inc.; Nobleton, Ontario: Irwin-Dorsey, Ltd.

RAPOPORT, A. (1966) Two-person Game Theory: The Essential Ideas. Ann Arbor:
Univ. of Michigan Press.

——— (1967) "Games Which Simulate Escalation and Deterrence." Peace Research
Reviews I (August): 1-76.

––– and M. GUYER (1969) "The Psychology of Conflict Involving Mixed-motive Decisions." Univ. of Michigan: Mental Health Research Inst.

––– and A. M. CHAMMAH (1965) Prisoner's Dilemma: A Study in Conflict and Cooperation. Ann Arbor: Univ. of Michigan Press.

RIKER, W. H. (1962) The Theory of Political Coalitions. New Haven: Yale Univ. Press.

––– and P. C. ORDESHOOK (1973) An Introduction to Positive Political Theory. Englewood Cliffs, N.J.: Prentice-Hall, Inc.

ROTHSTEIN, R. L. (1968) Alliances and Small Powers. New York: Columbia Univ. Press.

RUSSETT, B. M. (1963) "The Calculus of Deterrence." J. of Conflict Resolution VII (June): 97-109.

––– (1963) Community and Contention: Britain and America in the Twentieth Century. Cambridge, Mass.: M.I.T. Press.

––– (1968) "Components of an Operational Theory of International Alliance Formation." J. of Conflict Resolution XII (September): 285-301.

––– (1970) What Price Vigilance? The Burden of National Defense. New Haven: Yale Univ. Press.

––– and J. D. SULLIVAN (1971) "Collective Goods and International Organization." International Organization XXV (Autumn): 845-865.

SAMUELSON, P. A. (1954) "The Pure Theory of Public Expenditures." Review of Economics and Statistics 36(November): 387-390.

––– (1955) "Diagrammatic Exposition of a Theory of Public Expenditure." Review of Economics and Statistics 37(November): 350-356.

––– (1969) "Contrast Between Welfare Conditions for Joint Supply and for Public Goods." Review of Economics and Statistics 51(February): 26-30.

SANDLER, T. and J. CAULEY (1975) "On the Economic Theory of Alliances." J. of Conflict Resolution XIX (June): 330-348.

SCHELLING, T. (1960) The Strategy of Conflict. London: Oxford Univ. Press.

SHAFFER, S. M. (1975) "The Influence of Threat and Alliance Setting on National Defense Expenditures: NATO, 1950-1969." Unpublished Ph.D. dissertation, Univ. of Michigan.

SHIBATA, H. (1972) "Joint Production, Externality, and Public Goods." In R. M. Bird and J. G. Head (eds.) Modern Fiscal Issues: Essays in Honor of Carl S. Shoup. Toronto and Buffalo: Univ. of Toronto Press.

SHURE, G. H., R. J. MEEKER, and E. A. HANSFORD (1965) "The Effectiveness of Pacifist Strategies in Bargaining Games." J. of Conflict Resolution IX (March): 106-117.

SNYDER, G. H. (1971) " 'Prisoner's Dilemma' and 'Chicken' Models in International Politics." International Studies Quarterly 15(March): 66-103.

STEINER, P. O. (1970) "The Public Sector and the Public Interest." In R. H. Haveman and J. Margolis (eds.) Public Expenditures and Policy Analysis. Chicago: Markham Publishing Co.

WAGNER, R. H. (1973) "National Defense as a Collective Good." Paper prepared for delivery at the 1973 Annual Meeting of the Amer. Pol. Sci. Assn. New Orleans.

WOLFERS, A. (1959) "Collective Defense Versus Collective Security." In A. Wolfers (ed.) Alliance Policy in the Cold War. Baltimore: Johns Hopkins Press.

––– (1962) Discord and Collaboration: Essays on International Politics. Baltimore: Johns Hopkins Press.

––– (1968) "Alliances." In D. Sills (ed.) International Encyclopedia of the Social Sciences. Vol. I. New York: Macmillan and Free Press.

YPERSELE DE STRIHOU, J. M. van (1968) "Sharing the Defense Burden Among Western Allies." Yale Economic Essays 8(Spring): 261-320.

PART III

TRANSACTIONS IN THE INTERNATIONAL ARENA

Chapter 7

THE TECHNOLOGY OF
TRANSNATIONAL ENVIRONMENTAL EXTERNALITIES

V. KERRY SMITH
Resources for the Future

177-90

I. INTRODUCTION

Economics finds much of its historical roots in the fascination of eighteenth century philosophers with some special features of one form of social interaction—the market. That is, perfectly functioning markets were found to offer an interaction process in which an individual's marginal valuation for the goods or services involved was revealed through the mechanism of exchange. As a result any resources which were exchanged on such markets were necessarily allocated to their highest valued use. Thus "the invisible hand" assured an efficient resource allocation. Unfortunately, this fascination retarded interest in the practical significance of the effects of certain production and consumption activities which were not capable of direct accommodation by the actions of the private economic "actors" alone. These effects have been given a number of different labels—external economies and externalities being among the most common designations. An externality is said to occur when an economic entity's (consumer or firm) satisfaction or productive ability is influenced by factors whose levels are selected by other entities without concern or recognition of the effects to that party (or parties).[1] Examples of the failure to accord externalities proper attention abound in the early literature on price theory and welfare economics. One notable example is a seminal paper by Scitovsky in which he argued that:

> The examples of external economies given by Meade are somewhat bucolic in nature, having to do with bees, orchards, and woods. This, however, is no accident: *it is not easy to find examples from industry.* ... For more detailed discussion the reader is referred to Meade's article, which will, I think, convince him of the scarcity of technological external economies (Scitovsky, 1954: 144 [emphasis added]).

The growing concern over the quality of life, in general, and environmental degradation, in particular, during the late sixties and early seventies has

AUTHOR'S NOTE: Fellow, Quality of the Environment Division, Resources for the Future. Thanks are due Todd Sandler for suggestions related to this research.

stimulated renewed interest in all types of external effects.[2] The purpose of this paper is to consider the implications of the technical mechanisms generating environmental externalities in order to enhance our understanding of their effects in an international setting. While the discussion will focus on transnational externalities it has direct implications for localized external effects as well. The objective of the discussion is to indicate that some aspects of transnational externalities may be simplified by the inherent nature of the generation and transport mechanisms for them.

Following these introductory remarks the paper consists of four sections. Section II discusses the conventional treatment of production externalities and the implications of a generalization which reflects the important role of common property environmental resources in the context of a simple two country model. In Section III, the implications of revising this framework to impose separability restrictions of the nature of the production technology are outlined. Section IV outlines the relevance of these results to the problems associated with measuring the welfare losses associated with transnational externalities and to the literature on second best problems. Section V summarizes the conclusions of the paper, and their potential implications for policy.

II. PRODUCTION EXTERNALITIES: CONVENTIONAL PRACTICE AND A GENERALIZATION

Transnational externalities can stem from the interactions between economic entities of different countries in a variety of ways. d'Arge (1975) has recently offered a useful taxonomic framework based on their source and impact. That is, he defines his framework in terms of answers to two questions. Do the externalities originate in production or consumption activities and do they affect consumption or production activities?[3] For our purposes it is sufficient to focus on the production to production type of externality, which he has suggested are among the dominant current cases of transfrontier (or transnational) environmental externalities.

The most direct means of illustrating the central components of the conventional model (for this case) is in terms of the transformation functions for two countries.[4] We will assume that one country is the emitter (e) and the other the receptor (r). In addition, each country will be assumed to be capable of producing two marketable goods X and Y. These production activities in one country (e) generate the externalities (Z) which interfere with production in the second (r). Thus the situation can be described with their transformation functions in equations (1) and (2):

(1) $T_e(X_e, Y_e, R_e, Z) = 0$

(2) $T_r(X_r, Y_r, R_r, Z) = 0$

where R_e, R_r represent the resource endowments of each country available for production activities.[5]

As it stands this representation resembles the conventional two person production externality model. There are, however, some differences which only become apparent when we define the Pareto-optimal resource allocation conditions. In order to do so we must represent collective preferences in each country. For simplicity we shall use community utility functions to serve this end, recognizing the potential difficulties in relating community to individual preferences.[6] Equations (3) and (4) define these utility functions:

(3) $U_e = U_e(X_e, Y_e + Y_I)$

(4) $U_r = U_r(X_r, Y_r - Y_I)$

with Y_I designating the quantity of Y which exchanges in international trade between the two countries.[7]

Assuming these four relationships are all classically well-behaved, we can define the conditions necessary for a Pareto-optimal resource allocation as the first order conditions associated with maximizing the constrained objective function given in equation (5):

(5) $G = U_e(X_e, Y_e + Y_I) + \lambda[U_r(X_r, Y_r - Y_I) - \bar{U}]$
         $+ \theta_1[T_e(X_e, Y_e, R_e, Z)] + \theta_2[T_r(X_r, Y_r, R_r, Z)]$

The familiar necessary conditions[8] for a maximum of equation (5) are given in equations 6 and 7, in terms of the marginal rates of substitution (MRS) and transformation (MRT) in each country.[9]

A		B	
(6) MRS^e_{XY}	$= MRT^e_{XY}$	$= MRT^r_{XY}$	$= MRS^r_{XY}$
(7) MRT^e_{XZ}	$= - MRT^r_{XZ}$		

The first equation establishes the Pareto efficiency of free trade. That is, in the absence of trade we can expect each country seeking to allocate its resources efficiently will satisfy the A and B components of equation (6). Free trade assures that the exchange process leads (in the absence of differential bargaining power for either country) to an outcome consistent with the globally efficient conditions (i.e., A=B).

Equation (7) arises because the transnational externality, Z, is internalized through the statement of the objective function. Free trade will not lead to the satisfaction of this condition. Hence there is a clear rationale for concern over the appropriate international control mechanisms in the presence of transnational externalities. What differentiates this case (as described here) from that of the conventional treatment of two-party externalities is primarily the institutional difficulties associated with either bargaining or imposed solutions. There is unlikely to be much debate over the view that there are exceptionally difficult problems involved in the making the parties involved in international externalities take full account of the effects of their individual actions. Any appeal to the Coasian (1960) theorem, which states that a resource will be put to its highest valued use regardless of the initial assignment of rights to it, can be seriously questioned when we are dealing with rights to the services of international common property resources. Nonetheless, there are some aspects of the problem which have not been completely developed and offer the potential of modest simplifications in these complexities.

The first of these issues concerns the relationship between the patterns of use of the services of common property environmental resources and the magnitude of the external effects. Simply stated, how does the Z produced by country e get to country r? At first, one might suggest this is trivial for, after all, we should be able to define any functional relationship between the emissions and received external effect. Since this relation is a purely technical one (i.e., the result of a river tributary system, the pattern of air diffusion, etc.), it need not be given explicit consideration. Specifically, if the external effect received by country r is w and there is some relationship between w and the emission of country e, Z, as in equation (8), then we need only embed this relation in our transformation function for e as in equation (9):

$$(8) \quad w = f(Z)$$

$$(9) \quad \bar{T}_r(X_r, Y_r, R_r, w) = \bar{T}_r(X_r, Y_r, R_r, f(Z)) = T_r(X_r, Y_r, R_r, Z)$$

There are two problems with this penchant for simplification. First, $T_r(\ )$ need not satisfy the properties of a well-behaved transformation function. Moreover, this outcome can be shown to be completely consistent with a classically well-behaved $\bar{T}_r(\ )$ function. Second, it ignores the potential information available from $f(Z)$.

Consider the first of these objections. Page and Ferejohn (1974) recently noted the important role "environmental transfer functions," our f(Z), play in the policy making process with externalities:

> Important policy implications follow from the degree of convexity of the environmental transfer functions. The more concave are the g [transfer functions], the more likely we are to recommend all or nothing policy prescriptions (p. 457).

Scott's discussion of the problems associated with the economics of the international transmission of pollution is also related to this issue. He argues in favor of greater research directed to the role played by the common property resources receiving the emissions of residuals, and, in turn, responsible for their diffusion:

> ... instead of concentrating on the international trade consequences of alternative national systems of abating pollution from pulp and paper plants, economists should also be participating in research into how the riparian nations are going to organise a common water receptor, the ambient air, and international river or the ocean in order to achieve certain environmental rights (Scott, 1972: 261).

The problem, it seems, arises from a failure to recognize that the source of the external effect should be treated as a joint output with X_e and Y_e for the country responsible, and as an input for the country experiencing its effects. The nature of the transfer mechanism embodied in the common property environmental resource which receives the residuals determines the effect (w) transmitted to country r for given levels of emissions (Z).

The recognition of this role of the externality in the emitting and receiving countries forms the basis for our generalized view of transnational externalities. Thus the generalization does not arise because it is possible to specify a single functional statement which encompasses all cases without a great deal of specific features for any one of them. Rather it stems from a more complete accounting of the mechanisms involved in externalities. That is, the externalities discussed here arise because the firms in one country use the services of international common property resources to dispose of the residuals jointly produced in the fabrication of X and Y. By definition, a common property resource is one which does not allow for exclusion or discrimination with respect to access to its use (Krutilla and Fisher, 1975: 20-21). The transfer functions are then technical relationships which indicate how certain use patterns affect the services of these common property resources available to other economic agents. If we substitute for w as in equation (9) and deal with general specifications, then we are, in effect, ignoring the information these transfer relationships may have to offer. This point is most readily apparent when we consider the case of several emissions. For example, if we know that several pollutants combine to form photochemical smog, and this smog is the source of an externality to the receptor country, then the information associated with the environmental transfer function plays the same role as a separability restriction on $T_r(\ )$. More generally, it may also be possible to impose additional separability restrictions on $T_r(\ )$ and $T_e(\ )$ simply because we can view Z as a joint output for country e and as affecting an input to country r. As d'Arge aptly notes, an important aspect of measuring the effects of transfrontier externalities, particularly the wealth effects, is the manner in which the externality "enters production functions in both emitter and receptor nations" (1975: 404). We propose to discuss these issues in more detail in what follows.

III. A REVISED MODEL

In what follows we argue that it is possible to simplify the analysis of the consequences of transnational externalities with separability restrictions to the transformation function for the receiving country. These restrictions will arise from two sources:

(a) the environmental transfer functions describing the relationship between emissions and the "received" externality;
(b) the nature of the production process for the receptor country.

The first of these restrictions requires the presence of more than one residual by-product to the production process in country e.[10] Thus, if we amend equation (1) to conform to the specification given in equation (10) and assume the external effect is embodied in a single variable, w, then knowledge of the transfer function can simplify the analysis of the role of intervention to achieve an efficient resource allocation.

(10) $T_e^*(X_e, Y_e, R_e, Z_1, Z_2) = 0$

(11) $w = g(Z_1, Z_2)$

This point is readily seen when we compare the results of the maximization of equation (5) with revised constraints consisting of equations (10) and (12) versus equations (10), (11), and (13).

(12) $T_r^*(X_r, Y_r, R_r, Z_1, Z_2) = 0$

(13) $\overline{T}_r(X_r, Y_r, R_r, w) = 0$

In the first case, a Pareto-efficient allocation of resources requires equation (6) to be satisfied together with equations (14) and (15) as replacements for equation (7).

(14) $MRT^e_{XZ_1} = -MRT^r_{XZ_1}$

(15) $MRT^e_{XZ_2} = -MRT^r_{XZ_2}$

The second specification of the constraint set permits a direct relationship between $MRT_{XZ_1}{}^e$ and $MRT_{XZ_2}{}^e$ as in equation (16):

(16) $MRT^e_{XZ_1} = MRT^e_{XZ_2} \cdot \dfrac{g_{Z_1}}{g_{Z_2}}$

This point is so simple that it may be overlooked in addressing the practical problems associated with international environmental policy. For empirical analysis, measurement of the economic structure of production relationships and the implications of environmental externalities should be treated distinctly from the measurement of these transfer relations. Equally important, the definition of policy instruments and institutions to enforce them must reflect both economic and physical relationships. A concern for a more adequate description of the institutional requirements for a Pareto-efficient resource allocation led Plott and Meyer to describe the conventional treatment of public goods and externalities in much the same terms as we did at the outset. They noted:

> Production is the only basic activity in the standard characterization of a public good. Consumption is not a separate activity since it occurs automatically with production. If an irritant consumed by a person reaches him by means of some chain of events, e.g., irritant consumed depends upon the amount of smoke reaching him and thus upon the amount of smoke emission from the source, $C_i = C_i[s_i(X)]$, then the utility function is simply relabeled. *The intermediate consumption variables are eliminated and utility is expressed as a function of the amount of smoke produced at the source, e.g., $\tilde{U}_i\{C_i[s_i(X)]\} = \tilde{U}_i(X)$.* (Plott and Meyer, 1975: 65-66) [emphasis added].

This characterization, they argue, is "... close to being empty in content." Moreover, explicit treatment of the nature of the transfer mechanisms is found to be required for understanding the range of institutional alternatives feasible to attain Pareto-efficient resource allocations.[11] Thus the use of equations (10), (11), and (13) over (10) and (12) as the production constraints for a determining of Pareto-efficient resource allocation offers several advantages from the pragmatic perspective of policy making.

The second type of restriction must result from the inherent nature of the production relationships underlying the transformation functions and involves our ability to write the transformation function $T_r(\ )$ in a separable form. Recent advances in the testing of flexible functional forms in econometrics (see Christensen, Jorgenson and Lau, 1973; Brown, Caves and Christensen, 1975; and Bich and Smith, 1977) permit one to evaluate such separability restrictions empirically using either a transformation function or a joint output cost function. It is therefore reasonable to inquire into their advantages for the problems at hand. The central issue relates to whether $\overline{T}_r(\ )$ can be written as in equation (17)

$$(17) \quad \overline{T}_r(X_r, Y_r, R_r, w) = \tilde{T}_r(H(X_r, Y_r), R_r, w)$$

If it can, then equation (17) can be re-written with an input index and an output index distinctly identified as in equation (18).[12]

$$(18) \quad H(X_r, Y_r) - L(R_r, w) = 0$$

This restriction happens to be especially useful in the specification of joint output cost and profit functions corresponding to equation (18) (see Lau, 1969, Theorem XXIV and Corollary II of Theorem XXV as well as Hall, 1973).[13] Moreover, it has direct implications for the relationship between the Pareto-efficient conditions for goods exchanging in markets (i.e., X and Y) and the externalities (in this more general case with Z_1 and Z_2). The marginal rate of transformation between X and Y in the receiving country is independent of the level of the externality received. That is, the MRT_{XY}^r can be written as:

$$(19) \quad MRT_{XY}^r = \frac{\overline{T}_{rY}}{\overline{T}_{rX}} = \frac{\tilde{T}_H}{\tilde{T}_H} \cdot \frac{H_Y}{H_X} = \frac{H_Y}{H_X}$$

Thus a failure to satisfy the efficient conditions for the generation and dispersal of Z_1 and Z_2 in country r does not necessarily impact the domestic efficiency in the allocation of X and Y (i.e., segment B of equation (6)). In Section IV we explore the implications of this conclusion for the measurement of the welfare losses associated with transnational externalities and for second best policies.

IV. IMPLICATIONS

The measurement of the economic losses associated with externalities is a difficult problem both conceptually and operationally. When the externalities involved extend over national boundaries and the trade effects of various adjustment policies must be accounted for then the problems are compounded. Accordingly, it is not surprising that d'Arge has observed that if the resolution of such external effects results in shifts of the international prices of goods and services it can make the single emitter or receptor nation better or worse off (1975: 415). If, however, international prices can be assumed constant for the changes in externalities to be evaluated, then he argues, the corresponding wealth effects are related to the shift in the transformation function associated with the external effect. With our framework it is possible to directly relate such measures to the compensated demand for reductions in the externality. In order to do so it is convenient to use the equivalent representation of the transformation function—the joint ouput cost function.[14] This result follows from the duality principles between the production technology and cost function in the presence of cost minimizing behavior (see Shephard, 1953, and McFadden, 1977). Lau (1969) has shown that the joint output cost function corresponding to equation (17) is given by:

$$(20) \quad C_r(X_R, Y_R, P_R, w) = C_r(H(X_r, Y_r), P_R, w),$$

where the P_R equals shadow price of R. The previous analysis indicated, and it is easily demonstrated in this framework, that the domestic MRT for country r is independent of w. Thus using d'Arge's assumptions that international prices for X and Y remain fixed, the compensated inverse demand for reductions in w can be derived as:

$$(21) \quad \frac{\partial C_r}{\partial w} = u(H(\ ), P_R, w)$$

This relationship tells one how the expenditures necessary to maintain the "optimal" levels of X_r and Y_r in the presence of free trade would have to change when the externality changed. H( ) remains unchanged because a change in w does not affect the MRT and therefore the optimal levels of X_r and Y_r are fixed. Thus, d'Arge's observations provide a means of directly evaluating the marginal damages of the externality. It should be noted, however, that he did not require the separability assumption. The reason is straightforward—international prices are assumed fixed. The separability restriction allows one to say that u( ) is also the marginal damage function without trade. That is, the domestic supply conditions (i.e., MRT_{XY}^r) are invariant with respect to changes in w. Why then do we have to assume international prices are fixed? The answer emphasizes again the importance of recognizing the role the externalities play in each country. The Z's are joint outputs with X and Y for country e so that output separability of the transformation function would not assure that the MRT^e_{XY} would be fixed with changes in Z_1 or Z_2. Hence in this two country model, the international prices cannot necessarily be assumed independent of actions affecting Z_1 and Z_2. Separability of country r's transformation function identifies the source of the potential change to international prices as relating to the effects of compensation or charge schemes on e's MRT.

It is probably apparent that this discussion is also directly related to the theory of second best and piecemeal policy in the presence of externalities. The separability restrictions imposed here represent slightly more general formulations than those suggested by Davis and Whinston (1965). However, a recent paper by Dusansky and Walsh (1976) derives a more general class of separable objective and constraint functions which yield the overall conclusion that even in the presence of second best (Lipsey and Lancaster, 1956) constraints for so-called deviant commodities (i.e., our externalities) the conventional Paretian conditions for non-deviant commodities (our X and Y) continue to be optimal.[15]

Thus, these results taken together with our discussion of the potential reasons for separability restrictions permit a generalization of Negishi's (1972) theorem on second best conditions. His theorem proceeds as follows:

> In a second best problem, the Paretian conditions in the sense of equal marginal rates of substitution are still desirable for decision units *physically separable* from the deviant and the Paretian conditions in the sense of perfect competition and laissez faire remain untouched for decision units not only physically but also *pecuniarily separable* from the deviant (p. 156) [emphasis added].

Our extension suggests that these conditions can be expanded to include naturally separable and technologically separable restrictions. The first of these alternative ways of satisfying Paretian conditions in a second best world arises from taking direct account of the environmental transfer functions and the second from a recognition of the different role environmental externalities play for the emitter and receptor countries with the associated potential for further restrictions to the production technology.

V. SUMMARY

As the scope of man's production and consumption activities has expanded from the confines of a given geographic area to increasingly larger areas there appears to have been a corresponding increase in the environ-mental impacts of the residual by-products of these activities. The economic analysis of environmental externalities has tended to follow a similar progres-sion beginning with studies of externalities involving a small number of economic agents to cases where the nature of the environmental system appeared capable of defining boundaries which would "contain" the external effects (i.e., residuals management models for a river basin or air shed), and ultimately to problems involving many nations. In each case the expansion in scope, not surprisingly, resulted in a concomitant increase in the difficulty of the problems encountered in the development of workable policies.

This paper has argued within the context of a very simple model that there are often restrictions embedded in the technical mechanisms by which exter-nalities are generated that can serve to simplify the problems associated with designing policies to cope with environmental externalities. As we noted, Page and Ferejohn and Plott and Meyer have called for greater attention to the technology of the process of generation, dispersal and ultimate impact of some external effect of economic agents. The first of these authors com-mented on the problems transfer functions can introduce for the convexity conditions for conventionally defined solutions to externalities problems. The second set noted that the potential array of institutional mechanisms avail-able for inducing efficient resource allocation patterns is expanded with greater attention to the specification of this underlying technology of the externalities.

Both of these arguments can be considered in a more general context—namely how do we efficiently use information—economic, environmental or otherwise, in the development of public policies to redirect the allocation of resources. Whether a concern for the appropriate instrument or institution, the issues are similar and our point is that they are quite relevant to the special dimensions of transnational environmental externalities.

NOTES

1. For a detailed discussion of the concepts of externalities see Chapter One in this volume by Loehr and Sandler (1978). A clearcut review of the relationship between externalities and common property resources is also available in Krutilla and Fisher (1975) Chapter Two.

2. One widely cited evaluation of the adequacy of our natural resources (Barnett and Morse, 1963) anticipated the coming concern over environmental quality by noting:

> The problems we have just identified, [i.e., urban sprawl, conges-tion, pollution, disfigurement of the landscape, etc.] and others like them, have arisen because favorable technological changes, and the growth of output and population which they have made possible, have brought about certain unfavorable changes in other parameters

of our existence. Undesirable conditions have been created which it would be very costly for individuals and private enterprises to correct, or which exceed their capacity to act. Such conditions, therefore constitute social problems, which, if not solved deteriorate the quality of life (p. 261).

3. It is certainly possible to have the external effects from one set of activities in one country affect both production and consumption in another. For more details see d'Arge (1975: 401-402).

4. The transformation function describes the locus of alternative sets of outputs corresponding to vectors of inputs. It is simply another more general statement of the family of production possibility curves for a country. For further discussion see Hall (1973) and Lau (1969).

5. The T( ) functions are assumed to be continuous, twice differentiable, convex and closed in X, Y, R and Z in the nonnegative orthant. $T_e( )$ and $T_r( )$ are strictly increasing in X and Y and decreasing in R. $T_e( )$ is strictly increasing in Z while $T_r( )$ is not.

6. Community indifference curves do not provide a viable means of determining the relationship between individual utility and community welfare. They do, however, offer an acceptable means of describing community demands. As Samuelson noted:

> Community indifference curves between the totals of two goods . . . give us a 'demand relationship.' . . . *and essentially nothing more* (1956: 4).

7. We shall use X as our numeraire in the analysis which follows and assume that all transformation and utility functions display convexity properties which are consistent with the second order conditions for a constrained maximum of $U_e( )$ as in equation (5).

8. We require that the lagrangian constraints are satisfied and the multipliers are designated as follows:

$$\lambda \geq 0$$

$$\theta_1, \theta_2 \leq 0$$

9. The marginal rates of substitution and transformation are defined as follows:

$$MRS_{XY}^r = \frac{U_rY}{U_rX} \text{ and } MRT_{XY}^r = \frac{T_rY}{T_rX}$$

$$\text{with } U_{rX} = \frac{\partial U_r}{\partial X_r} ; T_{rX} = \frac{\partial T_r}{\partial X_r}$$

10. It should be noted that the potential for convexity problems does not require that there be more than a single residual. This requirement relates to being able to use the information to restrict the relationship between arguments of the transformation function for country r.

11. They argue that their efforts are devoted to "developing concepts, or characteristics of models, which, independent of optimality properties, can be identified as involving externalities" (Plott and Meyer, 1975: 67).

12. This statement requires that the conditions for the implicit function theorem are satisfied. See Lau (1969) for further discussion.

13. For an application of these same issues to problems associated with the household demand for public goods see Freeman and Smith (1977).

14. This simplification need not have been adopted for our results could have been derived in terms of the numeraire X. P_R in what follows is the shadow price implied by the given endowment of R to country r.

15. The term deviant is used to refer to those commodities where the necessary conditions for an efficient resource allocation are not satisfied. For example, if one held that equation (6) was satisfied but equation (7) was not, and the relationship between the MRTs for X and Z was given by:

$$MRT_{XZ}^e - kMRT_{XZ}^r = 0 \text{ for } k \neq 0, 1$$

then Z would be referred to as a deviant commodity.

BIBLIOGRAPHY

BARNETT, H. J. and C. MORSE (1963) Scarcity and Growth. Baltimore: Johns Hopkins University.

BICH, T. N. and V. K. SMITH (1977) "An Econometric Evaluation of Air and Water Residuals for Steam Generating Electric Plants." Unpublished manuscript.

BROWN, R. S., D. W. CAVES and L. R. CHRISTENSEN (1975) "Modeling the Structure of Production With a Joint Cost Function." Social Systems Research Institute, University of Wisconsin, Discussion Paper No. 7521.

CHRISTENSEN, L. R., D. W. JORGENSON and L. J. LAU (1973) "Transcendental Logarithmic Production Frontiers." Review of Economics and Statistics 55 (February): 28-45.

COASE, R. H. (1960) "The Problem of Social Cost." Journal of Law and Economics 3 (October): 1-44.

d'ARGE, R. C. (1975) "On the Economics of Transnational Environmental Externalities." In Economic Analysis of Environmental Problems, E. S. Mills (ed.). New York: National Bureau of Economic Research.

DAVIS, O. A. and A. B. WHINSTON (1965) "Welfare Economics and the Theory of Second Best." Review of Economic Studies 32(January): 1-14.

DORFMAN, R. (1974) "The Technical Basis for Decision Making." In E. T. Halfele (ed.). The Governance of Common Property Resources. Baltimore: Johns Hopkins University.

DUSANSKY, R. and J. WALSH (1976) "Separability, Welfare Economics and the Theory of Second Best." Review of Economic Studies 43(February): 49-53.

FREEMAN, A. M. III and V. K. SMITH (1977) "Household Production and Revealed Preference for Public Goods: A Comment." Unpublished manuscript.

HALL, R. E. (1973) "The Specification of Technologies With Several Kinds of Outputs." Journal of Political Economy 81(July/August): 878-892.

KRUTILLA, J. V. and A. C. FISHER (1975) The Economics of Natural Environments. Baltimore: Johns Hopkins University.

LAU, L. J. (1969) "Some Applications of Profit Functions." Memorandum No. 86 Research Center in Economic Growth, Stanford University (November).

LIPSEY, R. G. and K. LANCASTER (1956) "The General Theory of Second Best." Review of Economic Studies 24(February): 11-36.

LOEHR, W. and T. SANDLER (1978) "On the Public Character of Goods." In this volume.

McFADDEN, D. (1977) "Cost, Revenue and Profit Functions." In Production Economics: A Dual Approach to Theory and Applications, M. Fuss and D. McFadden (eds.). Amsterdam: North Holland.

NEGISHI, T. (1972) General Equilibrium Theory and International Trade. Amsterdam: North Holland.

PAGE, T. and J. FEREJOHN (1974) "Externalities as Commodities: Comment." American Economic Review 64(June): 454-59.

PLOTT, C. and R. MEYER (1975) "The Technology of Public Goods, Externalities and the Exclusion Principle." Economic Analysis of Environmental Problems, Universities–National Bureau Conference Series 26. New York: Columbia University Press.

SAMUELSON, P. A. (1956) "Social Indifference Curves." Quarterly Journal of Economics 70(February): 1-22.

SCITOVSKY, T. (1954) "Two Concepts of External Economies." Journal of Political Economy 17(April): 143-51.

SCOTT, A. D. (1972) "The Economics of International Transmission of Pollution." In Problems of Environmental Economics. Washington, D.C.: OECD.

SHEPHARD (1953) The Theory of Cost and Production Functions. Princeton: Princeton University Press.

WOODLAND, A. D. (1974) "Demand Conditions in International Trade Theory." Australian Economic Papers 13(December): 209-224.

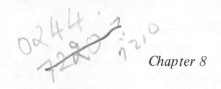

Chapter 8

ANALYZING INTERNATIONAL EXTERNALITIES:
THE CASE OF THE LAW OF THE SEA NEGOTIATIONS

R Y A N C. A M A C H E R
Arizona State University

R O B E R T D. T O L L I S O N
Virginia Polytechnic Institute
and State University

INTRODUCTION

The fourth session of the third United Nations Conference on the Law of the Sea (UNCLOS) ended on May 7, 1976.[1] This session represents the latest round of a continuing dialog between the diplomatic corps of more than 140 countries. The first UNCLOS which was held in 1958 produced four Conventions and numerous agreements. Despite all the activity, the four Conventions were nothing more than a codification of the customary international law on ocean usage.[2]

The second UNCLOS was held in 1960 with ambitious designs. The goal was to develop a new law of the sea treaty which would permit the nations of the world to recover the ocean's wealth and at the same time reduce the potential for conflict. Indeed, many legal scholars and statesmen argued, and continue to argue, that failure to reach agreement will produce chaos and conflict in the oceans.[3] This second UNCLOS ended without agreement.

Given the number of participants and the complexity of the issues, it should not be surprising that an acceptable treaty has not been realized. Indeed, a public choice approach to an examination of the voting rules, the issues, and the number of participants would lead one to predict the likelihood of failure to reach agreement.[4] It should also be pointed out that the failure to reach a treaty in each of the four sessions of the third UNCLOS has not plunged the world into "chaos or unmitigated disaster." In fact it seems legitimate to wonder if countries that now ignore customary international law would be constrained by any agreement that is produced by the UNCLOS.

Our major objective in this paper is to illustrate how economics can be useful in examining the international externalities and public goods aspects present in International Sea Law. Our purpose is not to discuss every issue involved in the negotiations but to illustrate how concepts from the economics of public finance and public choice can be used in analyzing the general types of problems that have emerged in the negotiations over Law of the Sea. We apply our approach to several specific issues in the Law of the Sea negotiations, including ocean resource exploitation, navigation, pollution, conservation and science. The general theme of our analysis will be that given the costs of reaching international agreement, it would seem wise to concentrate efforts at international agreement on those areas and at those levels in which agreements can make the greatest contribution. We develop in Section I a general methodological framework for analyzing international public goods and externalities. In Section II we review several of the main issues involved in the Law of the Sea negotiations. In Section III we analyze some UNCLOS issues in terms of the methodological framework developed in Section I. We offer some concluding remarks in Section IV.

WHICH LEVEL OF GOVERNMENT?

A methodological error that is often made in discussions of public policy is to assume that the discovery of market failure is sufficient to invoke an unexamined alternative (government). The error is that government action also produces externalities and is clearly not a perfect (costless) way to correct private market failures. In the context of the Law of the Sea negotiations, this error often takes the form of assuming that the finding of market failures implies that they should be internalized at the highest possible level of international agreement (the United Nations). Although economists make this mistake less readily than others, the economics profession is somewhat the blame for engendering the general idea that the simple application of Pigovian taxes and subsidies is a cure-all for market failure. In recent years, however, such writers as Buchanan (1961), Coase (1960), and McKean and Minasian (1966) have pointed out some of the problems with this simple Pigovian logic. At the international level this rush to internalize at the highest level can in particular obscure many of the advantages of bilateral and regional agreements to control externalities, and in a broad sense it simply ignores the costs of lost diversity where the amount of externality control desired varies widely among individual nations.

The economic theory of fiscal federalism focuses on the determination of optimal sized governmental units, which in turn is based on the principle of perfect correspondence. Perfect correspondence occurs when the jurisdiction that provides the public good or generates the public bad includes the entire set of homogeneous individuals who consume the good or bad.[5] This is clearly a theoretical, limiting case. A more realistic case of international externality is where benefits or costs taper off spatially from some point of origin and are not spread equally among the members of a given polity.[6] This type of benefit or cost incidence makes it necessary to examine the technical aspects of particular externality problems in determining the relevant level of government to regulate the externality. If all levels of consumption of the good or bad are considered, rigid application of perfect correspondence could lead to the determination of the consumption levels of most public goods at an extremely centralized level. Whenever the costs of creating correspondence exceeds the efficiency gains from centralized provision, such centralization is undesirable. In other words, most practical applications of the correspondence principle leads to consideration (over spatial patterns) of the trade-offs among the various cost and benefits of great conformity.

In practice, the application of the correspondence principle suggests the equating of the marginal costs and benefits from expanding the number of individuals in the relevant jurisdiction. Many trade-offs exist in arriving at the optimal jurisdiction size. Among those treated in the literature are diversity in individual demands (i.e., the decentralization theorem, Tullock, 1969b and Barzel, 1969), costs of collective decision making, (Tullock, 1969a) consumer mobility, (Tiebout, 1956; Buchanan and Wagner, 1970; and Buchanan and Goetz, 1972) governmental interdependence, (Tullock, 1969a and Pauly, 1970) and, in an explicit normative model, the equality of total utility over the issue set among the members of a polity (i.e., the equal-stake requirement, Mueller, 1971). The decentralization theorem emphasizes the optimality of local public goods supply where there is a diversity of individual demands for the good by place of residence and there are no economies to centralized provision of the public good. In effect, this argument suggests that the incentives for decentralization are likely to be greatest where the diversity in local demand is high. The trade-off involving the costs of collective decision-making stresses that there are administrative and voting costs to having multiple decision-making entities. Consumer or voter mobility causes special problems. In some respects, mobility increases the gains from decentralized decision-making since consumer-voters may locate as a function of their preferences for mixes of private and public goods. On the other hand, where such factors as congestion costs become important, mobility can be a mixed blessing to consumer-voters already living in a given polity. Governmental interdependence stresses the problems covered by externalities that occur across jurisdictional boundaries. This trade-off suggests decision making on a more centralized scale. Finally, the equal-stake requirement emphasizes the requirement that voting rights should be tailored to individual stakes in a collective decision.

A broad trade-off that we particularly wish to emphasize at the international level is that between diversity in individual (say country) demands for the control of international externalities and centralized procedures to internalize international social costs and benefits. If we take the economist's view of optimality as tailoring economic outcomes to fit individual preferences as closely as possible, then decentralized provision of public goods will typically be more efficient unless "lumpiness" of public investment causes centralized provision to have some inherent cost saving.

There has been a tendency in the literature to assume that efficiency in externality control requires the same tax-price for all communities (see Stein, 1971). This does not necessarily follow, and as stressed by the decentralization theorem where people have different tastes, fiscal mechanisms should be tailored to reflect this diversity (see Amacher, Tollison, and Willett, 1972). Much of this discussion centers on the question of factor mobility and stresses that where factors are immobile, different tax-prices will still be optimal where the costs of mobility are properly accounted for. Mobility does cause some special problems. Competition among local communities can lead to undercutting of tax prices to control local externalities to secure local industry. This is more likely to be a problem where local competition takes the form of bidding for tax havens (e.g., the location of corporate offices or the registry of a ship) than in the case of countries allowing differing amounts of ocean pollution. In domestic economies, as Sherman and Willett (1969) stress, there can be a problem of lowering pollution standards to bid for industry when there are local employment benefits. This is probably more of a problem within regions than among countries. Within regions substantial employment effects may exist from factor mobility because of resultant changes in aggregate demand. Among countries, where exchange rates can change, there may be sectoral impacts of industrial relocation, but there would be no problem of deficient effective demand causing additional long-run unemployment.

It is especially important to note that where costs and benefits taper off spatially varying benefit taxes (as stressed by Musgrave, 1969) can be employed. It is difficult, however, to conceive of a solution to tapering off externalities in terms of a workable voting system. Capricious outcomes can result where individuals with small interests in a spillover problem are given a full vote in the determination of the outcome. This sort of structure of voting rights can lead to intensity problems, where voting may not maximize social welfare. That is, partial taxation and equally weighted voting rights for tapering externalities can lead to capricious results. This is a particularly important point in UNCLOS issues.

To conclude this brief discussion we wish to emphasize that it is crucial to analyze specific externality problems with respect to the basic trade-offs involved in deciding at what level they should be handled. Basic questions that must be addressed would be a) the nature of the externality—does it exist, is it worth the cost of doing something about, and over what domain does it occur, and b) the efficiency of organizations designed to deal with the spillover.[7] It is possible that some of the externalities at issue in the Law of the Sea negotiations, when subjected to this sort of technical analysis, would appear to be best handled by bilateral or regional agreements at a far more decentralized level of decision-making than a conference of United Nations members, each with a full vote on all issues.

UNCLOS ISSUES

In broad terms, the Law of the Sea Convention is concerned with:

1. Limiting and defining the extent to which states can exercise sovereignty over use of the seas adjoining their coasts or exploitation of the resources in or under them.
2. Providing international rules for the exploitation of ocean resources beyond the areas subject to the control of the coastal states.

These conceptual concerns take real meaning only in the context of the actual issues under consideration in the Law of the Sea Conference. For convenience, the set of issues can be classified under four broad categories: Jurisdiction over Mineral Resources; Navigation; Pollution; and Conservation and Science.

JURISDICTION OVER MINERAL RESOURCES

Most states agree in principle that each coastal state should have sole control over the mineral resources of the ocean adjacent to that state and the revenues generated therein. This area has generally been identified with the nation's territorial sea; the real issue here is how far out this area of absolute control would extend. Similarly, most agree that beyond the area where nations have any control, there would be an international zone, but the issue here is what type, if any, of international authority should be established to govern activities in the deep sea bed. Advocates of an international authority have labelled such an organization the International Seabed Resource Authority (ISRA), but its powers remain in dispute. A third major area of the ocean comprises the area between the territorial sea and the international zone. This is often referred to as the Coastal Seabed Economic Area (CSEA) and is envisioned as an area where the coastal state would exercise control, but where it would do so under the guidance of some international rules and where some of the benefits of its resource exploitation would be shared by the international community. This latter notion has been termed revenue sharing.

To put the matter more concisely, the principal issues for negotiation concern the inner and outer boundaries where revenue sharing would take place, the international restrictions on national sovereignty in this area, and also the sort of international organization required to establish the property rights and to govern the activities of deep sea miners in the area beyond all national jurisdiction.

With respect to the outer boundary of coastal state jurisdiction, the nations which are land-locked tend to desire a narrow boundary, leaving more of the oceans under the jurisdiction of the international authority. Coastal states, in contrast, want control over as much as they can conscionably obtain, generally perceived as being the area out to 200 miles or the extreme edge of the continental margin, whichever is farther from shore. Similarly, land-locked countries (and even some coastal states whose continental margins are either not potentially rich in resources or which will not be exploited for a long time either because they are of low quality or the country does not possess the required technology) favor broad boundaries for the revenue sharing area and favor very high rates of revenue sharing. Countries with abundant resources and the technology for their exploitation tend to favor a very distant seaward limit before revenue sharing begins and low revenue sharing rates, with the inner and outer boundaries of the revenue sharing area being virtually coincident, hence almost eliminating the need for any funds transfer. The area between 200 miles and the end of the margin is sometimes mentioned as a region for revenue sharing. Many LDC's have been adamant that poor nations cannot be expected to share revenue from the sea with others. However, some countries, particularly the United States, have expressed a willingness to trade off wide boundaries and high revenue sharing for concessions on other issues.

Finally, developed countries, especially those possessing the technology to exploit manganese nodules, would find it in their best economic interest to have no international authority with substantive power to regulate deep sea mining activities.[8] These nodules contain copper, nickel, cobalt and manganese (as well as small quantities of other minerals). Cheap, efficient exploitation of nodules is in the interests of all countries consuming these minerals. LDC's, however, favor an international organization with very extensive powers to regulate deep sea mining activities and even discriminate among producers. They apparently seek a monopoly enterprise which alone would directly undertake the development of deep sea resources, erecting barriers to entry into the industry and perhaps even coordinating its activities with major land based producers, much as a cartel.[9] For the few LDC's and developed countries that are major copper, nickel, or cobalt producers, such an outcome is clearly in their self-interest. Other LDC's have neglected their self-interest as mineral importers in order to support the producers, presumably on grounds of Third World solidarity in the quest for the New International Economic Order in which all LDC's have cartel type organizations to protect their exports. Even if the deep sea minerals are not worth much in a present value sense, the principle of opposition to raw material cartelization can be served by developing policy for the deep sea bed based on sound economic reasoning.

NAVIGATION

Of the one hundred nineteen coastal states, only twenty-nine have territorial seas of three miles in breadth; of the ninety with territorial sea claims of greater than three miles, however, only eighteen have claims of more than twelve miles. One quite important aspect of the Law of the Sea treaty negotiations is a settling upon the internationally allowable breadth of territorial seas; not surprisingly, there seems to be quite general agreement that twelve-mile territorial seas are virtually inevitable.

A territorial sea is one in which the coastal state has unambiguous and extensive control. Not only does it have complete jurisdiction over the living and non-living resources in that area, but its complete control over navigation in that area is limited only by the customary international law doctrine of "innocent passage." Under innocent passage, the coastal state must allow passage through its territorial sea to any ship of a non-belligerent state, provided the ship has only an innocent purpose. The coastal state can set non-discriminatory navigation and safety rules, and can require prior notification whenever a ship desires passage. This doctrine is in effect currently, and encompasses those straits (such as Skagerrak) which lie entirely within one or more countries' territorial sea.

An issue of great importance is encompassed in this territorial sea question: the extension of coastal state territorial seas to twelve miles (which nearly all countries want) will place many of the most important of the world's navigable straits in territorial seas, for many of the high seas corridors through straits, which exist under the three-mile territorial sea, will be eliminated by the extension of coastal state authority. Such "closure" might have effects on both commercial and military vessels.

There are one hundred forty straits in significant use in world shipping. Two in particular, the Straits of Dover and the Strait of Gibraltar, collectively account for approximately 45.2 percent of the total dollar value of U.S. water-borne imports. This represented total trade of nearly $23 billion in 1972 (U.S. Maritime Administration, 1972). If territorial seas are extended from three to twelve miles, nearly every strait used for both commercial and military use will fall within territorial seas. Straits which are, for example, seven miles wide and whose adjacent states currently claim territorial seas of three miles would no longer have a high seas corridor of one mile in breadth, but would have two adjacent three and one-half mile territorial seas. Because ships passing through these straits would come under the explicit control of the straits' states, it is argued that the costs of shipping might be raised substantially. However, it is not clear that straits states would find it in their interests to limit use of their straits, even if lowcost methods of exercising stringent control were devised.

There are, in ascending order of severity, four levels of control which states may exercise with respect to the passage of vessels through their territorial straits: a) free transit, which grants the ship the equivalent of high seas freedom, b) innocent passage, c) strait transit toll, and d) closure. Of these, free transit is generally preferred by states with significant maritime interests; however, arguments can be made for innocent passage where there is a substantial amount of traffic or the strait is treacherous. Economic arguments could be offered for strait transit tolls as an allocation device in those instances where crowding is a significant problem.

The expansion of territorial seas to twelve miles, as is favored by most Law of the Sea treaty participants, is simply an internationally sanctioned expansion of property rights. The attempt to achieve a free transit through straits regime is analogous to arguing that passage through straits is essentially a free good which should be shared by all, for without that free good costs to all parties would be raised to such a prohibitively high level that water-borne commerce would fall significantly.

The security implication of the possible "closure" of straits has for some time significantly influenced, perhaps even dominated, positions on the Law of the Sea Conference. This issue, as many of the other issues in the negotiations, does not require international agreement. Using the U.S. case as an example, Robert Osgood has pointed out that U.S. nuclear strategic interests come down to protecting U.S. interests in only two straits, Gibraltar and the Indonesian Straits.[10] These strategic interests can be protected, as can interests in any other straits deemed important, by the same type of ad hoc modus vivendi that has protected U.S. interests in the past. The important point is that U.S. policy makers should not make concessions to reach a treaty compromise that are more "costly" to the U.S. than the present regime of favorable political relations with the few involved countries. We feel that failure to reach a treaty compromise will not present any added difficulties with regard to military interests that cannot be resolved through already existing institutional arrangements. Instead any difficulties can perhaps be resolved at less cost through bilateral arrangements.

POLLUTION

The UNCLOS also is addressing the problem of establishing minimum international ocean pollution standards. The rationale supporting the view that there should be a single international standard is that standards which vary widely from the coastal areas of one state to another would cause large increases in the shipping costs of international trade, as ships may have to travel substantially longer distances to avoid particularly stringent rules of a single coastal state which happens to border a trade route.

The position that, without uniform international standards, chaotic shipping conditions would result is dubious. The proponents of single standards argue that without a single standard, in particular, a vessel design and construction standard, countries are likely to impose bizarre standards, and that there would be no effective means by which coastal states neighboring those with very lax standards would be able to control pollution coming from adjacent waters. The first argument is weakened by the recognition that countries which behave in their rational self-interest will increase their own shipping costs substantially by imposing highly specialized pollution reducing vessel construction standards. To the extent that they are at wide variance with those of the rest of the world, their costs will increase more than proportionally. The second argument would be false if an effective liability system were established, under which polluters would be made to bear the full cost of environmental repair.

By requiring owners and operators to build ships with highly effective pollution abatement capability, nations could achieve significant reductions in oil damage, but the cost of implementing this technology could exceed the gains to society achieved thereby (See Amacher and Sweeney 1976b). Moreover, to the extent that a pollutionless coastal area is more valuable to a nation with higher income, the cost relative to the social benefit to, say, a less developed country could be far greater than for a country like the U.S. Furthermore, the same result as that attained by dictating a particular technology could conceivably be achieved through a system imposing liability for damages on the party responsible for pollution. The latter approach would have the advantage of avoiding undesirable hindrances to innovation and perhaps introduction of more effective pollution abatement equipment and procedures. It would also leave the choice of technology to those who could be expected to be most familiar with relative costs.

CONSERVATION AND SCIENCE

Fisheries' management poses a serious problem. Unlike most non-living resources fish move about, hence the establishment of property rights is substantially more difficult. Typically, ownership is established by capture, and thus the individual fisherman has no incentive to manage the fish stock as if he owned it.[11] Moreover, it is quite possible to deplete the stock of fish through overfishing, so that no fish or few fish remain for subsequent generations of fishermen (See Clark, 1973). It is likely that the problem with fish is serious enough to warrant international action. The Law of the Sea treaty seeks to deal with the issue but so far has achieved little success. However, there are many international organizations that are attempting to regulate various fish stocks and fisheries. While some of these have had some success in restoring depleted fish stocks, they have a uniformly poor record in exploiting the economic potential of the fisheries. Thus, there seems to be relatively little to be hoped for in any fisheries' agreement that might emerge as part of a treaty. Thus while we recognize the need for action we are not optimistic about the UNCLOS as a successful forum.

A second issue in this general class revolves around the freedom to conduct scientific research in the oceans and within the coastal state economic areas of other countries. This raises the question of the pure public goods nature of scientific research. If scientific research does not interfere with other ocean uses and is a pure public good, the fruits of which can, at least conceptually, be shared by all nations, then it is difficult to oppose freedom of scientific research. On the other hand, if the benefits of scientific research can be successfully and fully internalized by the research group or its national sponsors, then only altruism should motivate countries to allow the researchers to share freely in their explicit property rights, as would be the case if countries allowed full freedom of scientific research in their coastal state economic areas (supposing, as seems likely, that most states could unilaterally impose, say, a 200-mile CSEA) or in its shared rights, as in the ocean area under international control. Certainly, if another party wants to use something over which a nation has been given control by international agreement, or in which it shares control, then the using party should be willing to pay for its use.

ALTERNATIVES TO A UNCLOS[12]

As we have been indicating in the previous section, there are abundant forums and institutions already in existence to deal with most of the Law of the Sea issues. Most of the issues under consideration in the Law of the Sea negotiations are already within the province of customary international law or treaty, or less comprehensive regional and bilateral agreements. Proceeding systematically, note first that the Truman Doctrine asserts U.S. control over the non-living resources on the continental margin, and this doctrine has received general international sanction in the U.N. Convention on the Outer Continental Shelf (Geneva Convention) of 1958 where it was agreed that coastal states have jurisdiction over the non-living resources on their continental shelves out to a depth of at least two hundred meters or the technological limits of exploitation, whichever is further.

The one item within the general area of Jurisdiction over Mineral Resources where no policy now exists and where no body of customary law or convention exists has to do with the deep sea bed and its exploitation. No precedent exists for mining the ocean floor for commercial purposes, and it is here where the need for specific alternatives is most apparent and most pressing as several commercial operations (all involving U.S. firms) are under consideration.

Within the domain of navigational issues, there are bodies of law and diplomatic agreements governing the use of straits, there are conventions, agreements, and international organizations, principally the International Maritime Consultative Organization, which deal with ocean pollution, and there are numerous international understandings and declarations concerning the breadth of territorial seas. Indeed, the need for new and explicit policy initiatives on the part of the U.S. is not at all clear cut at present. Forums and institutions already exist for dealing with most of the potentially troublesome issues which may arise, not the least of which might be bilateral agreements to solve disputes on an ad hoc basis.

Pollution problems are not optimally solved by a uniform world standard. Unilateral, bilateral or multilateral imposition of liability where polluters are made to bear the full cost of environmental repair is likely the most effective method of internalization (See Cummins, Logue, Tollison, and Willett, 1975). With respect to fisheries resources, here again a large number of treaties, conventions, and organizations already exist and are active in attempting to control the over-exploitation of those resources. Since the U.S. already participates in these agreements, if the Law of the Sea treaty fails, the mechanisms are already in place to achieve substantially the same results hoped for in the comprehensive treaty. Accordingly, the speedy development of U.S. policy alternatives in this area does not appear to be a high priority item.

Finally, note that scientific research is currently taking place in the deep sea in an unimpeded atmosphere. Failure to reach agreement on a Law of the Sea treaty would likely not incite other countries to engage in novel and systematic harassment of these and future scientific expeditions.

By and large, one cannot help but notice that for most of the issues being taken up within the Law of the Sea, most governments already have a clearly defined policy. These policies range, of course, from formal participation in international treaties or organizations to bilateral arrangements, to agreement to follow customary international law, to implicit or unstated policies where it is presumed and expected that the international community will not challenge other countries' prerogatives, as for example, in the case of movement of military vessels through straits or in our conduct of scientific research.

Deep sea bed mining is one area where no policy exists and indeed where there is no experience or even observations on the behavior of countries. Moreover, the absence of a policy here is most glaring in that domestic firms which say they have the technical ability to explore and exploit manganese nodules deposits on the ocean's floor, complain that they are actually being prevented by uncertainty over policy from doing so.

An attractive alternative would be an attempt to extend principles developed in a lead country, say the U.S., through model domestic legislation to a formal agreement among a small group of countries with important interests in sea bed mining.[13] These countries, say the United States, the major OECD countries and perhaps the Soviet Union would agree to a standard of "good" international behavior in this area. This approach has much to recommend itself because a group of such countries could very likely set a standard which would not be violated because of their economic and military significance. If this policy were an enlightened policy, and one that provided for eventual participation by the LDC's, it could very quickly displace any "need" for a comprehensive treaty.

The primary benefit of negotiating an agreement among such a subset of the present Conference Nations is largely a result of the fact that the centralized manner in which the present negotiations are set, with such a large number of participants, many of whom have no major stake in oceans' questions, leads to very high decision costs. It is very difficult to reach agreement because the large number of participants makes trade-offs harder to consummate. Indeed the present composition of the negotiations, where voting power differs substantially from potential costs and benefits, results in either a less than optimal treaty or in no treaty at all. A reduction in the number of participants, particularly a reduction to those who have significant political, economic, and military interests in the sea, would likely speed the negotiations and produce a "better" agreement.

CONCLUDING REMARKS

We have used the present UNCLOS as a vehicle to argue that the discovery of an international externality is not sufficient to invoke a call for world governmental intervention. In short, we do not see chaos in the seas resulting from failure to reach a comprehensive treaty. Most problems can be dealt with by existing law or through existing forums. We do, however, feel that some policy is necessary with respect to deep sea bed mining. We have suggested that it is not necessary that this policy be developed in an all encompassing world forum, but rather by those countries that have significant economic interests in such policy.

NOTES

1. As James Johnston (1976) has so aptly noted, the session began on April Fool's Day 1976.

2. For a standard reference on this customary law see McDougal and Burke (1962).

3. For a representation of the view that "a continuation of the trend of recent years can only spell unmitigated disaster," see Friedman (1971: xi). For the opposite view, see the papers and discussion in Amacher and Sweeney (1976b).

4. For such a view see the paper by Robert D. Tollison and Thomas D. Willett in Amacher and Sweeney (1976b) and Johnston (1976).

5. For a definition see Oates (1972) and Musgrave (1969).

6. See Musgrave (1969: 296) for a clear discussion of the problem posed to the theory of fiscal federalism by tapering benefits and costs.

7. Sandler and Cauley (1977) examine in detail the design of supranational structures to optimally internalize relevant externalities. In particular they look at the relevant trade-offs in design of the institution.

8. For a thorough analysis of the potential problems of a stringent regulation see Logue, Sweeney and Petro (1975).

9. For an eloquent criticism of such an international monopoly, see the remarks of Northcutt Ely in Amacher and Sweeney (1976b) and for a discussion of the potential for cartels without an ISRA see Amacher and Sweeney (1976a).

10. For an in-depth discussion of U.S. security interests in the Law of the Sea, see Robert Osgood, "U.S. Political and Military Interests in Ocean Law" in Amacher and Sweeney (1976b).

11. This is often referred to as the common pool problem. See Sweeney, Tollison, and Willett (1974).

12. For a detailed consideration of alternatives available for U.S. policymakers, see Amacher, Logue and Sweeney (1976).

13. As early as 1973 former Secretary of State, Dean Rusk, called for such multilateral action by a subset of developed countries. Hearings (1973).

BIBLIOGRAPHY

ALEXANDER, LEWIS M. (ed.) (1972) Law of the Sea: A New Geneva Conference. Kingston: University of Rhode Island.

AMACHER, RYAN C. (forthcoming) "Eastern Europe's Economic Stake in the Law of the Sea Negotiations." Pp. in J. Brada (ed.) East-West Business: Theory and Evidence. Bloomington: Indiana University Press.

AMACHER, RYAN C. and RICHARD JAMES SWEENEY (1976a) "International Commodity Cartels and the Threat of New Entry: Implications of Ocean Mineral Resources." Kyklos 29, 2:292-309.

AMACHER, RYAN C. and RICHARD JAMES SWEENEY (eds.) (1976b) The Law of the Sea: U.S. Interests and Alternatives. Washington: American Enterprise Institute.

AMACHER, RYAN C., DENNIS E. LOGUE, and RICHARD JAMES SWEENEY (1976) "Coping with the Failure of the Law of the Sea Conference: A U.S. Perspective." U.S. Treasury, mimeographed.

AMACHER, RYAN C., ROBERT D. TOLLISON, and THOMAS D. WILLETT (1972) "The Economics of Fatal Mistakes: Fiscal Mechanisms for Preserving Endangered Predators." Public Policy 20, 3:411-441.

BARZEL, YORAM (1969) "Two Propositions on the Optimum Level of Producing Public Goods." Public Choice 7(Spring): 24-37.

BUCHANAN, J. M. (1961) "Politics, Policy, and the Pigovian Margins." Economica 29(February): 17-28.

——— and CHARLES J. GOETZ (1972) "Efficiency Limits of Fiscal Mobility: An Assessment of the Tiebout Model." Public Economics 1, 1:25-44.

——— and RICHARD WAGNER (1970) "An Efficiency Basis for Federal Fiscal Equalization." In J. Margolis (ed.) The Analysis of Public Output. New York: Columbia University Press.

CLARK, COLIN (1973) "Profit Maximization and the Extinction of Animal Species." Journal of Political Economy 81, 4:950-972.

CLARKSON, K. (1974) "International Law, U.S. Seabeds Policy and Ocean Resource Development." Journal of Law and Economics 17, 1:117-142.

COASE, RONALD (1960) "The Problem of Social Costs," Journal of Law and Economics. (October): 1-44.

COMMITTEE ON COMMERCE (1974) The Economic Value of Ocean Resources to the United States. Washington: U.S. Senate.

CONFERENCE ON CONFLICT AND ORDER IN OCEAN RELATIONS (1974) Perspectives on Ocean Policy. Washington: Johns Hopkins School of Advanced International Studies.

CUMMINS, PHILLIP A., D. E. LOGUE, R. D. TOLLISON, and T. D. WILLETT (1975) "Oil Tanker Pollution Control: Design Criteria vs. Effective Liability Assignment." Journal of Maritime Law and Commerce 7, 1:169-206.

FRIEDMAN, WOLFGANG (1971) The Future of the Oceans, New York: George Braziller.

HEARINGS BEFORE THE SUBCOMMITTEE ON MINERALS, MATERIALS, AND FUELS, PART 2. (1974) Washington: U.S. Government Printing Office.

HEARINGS ON S. RESOLUTION 82. (1973) Senate Subcommittee on International Organizations and Movements. Washington: U.S. Government Printing Office.

JOHNSTON, JAMES L. (1976) "The Likelihood of a Treaty Emerging From the Third United Nations Conference on the Law of the Sea." U.S. Treasury, mimeographed.

KNIGHT, H. G. (1974) "Treaty and Non-Treaty Approaches to Order in the World Ocean." Perspective on Ocean Policy. Washington: U.S. Government Printing Office.

LAYLIN, G. (1973) "The Law to Govern Deepsea Mining Superseded by International Agreement." San Diego Law Review 27, 3:14-39.

LOGUE, D. E., R. J. SWEENEY, and B. N. PETRO (1975) "The Economics of Alternative Deep Sea Bed Regimes." Marine Technology Society Journal 17,1: 10-20,

McKEAN, R. N. and J. R. MINASIAN (1966) "On Achieving Pareto Optimality—Regardless of Costs," Western Economic Journal 4,3: 17-30.

MUELLER, DENNIS C. (1971) "Fiscal Federalism in a Constitutional Democracy." Public Policy 19, 4: 567-594.

MUSGRAVE, RICHARD (1969) Fiscal Systems. New Haven: Yale University Press.

OATES, WALLACE E. (1972) Fiscal Federalism. New York: Harcourt Brace Jovanovich, Inc.

OVERSEAS PRIVATE INVESTMENT CORPORATION (1971) Political Role Investment Insurance Handbook Washington: U.S. Government Printing Office.

PAULY, MARK (1970) "Optimality, 'Public' Goods, and Local Governments: A General Theoretical Analysis." Journal of Political Economy 78, 3: 572-585.

SANDLER, TODD and JON CAULEY (1977) "The Design of Supranational Structures: An Economic Perspective." International Studies Quarterly 21, 2:

SHERMAN, R. and T. WILLETT (1969) "Regional Development, Externalities and Tax-Subsidy Combinations." National Tax Journal 22, 2: 158-171.

STEIN, J. (1971) "The 1971 Report of the President's Council of Economic Advisors: Micro-Economic Aspects of Public Policy." American Economic Review 61, 4: 531-537.

SWEENEY, R. J., R. D. TOLLISON, and T. D. WILLETT (1974) "Market Failure, The Common Pool Problem, and Ocean Resource Exploitation." Journal of Law and Economics 17, 1: 179-192.

TIEBOUT, CHARLES M. (1956) "A Pure Theory of Local Expenditures." Journal of Political Economy 64(October): 416-424.

TULLOCK, GORDON (1969a) "Federalism: Problems of Scale." Public Choice 6(Spring): 54-70.

TULLOCK, GORDON (1969b) "Social Cost and Government Action." American Economic Review 59, 2: 189-197.

Chapter 9

NATURAL RESOURCE TAXATION, TAX EXPORTATION, AND THE STABILITY OF FISCAL FEDERALISM

W I L L I A M E. M O R G A N
University of Wyoming

R O B E R T B. S H E L T O N
Resources for the Future

In a recent contribution to fiscal federalism, Sandler and Shelton (1972) examine the implications of tax exportation on the stability of fiscal federalism. Utilizing a two-good (private and public), two-region general equilibrium analysis, they specify necessary and sufficient conditions for stability when regions experience public good spillins and have the power to export part of their taxes.

This paper adopts the general equilibrium formulation used by Sandler and Shelton, but extends their analysis. One of the weaknesses of their study is that they assumed exportation to occur without examining the internal regional production effects. This paper corrects this defect. Secondly, this paper extends the analysis to include natural resource production which is an input to private good production. Given the recent policy concerns regarding natural resource development, particularly energy resources, and given that natural resources are a convenient mechanism for exporting a portion of a tax base, the analysis here has important and timely policy implications. (For discussion and test of the proposition that regions use natural resources as a mechanism for exporting taxes, see Hogan and Shelton, 1973; Shelton and Morgan, 1977.) Other studies of regional tax exportation include McLure (1964; 1967; 1969; 1970).

Two production situations are examined—private good and an exhaustible natural resource, and private good and public good. Although the natural resource is exhaustible, it is assumed that current production is small relative to the total stock of the natural resource. Moreover, the natural resource does not provide direct utility to the consumer. In the analysis it is also assumed that one region's endowment of the natural resource relative to the composite

AUTHORS' NOTE: The thoughtful comments and suggestions of Ralph d'Arge, Jack Mutti and Todd Sandler are gratefully acknowledged.

factor, capital-labor, is larger than that of the other region. Interregional trade is examined with and without factor mobility assumed. The production functions employed in the production of the natural resource, private, and public goods in both regions are assumed to be linearly homogeneous. In addition, it is assumed that the benefits of public goods are considered homogeneous regardless of origin and that the spillovers are proportional to public good production. Finally, membership in the federation is assumed to be voluntary; i.e., a region may secede from the federation if its welfare position is lowered because of membership.

The paper is divided into four sections. Section I investigates interregional trade of the natural resource with a severance tax and factor mobility. Section II presents the case of trade of the natural resource with a severance tax and trade of the private good with an excise tax and no factor mobility. The analysis is extended in Section III and the effects of taxation on private and public sector production are investigated. Section IV consists of a summary and conclusions.

I. TRADE OF NATURAL RESOURCE WITH SEVERANCE TAX AND FACTOR MOBILITY

Figure 1a depicts the production possibilities curve for region I and shows trade-off between a private good and a natural resource, with the original, no interregional trade production possibilities curve being shown along $P_1 A P_1'$. The production possibilities curve slopes upward from P_1 to A because the natural resource is an input into the production of the private good; i.e., it requires OR_1 of the natural resource for the production of $R_1 A$ of the private good. The production possibilities curve from A to P_1', of course, has the usual shape. With no interregional trade, region I would produce at a point A, since this is the maximum possible amount of the private good production given the region's factor endowments. If trade were possible between region I and region II, region I would move down along the production possibilities curve $P_1 P_1'$ from A, to say B_1. Given the export of the natural resource to region II, region I would receive money, assuming no trade of a private good, which is used to buy factors of production from region II; e.g., the composite factor capital-labor, would shift out the production possibilities curve to $P_2 P_2'$. Given the increase in the production possibilities curve, region I would be on its new production possibilities curve at some point like B_2.[1]

Assuming initial equilibrium at B_2, suppose that region I desires to finance a public good by levying a severance tax. The severance tax is a tax on the production (extraction) of the natural resource. An example of a region

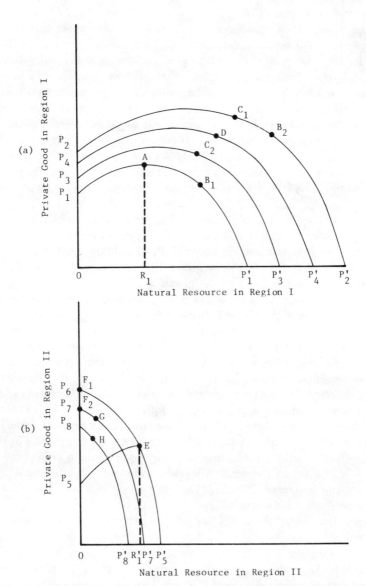

Figure 1: Trade of Natural Resource with Severance Tax (factor mobility)

financing a public good through a severance tax would be a major coal producing state in the Rocky Mountain region, e.g., Montana or Wyoming, financing part of higher education in the state through a coal severance tax (Shelton and Morgan, 1977).

The effect of the severance tax will change relative prices between the private good and the natural resource, which would move production from say B_2 to some point C_1. Furthermore, the severance tax will withdraw resources from both the production of the private good and the natural resource, which will be utilized in the production of the public good.[2] Since the severance tax withdraws resources, the production possibilities curve is reduced from $P_2 P_2'$ to $P_3 P_3'$ and production would be at some point C_2. However, assuming that part of the tax is exported through higher prices for the natural resource which is exported to region II, the production possibilities curve would not shift in by the full amount of the tax. Production possibilities curve $P_4 P_4'$ represents the "net" curve, with production indicated at point D.

Region II is depicted in Figure 1b. The production possibilities curve is similar to the production possibilities curve in region I. The initial production possibilities curve is shown by curve $P_5 P_5'$. Equilibrium without trade is shown at point E on $P_5 P_5'$ which requires OR_1' of the natural resource for the production of $R_1' E$ amount of the private good. The effect of trade in the natural resource must increase the production possibilities curve for the private good for region II, and this is indicated by $P_6 P_5'$, but with factor mobility (purchase of factors by region I) would lead to a shifting in the production possibilities curve to say $P_7 P_7'$ and production at some point F_2.

It is important to note that after trade occurs the production possibilities curves are shown without the hump. It has been assumed that the relative price difference between the imported natural resource as compared to the domestically produced natural resource results in the hump being to the left (outside) of the box. Stated differently, it is possible that region II would not produce any of the natural resource. An alternative assumption would be that the price differential is not as large and that region II would always produce some of the natural resource. With this assumption $P_5 E P_5'$ would shift upward and inward and the new production possibilities curves would have the same shape as the no-trade curve.

The effect of the severance tax in region I will of course change the relative prices in region II, and this will shift production from say F_2 to some point G. Furthermore, with the decrease in factors as a result of the severeance tax, the production possibilities curve shifts to $P_8 P_8'$ and production would take place at some point H. Point H, of course, represents increased production of the private good over the initial equilibrium at point E, or

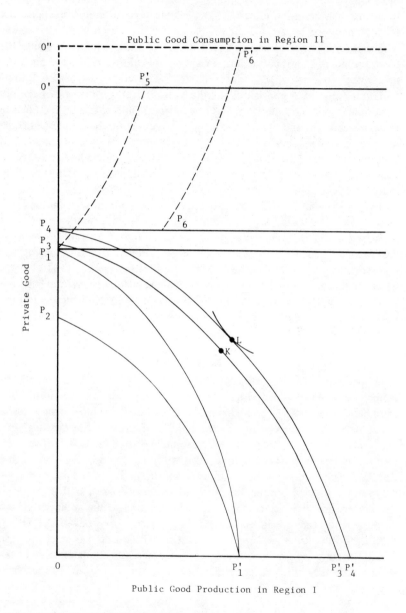

Figure 2: **Public Good Production in Region 1 and Spillin in Region II (factor mobility)**

region II would not participate in trade given no production of the public good in region I.

Figure 2 shows the production possibilities curve for the private good and for a public good in region I and region II. The production possibilities curve is inverted for region II and is placed on top of the production possibilities curve for region I. In this manner production spillovers of the public good can be noted.

Turning first to region I, $P_1 P_1'$ is the hypothetical production possibilities curve that would exist between the private good and the public good before trade. Since, by assumption, there is no production of the public good, the initial point would be at OP_1 production of the private good in region I and $O'P_1$ production of the private good in region II. The initial effect of trade on the production possibilities curve in region I would be to shift the curve to $P_2 P_1'$. There is no shift in the production possibilities curve along the horizontal axis since the natural resource is not an input into the public good. If the natural resource were an input into the public good, e.g., natural resources are an input into various types of military hardware for national defense, the production possibilities curve would also shift in along the horizontal axis.

The increase in factors as the result of exporting the natural resource would have the effect of shifting the production possibilities curve out to $P_3 P_3'$. The effect of the severance tax and producing the public good would be to shift production along the production possibilities curve $P_3 P_3'$ to some point K. The effect of the exportation of the severance tax would be to shift the production possibilities curve out to $P_4 P_4'$ and production would be at some point L. At this point the community indifference curve and the region's production possibilities curve are tangent. Point L indicates the equilibrium point for region I. However, the presence of spillovers will usually affect output decisions regarding the public good, and therefore, the final equilibrium point must be derived by examining reaction curves. In the case being examined here, the public good is being produced in only one region and therefore reaction curves are not necessary to determine equilibrium.

The hypothetical production possibilities curve for region II is shown as the dotted line $P_1 P_5'$. Also, shown is the amount of the spillin from the production of the public good in region I and gains from trade. This is depicted by the line $P_6 P_6'$. It is important to note that potential production of the private good for both regions has increased as a result of trade of the natural resource—by $P_1 P_4$ for region I and by the difference between $0'0''$ and $P_1 P_4$ for region II.

II. TRADE OF THE NATURAL RESOURCE WITH A SEVERANCE TAX, TRADE OF THE PRIVATE GOOD WITH AN EXCISE TAX AND NO FACTOR MOBILITY

Figure 3a shows the production possibilities curve of region I, with the original, no-trade production possibilities curve being $P_1 A P_1'$. This is the identical production possibilities curve found in Figure 1a. Initial equilibrium is again at point A which represents maximum production of the private good with no trade. Introducing trade between regions I and II will move region I down its production possibilities curve from point A to point B. The introduction of the severance tax initially will move production from B to C_1, due to the change in relative prices and, of course, shift the production possibilities curve to $P_2 P_2'$. Final production will be at some point like C_2 and consumption will be at D.

Turning to Figure 3b, the initial production possibilities curve is $P_3 P_3'$. Trade in the natural resource will shift region II's production possibilities curve to $P_4 P_3'$, with production being at some point F. As in the case of factor mobility, it has been assumed that the relative price differentials between the imported natural resource as compared to the domestically produced natural resource results in the hump being to the left (outside) of the box. Once again, the effect of the severance tax will change relative prices and move production back toward G. Given trade in the two goods and no factor mobility, associated with any production possibilities curve will be a consumption possibilities curve such as $C_2 E$ and corresponding with production at point G would be a point H on the consumption possibilities curve.

Now suppose that region II desires to produce a public good and has decided that this will be financed through an excise tax levied on the private good. The effect of the excise tax will be to change relative prices between the natural resource and the private good (denoted by a move from G to I), and this would alter production along a lower production possibilities curve $P_5 P_5'$ to some point, say J. Associated with J, of course, is a point on a lower consumption possibilities curve with final equilibrium being at point K.

Returning to Figure 3a, the effect of the excise tax will be to change the relative prices between the private good and the natural resource which would alter production along production possibilities curve $P_2 P_2'$ from C_2 to L. This would be associated with a lower consumption possibilities curve since part of the excise tax is being imported and consumption would be at some point M.

Figure 4 represents the inverted box diagram which was found in Figure 2. Turning first to region I, the effect of trade would be to create a consumption possibilities curve $C_1 P_1'$ which would be associated with production possibilities curve $P_1 P_1'$.[3] Assuming that we are initially at point A, we can demonstrate the effect of an increase in the severance tax to finance the public good

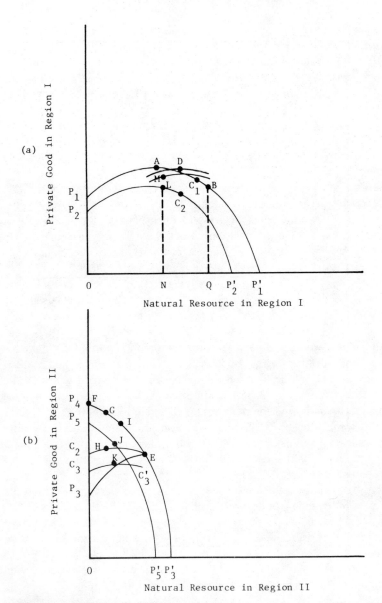

Figure 3: Trade of Natural Resource with Severance Tax and Trade of Private Good with Excise Tax (no factor mobility)

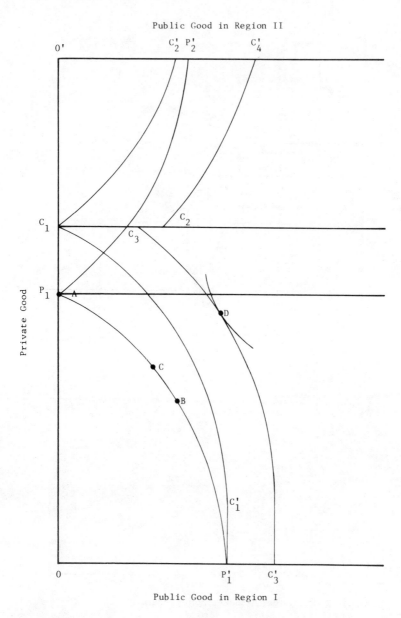

Figure 4: Production of Public Goods in Both Regions with Spillovers

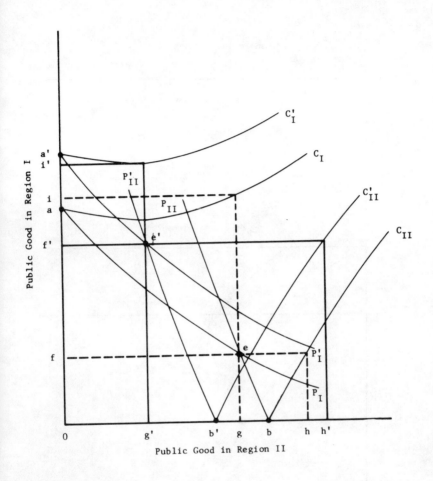

Figure 5: Reaction Curves Associated with Figure 4

in region I and the levy of an excise tax in region II to finance the public good. The severance tax in region I would move production from A to B along P_1P_1'. The effect of an excise tax levied in region II would be to move production in region I from point B to point C on curve P_1P_1'.

The production of the public good in region I of course will create spillovers in region II and vice versa. Looking at region II, the after-trade production possibilities curve should be P_1P_2' and the corresponding consumption possibilities curve would be C_1C_2' and C_2C_4' would represent the consumption possibilities including the spillin from region I. In region I the consumption possibilities curve after the spillin would be represented by C_3C_3'. Point D denotes the point of tangency of region I's community indifference curve and its consumption possibilities curve. In order to find the final point of equilibrium the reaction curves must be examined, which are depicted in Figure 5.

Figure 5 demonstrates the reaction curves associated with Figure 4. (For a more complete explanation of the reaction curves associated with tax exportation see Breton, 1970, and Sandler and Shelton, 1972: 739-743.) The initial no-tax exportation, no-public good spillover situation will result in 0b production of the public good in region II and 0a production of the public good in region I. The net effects of the tax exportation are shown as moving the reaction curves inward for region II and upward along the vertical axis for region I. This indicates that region I has an advantage in terms of tax exportation over region II. (It should be stressed that the original situation represents a no-tax exportation situation and not a no-tax situation.)

The curves marked C represent the consumption curves, the curves marked P represent the production curves in each region which is associated with levels of production in the other region. In order to determine the various equilibrium values of production, it is necessary to draw a horizontal line from D down to C_1P_1' in Figure 4 and then a vertical line down to the original production possibilities curve P_1P_1'. Tracing all of these equilibrium values of consumption and production will give you the values for the path along the production and consumption reaction curves in Figure 5. Equilibrium will be at e' in Figure 5 with consumption at i' and production at f' in region I and consumption at h' and production at g' in region II. The reaction curves are drawn assuming some level of taxation in both regions. Of course, neither region would impose a tax unless its welfare position is increased as a result of the tax.

III. THE EFFECTS OF TAXATION ON PRIVATE
AND PUBLIC SECTOR PRODUCTION

The general effects of severance taxes were discussed in the previous section. In the case of factor mobility, the severance tax in region I changed relative prices and altered production in favor of the private good which was denoted by movement along the production possibilities curve (Figure 1). Also, the tax resulted in resources being withdrawn from private production which was depicted by an inward shift of the production possibilities curve. Finally, it was noted that if tax exportation occurs, the production possibilities curve will not shift in by the full amount of the tax. However, it should be noted that region I would adopt a severance tax only if demand for the natural resource in region II is price inelastic, for adopting a severance tax with elastic demand in region II would decrease the total resources (factors of production) withdrawn from region II. If demand were elastic in region II, region I would impose an income tax in order to finance the public good.

The adoption of the severance tax in region I creates a price distortion, but in the case presented here the distortion is somewhat more complex. In the usual case where the production possibilities diagram depicts the trade-off between two final goods, remedying a price distortion on one of the goods would call for the adoption of an excise tax on the alternate good. While the natural resource can be viewed as a "final" good on the downward sloping portion of the production possibilities curve, it is nevertheless an input into the private good produced in region I and changing the price for export also changes the price faced by domestic users. Therefore, depending on factor substitution, the adoption of a severance tax might have to be coupled with proportional taxes on other factors in order to lessen the factor input price distortion which can be depicted as a greater inward shift of the production possibilities curve. However, adopting such a tax policy may slow the resource withdrawal from region II. For example, the flow of labor from region II will be slowed if the real wage is reduced by taxation in region I. Therefore, region I must face the trade-off between the increased resource flow from region I and factor input distortion.

Region II may be better off levying an income tax than an excise tax in order to finance a public good, since there is no offsetting beneficial income effect from tax exportation. However, an income tax will increase labor mobility since labor will migrate until the real wage is equal in the two regions and this would increase the negative income effect. The income effect resulting from migration might more than offset a distorting price effect of levying an excise tax on the private good.

In the case of no factor mobility once again, depending on the degree of exportation, region I is better off levying a severance tax, coupled with taxes on other factors, but now region I does not face the problem of slowing resource flows from region I by lessening factor price distortion through taxation of the other factors. However, region II has more incentive to adopt an excise tax, since part of the tax is exported to region I.

Two further important tax issues are the effect of the severance tax on natural resource production and the effect of tax exportation on public good production when public good spillovers occur. The conventional economic argument is that a severance tax will reduce the rate of extraction because the present value of the mineral yet to be extracted will be reduced (Lockner, 1965). In the present study, the imposition of the severance tax resulted in a reduction in natural resource output in the region imposing the tax (region I) because of a price effect and a negative income effect[4] (Figures 1 and 3). When the excise tax was imposed by region II, a further reduction in natural resource output occurred in region I because of the price effect and the income effect resulting from tax importation. The reduction in natural resource production in region I due to the severance tax and excise tax is denoted by NQ in Figure 3a. Of course, natural resource production with trade and taxes still exceeds production before trade.

The effects of tax exportation on public good production can best be illustrated by examining the polar cases—zero tax exportation and complete exportation of the severance tax. Zero tax exportation could occur: (a) because the natural resource is not exported; or (b) because of the inability of the producer to export the tax; e.g., lack of economic power or a perfectly competitive market. Regarding the latter, and assuming factor mobility in the taxing region, relative prices are distorted in favor of the nontaxed good (i.e., the private good) and the production possibilities curve shifts in by the total amount of the tax. The public good is produced and the other region (in our example, region II) receives public good spillins but does not incur tax importation. In region II the marginal benefits from the spillovers exceed the marginal tax which is zero. The result, of course, is public good underproduction in the taxing region.

Complete exportation of the tax is impossible in our example because the natural resource is an input to the private good which is consumed in the taxing region. However, the larger the share of the tax which is exported, the closer the after-tax production possibilities curve is to the pretax curve. Also, more of the public good production in the taxing region (region I) is being financed by region II. If marginal taxes paid by region II exceed the marginal benefit of spillovers from region I, overproduction of the public good will occur. It is important to note that the federation can remain stable even if tax importation exceeds the benefits from public good spillins. What is necessary for stability is that gains from trade plus the benefits from public good spillins are at least equal to the costs of tax importation. Optimal production of the public good (both regions combined) will occur when the marginal benefit of the spillover equals the marginal costs of the public good to region II in the form of tax importation. This would be only one of numerous possible outcomes resulting from negotiation between the two members of the federation.[5] Tax exportation can compensate the producing region for public good spillovers and lead to a more optimal level of public good production.

The results are similar assuming no factor mobility. With no factor mobility, the greater the share of the tax exported, the less the net inward shift in the production possibilities curve in the taxing region and the higher the consumption possibilities curve attainable.

IV. SUMMARY AND CONCLUSIONS

This paper examines the effects of taxation on private and public sector production using a general equilibrium framework. The paper extends the literature regarding allocation of resources in a federal structure when public good spillovers and tax exportation occur. The previous literature assumed exportation to occur but did not examine the internal regional production effects. Furthermore, this paper extends the analysis to include natural resource production which is an input into private good production. Since natural resources are a convenient and important mechanism for exporting taxes, an analysis of the potential effects of natural resource taxation has important implications for tax policy, particularly when considered in a federal structure.

Two production situations are examined—natural resource and private good, and private good and public good. Section I investigates interregional trade of the natural resource with a severance tax and factor mobility. Section II presents the case of trade of the natural resource with a severance tax and trade of the private good with an excise tax and factor immobility. These sections illustrate the income effects of trade, the price and income effects of taxation and identify the conditions necessary for stability of the federation. Also, the trade-offs between private and public good production and private and public good consumption, and the effects of public good and tax spillovers are demonstrated.

Several interesting implications regarding tax policy are developed with the assumptions specified. In the case of factor mobility, the adoption of a severance tax creates an unusual type of price distortion because the natural resource is an input into private good production in the taxing region. Therefore, a severance tax might be coupled with proportional taxes on the other factors in order to lessen factor input price distortion. However, taxation of factor inputs slows resource withdrawal from the other region and the taxing region must consider the trade-off between increased resource flows from the other region and factor input distortion. The other region may be better off levying an income tax than an excise tax in order to finance a public good because there is no beneficial income effect from tax exportation. This region must consider the trade-off between out-migration of resources caused by an income tax and price distortion caused by an excise tax on the private good.

The results are similar with factor immobility. However, the region imposing the severance tax is not concerned with the slowing of resource flows from the other region caused by taxation of factor inputs. Also, the other region has more incentive to adopt an excise tax because part of the tax is exported.

The paper demonstrates with the assumptions specified that a severance tax will reduce natural resource production because of price and income effects. Natural resource production in the region imposing the severance tax will be reduced further if the other region imposes an excise tax on the private good.

Public good overproduction as well as underproduction can occur without jeopardizing the stability of the federation because of gains from trade. In the original paper (Sandler and Shelton, 1972) the federation would remain stable only with public good underproduction or optimal production. If overproduction occurred, the marginal taxes paid by the other region through tax importation would exceed the marginal benefits from public good spillins and the federation would be unstable. With gains from trade the federation can remain stable. For stability, it is necessary that gains from trade plus benefits from public good spillins are at least equal to the costs of tax importation. In the case of underproduction of the public good, tax exportation can compensate the producing region for public good spillovers and lead to a more optimal level of public good production (more optimal for both regions combined).

NOTES

1. For simplicity, it is assumed that the production possibilities curve shifts out so as to preserve the slope along a ray from the origin; i.e., a homothetic shift.

2. Throughout the analysis it is assumed that some of the resources utilized in the production of the public good are withdrawn from the region imposing the indirect tax (in this case region I). Stated differently, the real resources generated from the other region (region II) through tax exportation are not sufficient to produce the amount of public good desired in the region imposing the tax and maintain private sector production at the pretax level. As a result, the production possibilities curve in the taxing region always shifts inward after the indirect tax is imposed. The social welfare function which is represented by the community indifference curve shown in Figure 2 determines how much of the public good region I wants to produce relative to the private good.

3. The consumption possibilities curve for region I, C_1P_1', undergoes a vertical displacement and becomes a strait line at C_1', because once region I has produced all of the public good possible, it will still have C_1' $P_1' = P_1C_1$ of the private good available. Since resources are immobile, region I can only buy private goods from region II.) Similarly, the production possibilities curve for region II becomes vertical at $0'$, (i.e., outside the box). For a discussion of this point see Greene (1975).

4. The reduction in natural resource production occurs because of the assumptions made regarding the degree of tax exportation and public good demand in region I

relative to real resources generated from the other region by the severance tax (fn. 2). Under other assumptions natural resource production could increase after the severance tax is imposed because the positive income effect (denoted by an outward shift of the production possibilities curve) could offset the price effect. This type of situation was not considered in the analysis because the stability of the federation is jeopardized.

5. Two types of behavior have been assumed in the literature dealing with federalism—neutrality and cooperation. The former assumes that members of one jurisdiction simply adjust to the spillins resulting from actions of members of another jurisdiction. The latter assumes that members react to the spillins and negotiate and bargain. For a discussion of these assumptions, see Breton (1970: 883-885).

BIBLIOGRAPHY

BRETON, A. (1970) "Public Goods and the Stability of Federalism." Kyklos 23, 4: 882-902.

GREENE, K. V. (1975) "Fiscal Federalism, Spillovers, and the Export of Taxes: A Comment." Kyklos 28, 2: 412-418.

HOGAN, T. D. and SHELTON, R. B. (1973) "Interstate Tax Exportation and States' Fiscal Structures." National Tax Journal 26, 4(December): 553-564.

LOCKNER, A. (1965) "The Economic Effect of the Severance Tax on Decisions of the Mining Firm." Natural Resources Journal 5, 1(January): 468-485.

McLURE, C. E. (1964) "Commodity Tax Incidence." National Tax Journal 17, 2(June): 187-204.

――― (1967) "Interstate Exporting of State and Local Taxes: Estimates for 1962." National Tax Journal 20, 1(March): 49-77.

――― (1969) "The Interregional Incidence of General Regional Taxes." Public Finance 24, 3: 457-483.

――― (1970) "Taxation, Substitution and Industrial Location." Journal of Political Economy 78, 1(January-February): 112-132.

SANDLER, T. M. and SHELTON, R. B. (1972) "Fiscal Federalism, Spillovers and the Export of Taxes." Kyklos 25, 4: 736-753.

SHELTON, R. B. and MORGAN, W. E. (1977) "Natural Resource Taxation, Tax Exportation and Regional Energy Policies." Natural Resources Journal 17, 2 (April): 261-282.

TRANSACTIONS NETWORKS, ECONOMIC GROWTH, AND INCOME DISTRIBUTION

THOMAS D. CROCKER
University of Wyoming

INTRODUCTION

It is widely acknowledged in the national and regional development literature that outside investment has been and is likely to remain a major growth stimulant in less developed areas that historically have been more or less autarchic. However, in the more sociologically oriented parts of the national development literature, dismay is often expressed about the fate of the majority of the native populations whose countries are experiencing large scale foreign investment. Similar concerns are now being expressed for those rural agricultural areas of the United States likely to be impacted by substantial energy or recreational developments.[1] Although those stating these concerns consistently cite the breaking down of the traditional social fabric and the inability of much of the native population to compete with sophisticated and wealthy outsiders, little effort appears to have been devoted to exploring in a logical fashion the underlying causes of the traditionalists' difficulties. It is frequently noted that existing growth models serve to direct policies toward typically included variables such as the volume of imports and the endowment of capital goods, thereby diverting attention away from possible significant repercussions of outside investment upon social and personal attitudes, business and government conduct, and social and geographical mobility. The purpose of this paper is to present and briefly explore one partial equilibrium, long-run framework capable of providing some insight into the underlying causes of social disruption. Changes in the distribution of income between social classes are shown to be at least partially dependent upon differences across classes in the costs of participation in transactions networks specialized in the exchange of particular kinds of goods and services. It is concluded that foreign investments typically thought to promote economic growth in less-developed areas can, by altering societal choices over

AUTHOR'S NOTE: Todd Sandler has made several worthwhile suggestions that have improved both the style and substantive content of this paper.

a broad variety of public goods, bring about perverse results. The perspective of the paper is an adaptation of Brunner and Meltzer (1971), while the analytical tools employed draw heavily from Lipsey and Rosenbluth (1971).

I. THE CONCEPT OF A TRANSACTIONS NETWORK

Legal scholars are sometimes heard to refer to the law as a bundle or network of rights defining, often through the intermediation of physical goods, the reciprocal relation of one human to another.[2] The definition has always seemed to me to be a particularly apt description of a social system; that is, a social system is a bundle or network of market and nonmarket sanctions and customs defining the reciprocal relations among men. These networks of sanctions and customs serve two purposes: (1) they provide a set of signals that convey the meaning of one individual's activities to another individual; and (2) they bound the question of deciding how to decide to respond to these signals. In short, these sanctions and customs, along with existing communications and transportation technologies, define feasible market and nonmarket transactions possibilities. Since the use of a network by one individual will often not influence its availability for a number of other individuals (an exchange, in accordance with the laws of the land, of my cash for a six-pack of Budweiser will not affect the availability of similar exchange opportunities for other individuals); and since the aforementioned reciprocity feature requires the nonexclusion, rather than the exclusion of others, a transactions network can legitimately be viewed as having public good features. Furthermore, the sanctions and customs of the network are prerequisites for exchange because they give content and interpretation to exchange for all actual and potential network participants. The provision of content and interpretation is simply the provision of information. Use of information by any one individual does not reduce the available stock. Moreover, as Marshall (1974) and others have shown, except under conditions where redistributions of existing wealth are the motivating force, it is generally in the individual's best interests to make other individuals aware of exchange opportunities.

Networks have been differentiated across locales according to the exigencies of the native population and its historical antecendents. Usually viewed as the polar extremes of organizing principles for societies is the extended family, in which substantial own-consumption reducing transfer payments are frequently and voluntarily made across individuals whose only ties may be geographical proximity, and the nuclear family, in which these frequent and voluntary transfers are limited to one's mate and children. These transfers are not limited to resources already in hand but also may include abstinence from activities that detract from the available resources of other family members. Replacing transfer payments or grants in the nuclear family society are markets in which pecuniary prices tied to explicit contractual obligations serve as the dominant means of conveying information and providing incentives. The sole power of the individual to participate in trade is derived from the ownership of property, and the only possible transaction outside the nuclear family is the exchange of promises or transfers of rights to ownership via a contract.[3]

Eisenberg (1976) has recently contributed to the clarification of the essential differences between nuclear and extended family societies. He describes the nuclear family society as using organizing principles based on rather inviolable "rights" and therefore adjudication of disputes, while the extended family is based on negotiation and compromise. Negotiation is graduated, accommodative, and intimate; adjudication is binary, and because it is strongly dependent upon agents to gather information, to make decisions, to establish contracts, and to settle disputes, its highly stylized norms often embody less than the sum total of principles the trading parties consider to be potentially applicable. When disputes exist, the linear nature of adjudication, in contrast to negotiation, makes it difficult or impossible to develop and test hypotheses, the choice of remedies is more constrained, and the disputants are sharply limited in both the content and the form of their participations.

Perhaps the major feature distinguishing the extended family society is the relative paucity of substitute transactors in the former. Since communication and transport systems in the former are usually not technologically sophisticated, the flow of goods, capital, and labor within the nation or region is more costly and therefore fragmented. Because substitute trading partners are not readily available, individuals in the extended family society have ongoing relations requiring regular dealings with each other over long periods of time on many issues that cannot be known in advance. Few, if any, exchanges are masked by anonymity with each party to an exchange transacting with an agent who hopes to make his fortune by selling and buying the promises of the parties to deliver future goods. Breaching of accepted sanctions and customs, if not necessarily more easily detected, is, once detected, certainly more readily penalized, since the breacher has no alternative trading partners to whom to turn.

The frequent use of agents and forward contracts in the nuclear family society introduces a further distinctive difference between it and the extended family society. Agents make their fortunes by practicing temporal and/or spatial arbitrage rather than by producing and/or consuming. The agent may buy a promise to deliver goods from a certain producer. This promise may then be sold to another agent in exchange for the promise of the second agent to pay the first agent a money sum upon actual delivery of the goods. In turn, the second agent may sell his contract to yet another agent. The arbitrage process, in effect, creates through a chain of transactions a set of assets, the value of each of which is contingent upon the fulfillment of promises to deliver the originally contracted for goods at the agreed upon dates. These arbitrage created assets (forward contracts) are valuable if and only if the agents' expectations about the fulfillment of contracts are realized. If only one agent fails to fulfill the terms of his contract, the value of the arbitrage assets held by all other agents in the chain will be negated. The gains to the agent who breached the contract could be exceeded by the losses incurred by the victims of the breach. Of course, if contract breaching becomes excessive, agents will take defensive postures by taking out insurance, holding inventories, integrating vertically backward to original sources of supply, and perhaps even adopting limited forms of the extended family society, e.g., establishing licensure as a necessary condition for assuming the agents' role.

One could extend the list of distinctive differences between nuclear and extended family societies. For our purposes, however, it is only important that one be able to characterize them in terms of their transactions networks and that differences in the transactions networks be admitted. Although the issue is not of central concern to this paper, an explanation of the causes of the differences could start from the increase in the feasible set of trading partners arising from advantages in endowments of communication and transportation facilities. One would then show how the exhaustion of all Pareto-relevant trading opportunities with the larger market size requires the adoption of a different transactions network than with smaller market sizes. Williamson (1975) is particularly instructive in this regard.

II. ECONOMIC GROWTH AND CHOICE OF A TRANSACTIONS NETWORK

The import of advanced technology into less developed locales often starts with what appears to be a desirable bargain with a multinational corporation. This initial bargain frequently leads to a continuing relationship with the parent company of the corporation. As Krueger (1974) has pointed out, often there are close ties between those who develop the technologies and those who choose what is to be imported. The aggregate employment effects of adopting capital-intensive technologies in economies where labor is plentiful have long been recognized; only recently, however, has major concern been expressed about the influence of this advanced technology upon the pattern of income distribution in the importing labor-rich country.[4] The shares of national income accruing to capital and skilled labor are said to be increased, and the location and organization of production is viewed as urban-biased. Pockets of very high wealth are created having production and consumption patterns bearing little semblance to those available to the great majority of the population. Finally, the prospect of ultimately gaining admission to these pockets of wealth is thought to contribute to a rural to urban migration that often concludes in the marginalization and impoverishment of the general work force along with the concentration of resources, information, and political power in the hands of privileged minorities.

Consider a less developed nation or region in which a multinational corporation has recently made an advanced technology, capital intensive, and substantial (from the importing nation's or region's perspective) investment. Concomitant with this investment is the training of a carefully selected portion of the nation's work force to operate the technology. The pay scales of this selected portion are strongly influenced by international norms, if not completely determined by them.

Assume, for simplicity, that all the nation's inhabitants have identical preference orderings. These inhabitants do, however, have differing endowments of human capital as well as varying degrees of familiarity with the trading opportunities made available by the introduction of the new technology. Differences in familiarity arise because of variations among individual inhabitants in the kinds of goods and services bought and sold, as well as differences in the frequencies with which these purchases and sales occur. Further assume that the only factor transactions in which these inhabitants participate are sales of their personal labor. Viewed as preference orderings, the inhabitants are therefore indistinguishable from one another; they are, however, distinctive as sellers of labor because of differences in their production skills and stocks of information about labor exchange opportunities. One group of inhabitants, all of whom are nuclear family members, specializes in labor exchanges involving the production of TV sets, plastics, psychology majors and other accoutrements of advanced industrial nations. The other inhabitant group, composed of extended families, specialize in labor exchanges involving production of subsistence foods, cottage goods, ceremonies and festivals, and similar items. There are thus two bundles of goods, modern and traditionalist, and two transactions networks, each network being partially specialized with respect to facilitating labor exchanges for a particular bundle. An inhabitant can move from one network to another but only at an increasing marginal cost in acquiring information about transactions networks different from that in which he initially resided.

In Figure 1, the N-ray represents the quantity of modern (M) and traditionalist (T) goods that can be obtained for a given expenditure on resources used to consummate a labor transaction in the nuclear family transactions network. Absolute market prices of M-goods and T-goods are assumed constant within any single network. Any particular distance along the ray is inversely proportional to the resource cost of executing a normalized labor transaction. The expected price at which the labor transaction occurs is assumed to be linearly and negatively related to the cost of executing the transaction.[5] The E, or extended family transaction network, ray is constructed in the same fashion as the N-ray. Thus in Figure 1, if the individual participates in a given network, the bundle of M and T-goods he will be able to acquire is dependent only upon the cost to him of arranging and participating in transactions for the sale of his labor.

The frontiers ab and a'b in Figure 1 represent different linear combinations of M and T attainable with the two networks. They are transaction possibility frontiers. Combinations lying outside the N-E cone are unattainable because no network exists by which they can be acquired. The distances ab and a'b will vary directly with the degree of dissimilarity between the two networks, i.e., the extent to which features found in one are absent in the other. Note that, as drawn, the E-network has an absolute advantage along the a'b frontier. The U-curve is an indifference function drawn as if both M and T-goods have diminishing marginal rates of substitution.

With the introduction of new technologies or with increases in real incomes, the transactions frontier can move outward and/or its slope can be

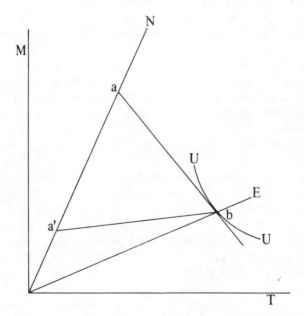

Figure 1: Optimal Transactions Network

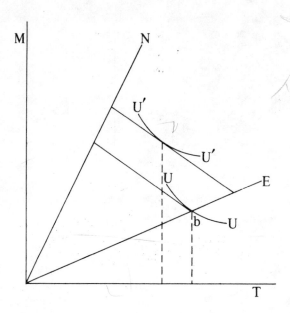

Figure 2: Superior Goods and Network Choice

altered. This can result in changes in both the combination of goods chosen as
well as the extent to which one network or the other is used. In Figure 2, for
example, T-goods have become inferior and therefore have a negative income
elasticity; the increase in real income represented by the shift of the transactions frontier from ab to a'b' actually leads to reduced consumption of
T-goods. Additionally, the increase in real income, which in this example does
not even involve a change in the relative costs of executing transactions in the
two networks, has caused the use of the E-network to decline. Not only have
the T-goods become inferior, the E-network, which specializes in the production and exchange of T-goods, is now also inferior.

Inferiority of the E-network does not require that the T-goods be inferior.
Figure 3 illustrates this. To show that a network may be inferior even though
the goods in which it is specialized are normal, an unconstrained income
transactions line, I, is constructed in Figure 3b. This is accomplished by
extending the transactions frontiers in Figure 3a to the axes and permitting
income to vary over all levels. The tangencies of the indifference functions
with the transactions frontiers then trace out an income transactions line
unconstrained by the unavailability of labor sales networks in which income
can be earned to acquire M or T-goods.

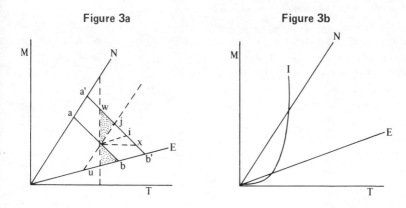

Figure 3: An Income Transactions Line

Now permit the income transactions line to intersect v in Figure 3a. Assume that the individual arrives at v by first selling enough labor in the E-network to get him from the origin to u, and then participating in the N-network enough to take him from u to v. The (T,M) combination of goods the individual acquires is thus defined. Now, due perhaps to technological improvements, the transactions frontier moves outward from ab to a'b'. As it moves outward, construct lines through v to cut a'b' at w and x. Then uw is parallel to the M-axis and vx is parallel to the T-axis. Any combination of (T,M) within this new set of axes therefore represents an unambiguous improvement in the individual's and the society's utility, given that both goods are normal.

Next draw a line through v that is parallel to the N-ray. This line intersects a'b' at j. A similar line through v and parallel to the E-ray intersects a'b' at i. Movement from ab to a'b' along the vj line implies that only the nuclear family transactions network is being used to execute the increased labor transactions necessary to obtain the wherewithal to acquire the larger bundle of M and T-goods. This is because the ratio in which the goods are acquired along vj is identical to the ratio in which they are acquired in the N-network. If, instead, the movement from ab to a'b' were along vi, only the E-network would be used.

Now presume that in addition to going through v, the income transactions line goes through wj, where w lies on a'b' but above j. This implies that over the increases in real income represented by the shift from ab to a'b', the E-network has become inferior, even though T-goods continue to be normal. The E-network, in effect, has a negative income elasticity of demand. For various income changes, the shaded area of Figure 3 represents those combinations of (T,M) goods for which the extended family transactions network will be inferior, although (T,M) goods are normal. More precisely, the E-network will be inferior if the slope at v of the income transactions line exceeds the slope of the N-ray. In other words, the E-network will be inferior if the income elasticity of demand for M-goods is high enough relative to the same elasticity for T-goods.

Over time it is conceivable that the N and E-networks will adapt to each other by adopting certain traits of the other. For example, the E-network may become more sensitive to the sanctions and customs of the traditionalists. This convergence of the two networks can be represented by a coming together of the N and E-rays in Figure 3a. As the two rays approach each other, the line segment ji must be reduced. This shortening of the ji segment implies that the likelihood of an income transactions line passing through ji is also reduced. Given that the income elasticity of demand for modern goods is substantially higher than for traditional goods, the alteration of extended family networks by having them adopt certain features of nuclear family networks (or the softening of N-networks by making them more like E-networks) can only hasten the demise of the E-network. The comparative advantage of the N-network in executing labor sales permitting the acquisition of M and T-goods is enhanced.

Even a decline in the resources cost of executing transactions in one network relative to the costs in the other does not guarantee greater use of the former network. Changes in these relative costs may occur, for example, because of a technological change or the receipt of information specialized to only one network. In Figure 4, the resource cost of executing labor transactions in the E-network has declined, as indicated by the movement of the transactions possibility frontier from ab to ab'. As before, let the income transactions line pass through v, and draw a vertical line through v to pass through ab' at w. If the T-goods are normal, the substitution effect of this reduction in the resource costs of executing transactions via the E-network must increase consumption of T-goods and reduce consumption of M-goods, the income effect increases both, and equilibrium must be in the range wb'. Now draw a line through v and parallel to the N-ray. As in Figure 3, movement along this line implies that only the N-network is being used to execute the increased labor transactions necessary to acquire the goods. If the income transactions line falls on the wj line segment, the E-network, in spite of and as a result of the reduction in the cost of using it, would be used less than it previously had been. The reason this could occur is because the reduction in the cost of using the E-network brings about an increase in the individual's real income. If his income elasticity of demand for M-goods relative to T-goods is sufficiently high, he will switch his resource savings in

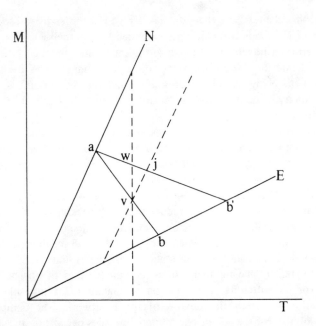

Figure 4: Changing Costs of Network Participation

the E-network (the T intensive network) to the N-network (the M intensive network) in order to be able to obtain more of the M-good. If consumption is to be carried to the right of j in Figure 4, the substitution effect must be very strong when the income elasticity of demand for M-goods is much greater than for T-goods. In effect, the argument of this paragraph shows that a Giffen network can exist. Geometrically, all that is required is for the slope of the income transactions line to be greater than the ratio, as given by the slope of the N-ray, in which the N-network executes labor transactions permitting the acquisition of M-goods and T-goods.

III. TRANSACTIONS NETWORKS, PUBLIC GOODS, AND MARKET SIGNALING

The analysis of Figure 4 in the previous section justified the adoption of a skeptical (or at least cautious) attitude toward proposals similar to Todero's (1969) in which traditionalist rural populations are to be subsidized in order to slow rural migration to the urban areas of less developed countries. One can by no means unequivocally conclude that such subsidies will enhance the relative attractiveness of the traditionalist life. In fact, they may substantially detract from this relative attractiveness and therefore hasten the migration from rural to urban areas as well as accelerating the substitution of modernist for traditionalist ways.[6]

If increases in real income differentially affect the extent to which particular transactions networks are used and if the resource costs of using these networks decline with frequency of use, those who are specialized in the network the costs of which have declined will find that their incomes have increased relative to those individuals specialized in less well situated networks. For both groups of individuals, the advantages of one network relative to another may have increased, although the benefits to the more historically specialized group or the more adaptive group will have increased relatively more. This result is readily illustrated in Figure 5, where the transactions frontier has shifted from ab to a″b″ for the nuclear family group and from ab to a′b′ for the extended family group. Members of the latter are able to execute fewer labor sales: thus they receive smaller incomes and settle upon a lower indifference function.

In effect, a foreign private or governmental investment has brought about a substitution of one network for another and therefore a substitution of one

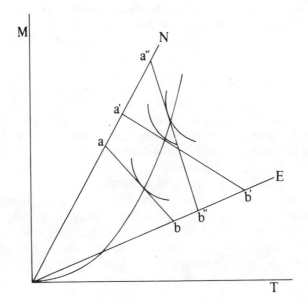

Figure 5: Division of Network Gains from Trade

public good for another. Moreover, to the extent that some measure describing the general distribution of income enters individuals' utility functions, this foreign-induced substitution of public goods has influenced the character of another public good, income distribution.[7] One might, in addition, speculate that the network substitution could affect the society's supply decisions for other public goods. For example, given that the impact of public goods upon transactions costs differs across networks, the actors in an N-network are under most circumstances more liely to be willing to fund a highway than a communal meeting hall. Finally, the foreign-induced network substitution may alter the observable traits of individuals and therefore the form of the culture of the country. Since cultural traits such as attitudes toward work are to some positive degree nonrivalrous and not entirely susceptible to the prevention of imitation by others, the character of another public good can be affected. If cultural traits are learned, an intergenrational public goods aspect is introduced.

Most of the aforementioned influences of network substitutions upon the choice of public goods are fairly obvious. The influence of these foreign-induced substitutions upon local culture may, however, be less so, and might, in fact, appear a bit farfetched. Nevertheless, a process by which these cultural changes can occur is easily sketched.

If, as in Figure 5, the rewards to the nuclear group are initially greater than the rewards to the extended group, the latter might be expected to try to adopt modes of behavior allowing them to participate with lower transactions costs in the N-network. In doing so, individuals in the extended group are making decisions about the allocation of their efforts prior to actual trade. However, if only because the nuclear group is the major initial local beneficiary of the foreign investment and will therefore usually have greater wealth, greater familiarity with, and thus better access to the government levers defining the scope for individual and collective initiative, it can do much to maintain its initial advantage in the transactions costs of participating in the N-network. In particular, assuming that markets are not utterly perfect, the nuclear group can reasonably be expected to recognize that there will be a rent or surplus associated with any particular trade and that network rules can influence the division of that rent or surplus. Rules which alter the expected division of gains from trade will also alter, before the trade actually occurs, the allocation decisions of the potential parties to the trade. Individual behavior in the search for and the anticipation of trade will be changed. The incentive structure of each group takes on a form that causes efforts to be directed toward these enterprises where the group's expected rents or surpluses will be maximized. If these rents or surpluses appear greatest in enterprises having little potential for ultimate entry into the class that molds the N-network (e.g., "street" businesses), what was once the extended group can be relegated to the position of a permanent underclass. In essence, members of the extended group choose to specialize in what appears to the original N-network members as the less desirable components of the N-network. Once having adopted the behavioral traits necessary for success in these less desirable components, any of the market signaling phenomena discussed by Spence (1973) and Starrett (1976) can serve as the basis for the permanently greater (relative to the original N-network members) N-network transactions costs borne by members of what was formerly the extended group.

In summary, any one of a number of common international trade instruments (e.g., multinational corporations, foreign aid, grants, etc.) frequently associated with explicit market-oriented modes of organization intended to promote economic growth can result in the substitution of one public good, a nuclear family transactions network, for another public good, an extended family network. The mix of public goods in the society can therefore be altered in deep and pervasive ways. Perhaps more important, are the possible distributional consequences stemming from the higher relative transactions costs faced by most former adherents of the E-network. By hypothesis, those who initially gain by participating in the N-network acquire, among other things, the ability to mold the rules and customs of this network so that the division of gains from trade perpetuates their initial advantage. This can be accomplished by structuring the incentive system of the extended family group in a fashion assuring that it appears disadvantageous to compete in trades with the leaders of the N-network. Thus, unless care is taken to assure continuing access of all segments of a population to all enterprises within the N-network, it is by no means clear that the contributions of international investments to the economic growth of less-developed locales are unqualified blessings. In fact, by starting a process that can lead to restrictions of the trade opportunities available to large segments of native populations, such investments can impose uncompensated social costs upon these segments. The restrictions serve only to transfer wealth from one population segment to another.

NOTES

1. On national economics, see Hagen (1962: 185-217), and on the United States, see VanderMeulen and Paananen (1976).

2. See Posner (1972), for example. Polinsky (1974) is an interesting critique by an economist of the perspective.

3. For a distinctive economic analysis of transfers within the family, whether nuclear or extended, see Becker (1974). This paragraph is intended to describe the dominant tendencies of each society. It does not deny the existence of altruism, although in accordance with Becker (1974), one might explain such behavior in terms of expectations of future rewards. Altruism, in addition, may very well differ between the two

society types according to the frequencies of contacts among certain individuals, the number of individuals in the entire network, the lengths of representative transactions chains, and other factors.

4. See Jolly (1974), for example.

5. The assumption of linearity has no basis other than analytical convenience. However, the negativity assumption can be justified with a model that has the sample of job opportunities from which the individual can draw increasing with reduced resource costs of executing a labor sales transaction. It is elementary in probability theory that an increasing sample size reduces the variance of a probability distribution. If reductions in variance are monotonically related to declines in the individual's uncertainty about the wage he can expect and if the individual is risk averse, a reduction in the costs of executing labor sales will increase his effective expected price for the transaction. Moreover, the increased sample size implies that the best offer the individual will receive, assuming that job offers do not decay, cannot be less than with a smaller sampling of employment opportunities. For a survey of existing models constructed along these lines, see Rothschild (1973).

6. Although it will not be attempted here, a reasonable model in which rural to urban (extended family to nuclear family) migration actually increases the absolute cost, for those who remain, of using the extended family network should not be too difficult to construct.

7. Income distribution, to the extent it enters individuals' utility functions, can readily be viewed as an externality question rather than a public good question. If the identity of others who receive income matters to an individual, the externality approach appears more analytically interesting. In the public good model, Pareto-efficiency requires that a good be produced such that marginal cost equal marginal gain; in the externality model, the further condition is imposed that the total marginal gain be the same no matter who receives the goods. It is thus the exclusion principle that distinguishes the two models. In the public good model, everyone derives utility from an output once it is produced. In the externality model, once output is produced, the individuals who enjoy it (e.g., individual; and all those who are able to identify j and are also concerned with his consumption) depends upon the amount they are willing to pay. Prices are therefore able to exclude groups of people in the externality model.

BIBLIOGRAPHY

BECKER, G. S. (1974) "A Theory of Social Interactions." Journal of Political Economy 82(November/December): 1063-1094.
BRUNNER, K. and A. H. MELTZER (1971) "The Uses of Money: Money in the Theory of an Exchange Economy." The American Economic Review 61(December): 784-805.
EISENBERG, M. A. (1976) "Private-orderings Through Negotiation." Harvard Law Review 89(February): 637-681.
HAGEN, E. E. (1962) On the Theory of Social Change. Homewood, Illinois: The Dorsey Press, Inc.
JOLLY, R. (1974) "International Dimensions." Pp. 158-182 in H. Chenery, M. S. Ahluwalia, C. L. G. Bell, J. H. Duloy, and R. Jolly [eds.] Redistribution with Growth. London: Oxford University Press.
KIPSEY, R. G. and G. ROSENBLUTH (1971) "A Rehabilitation of the Giffen Good." The Canadian Journal of Economics 4(May): 131-163.

KRUEGER, A. O. (1974) "The Political Economy of the Re.t-seeking Society." The American Economic Review 64(June): 291-303.

MARSHALL, J. M. (1974) "Private Incentives and Public Information." The American Economic Review 64(June): 373-390.

POLINSKY, A. M. (1974) "Economic Analysis as a Potentially Defective Product: A Buyer's Guide to Posner's 'Economic Analysis of the Law'." Harvard Law Review 87(June): 1655-1681.

ROTHSCHILD, M. (1973) "Models of Market Organization with Imperfect Information: A Survey." Journal of Political Economy 8(November/December): 1283-1308.

SPENCE, M. (1973) "Job Market Signaling." The Quarterly Journal of Economics 87(August): 355-374.

STARRETT, D. (1976) "Social Institutions, Imperfect Information, and the Distribution of Income." The Quarterly Journal of Economics 90(May): 261-284.

TODARO, M. P. (1969) "A Model of Labor Migration and Urban Unemployment in Less Developed Countries." The American Economic Review 59(March): 138-148.

VANDERMEULEN, A., Jr. and O. H. PAANANEN (1976) Selected Welfare Implications of Rapid Energy-Related Development Impact. Working Paper No. 143. Laramie, Wyoming: University of Wyoming (November).

WILLIAMSON, O. E. (1975) Markets and Hierarchies: Analysis and Antitrust Implications. New York: The Free Press.

BIOGRAPHICAL STATEMENTS

EDITORS

WILLIAM LOEHR is an Associate Professor and Associate Dean at the Graduate School of International Studies, University of Denver. He received his Ph.D. in economics from the University of Colorado. His published works include papers in *Kyklos, International Organization, Journal of Common Market Studies* and elsewhere. He helped edit the first volume in Sage Series on Comparative Political Economy.

TODD SANDLER is an Associate Professor of Economics at the University of Wyoming. He received his Ph.D. in Economics in 1971 at the State University of New York at Binghamton. During the 1977-1978 academic year, he was on leave as a visiting scholar at the Institute of Social and Economic Research at the University of York, United Kingdom, where he was supported by a NATO Postdoctoral Fellowship in Science. His current research deals with alliances and other supranational structures. His publications include papers in *Kyklos, Journal of Economic Theory, Journal of Conflict Resolution, International Studies Quarterly, Southern Economic Journal* and elsewhere.

AUTHORS

RYAN C. AMACHER is an Associate Professor of Economics at Arizona State University. He received his Ph.D. in 1971 from the University of Virginia. His publications include *Yugoslavia's Foreign Trade* and articles in the *American Economic Review,* the *Journal of Political Economy, Kyklos, Economic Inquiry,* and *Public Choice.* He is a co-editor of *The Economic Approach to Public Policy* and *The Law of the Sea.*

JON CAULEY received his Ph.D. in economics in 1970 from the University of Colorado. Presently, he is an Assistant Professor of Economics at the University of Hawaii at Hilo. His publications include articles in *Public Finance, Journal of Conflict Resolution,* and *Futures.*

THOMAS CROCKER was born in Bangor, Maine, received his bachelor's degree from Bowdoin College, and the Ph.D. from the University of Missouri—Columbia. He has previously taught at the University of Wisconsin and the University of California and has been at the University of Wyoming since 1975. His research interests are in resource and environmental economics and the economics of the law.

ALLAN C. DeSERPA is an Associate Professor of Economics at Arizona State University. He received his Ph.D. at the University of California, Santa Barbara, in 1970. His published works include articles in the *Economic Journal,* the *Canadian Journal of Economics,* the *Scottish Journal of Political Economy,* and *Economic Inquiry.*

ROGER HANSON was a Visiting Associate Professor of Political Science at Reed College and now works for Mathematica Policy Research, Inc. He received his Ph.D. from the University of Minnesota. His prior publications include essays in *American Journal of Political Science, Western Political Quarterly* and *Law and Society.*

STEPHEN K. HAPPEL is an Assistant Professor of Economics at Arizona State University. He received his Ph.D. in economics from Duke University in 1976, with major fields in population economics and economic development.

ELSIE KNOER received her Ph.D. in economics in 1977 from the University of Kansas. Presently, she is an Assistant Professor of Economics at Arizona State University in Tempe.

WILLIAM E. MORGAN is a Professor of Economics and Head, Department of Economics at the University of Wyoming. His publications include articles in the *Southern Economic Journal, Natural Resources Journal* and the *Annals of Regional Science.*

STEPHEN M. SHAFFER received his Ph.D. in Political Science from the University of Michigan in 1975. He is Assistant Professor of Political Science at the George Washington University. He has also taught at Michigan and the Graduate School of International Studies at the University of Denver. His current research focuses on patterns of international cooperation in science and technology.

ROBERT SHELTON is Associate Professor of Economics and Director of the Institute for Policy Research at the University of Wyoming. He has served as a Brookings Economic Policy Fellow and is currently on the Editorial Board of the *Journal of Cultural Economics*. He has published in such journals as the *Journal of Political Economy*, *National Tax Journal*, *Economic Inquiry* and *Public Choice*.

V. KERRY SMITH is a Fellow in the Quality of the Environment Division, Resources for the Future, Washington, D.C. He received his A.B. and Ph.D. degrees from Rutgers University. His current research concerns the economics of natural resource scarcity. Dr. Smith is the author of books on Monte Carlo Methods, Congestion Costs and the Economics of Air Pollution. His papers have appeared in the *Journal of the American Statistical Association*, *Econometrica*, the *Journal of Political Economy* and others.

ROBERT D. TOLLISON is a Professor of Economics at Virginia Polytechnic Institute. He received his Ph.D. from the University of Virginia in 1969. His publications include articles in the *American Economic Review*, the *Journal of Law and Economics*, the *Quarterly Journal of Economics*, *Economica*, the *Journal of Political Economy*, and the *Review of Economics and Statistics*. He has co-edited *The Theory of Public Choice* and the *Economic Approach to Public Policy*.